China's Transitional Economy

Studies on Contemporary China

The Contemporary China Institute at the School of Oriental and African Studies (University of London) has, since its establishment in 1968, been an international centre for research and publications on twentieth-century China. *Studies on Contemporary China*, which is sponsored by the Institute, seeks to maintain and extend that tradition by making available the best work of scholars and China specialists throughout the world. It embraces a wide variety of subjects relating to Nationalist and Communist China, including social, political, and economic change, intellectual and cultural developments, foreign relations, and national security.

Editorial Advisory Board:

Dr R. F. Ash
Mr B. G. Hook
Professor C. B. Howe
Professor Bonnie S. McDougall
Dr David Shambaugh
Professor Lynn T. White III
Dr Jonathan Unger

Volumes in the Series:

Art and Ideology in Revolutionary China, *David Holm*
Economic Trends in Chinese Agriculture, *Y. Y. Kueh and R. F. Ash*
In Praise of Maoist Economic Planning, *Chris Bramall*
Chinese Foreign Policy: Theory and Practice, *edited by Thomas W. Robinson and
    David Shambaugh*
Economic Reform and State-Owned Enterprises in China 1979–1987, *Donald A. Hay,
    Derek J. Morris, Guy Liu, and Shujie Yao*
Rural China in Transition, *Samuel P. S. Ho*
Agricultural Instability in China 1931–1991, *Y. Y. Kueh*
Deng Xiaoping: Portrait of a Chinese Statesman, *edited by David Shambaugh*
Greater China: The Next Superpower?, *edited by David Shambaugh*
The Chinese Economy under Deng Xiaoping, *edited by R. F. Ash and Y. Y. Kueh*
China and Japan, *edited by Christopher Howe*
The Individual and the State in China, *edited by Brian Hook*
China's Legal Reforms, *edited by Stanley Lubman*

China's Transitional Economy

Edited by

ANDREW G. WALDER

OXFORD UNIVERSITY PRESS
1996

Oxford University Press, Walton Street, Oxford OX2 6DP

Oxford   New York

Athens Auckland Bangkok Bogota Bombay
Buenos Aires Calcutta Cape Town Dar es Salaam
Delhi Florence Hong Kong Istanbul Karachi
Kuala Lumpur Madras Madrid Melbourne
Mexico City Nairobi Paris Singapore
Taipei Tokyo Toronto

and associated companies in
Berlin Ibadan

Oxford is a trade mark of Oxford University Press

Published in the United States
by Oxford University Press Inc., New York

British Library Cataloguing in Publication Data
Data available

Library of Congress Cataloging in Publication Data
Data available

ISBN 0-19-829097-7

Printed in Great Britain
on acid-free paper by
Biddles Ltd., Guildford & King's Lynn

To my grandmother, Mabelle Lanegran Frederick
and the memory of my grandfather, Floyd J. Frederick

Preface

During the 1990s China's transitional economy has become a subject of broad interest well beyond the community of China specialists. As one of the world's fastest growing economies for well over a decade, and by some measures destined soon to become the world's largest, it holds broad interest for academic economists and international agencies. This interest is enhanced by China's obvious relevance for vigorous policy debates about what is to be done to stimulate recovery and sustained growth in the economies of the post-communist world. Where in 1989 the consensus appeared to urge a policy of rapid privatization, trade and foreign exchange liberalization, and rapid stabilization through drastic cuts in subsidies and the money supply, China's economic dynamism appeared to result from strategy that ignored such advice.

Why has China's transitional economy performed so differently from those of Eastern Europe and the former Soviet Union? Did China start its reform under different conditions and with different historical legacies that have proved to be advantages? Do China's rapid growth rates serve to mask underlying problems that will eventually haunt the future? How successful have China's reforms been, after all? What are the implications of China's rapid growth for policy and economic analysis regarding the transitional economies of Eastern Europe?

This volume was motivated by the realization that the most important debates about these issues were being carried out in specialized economics journals that most China specialists do not read, or in conferences at which few China specialists are in attendance. And some of the more important questions hinge on technical analyses that are not accessible to those without professional training in economics. The readers of The China Quarterly, many of whom find it necessary to arrive at an informed position about China's transitional economy, need to be aware of what is being said about the prospects for China's transitional economy outside the China field—to learn from these discussions, and also to critically evaluate them. With the generous support of The China Quarterly, the authors in this volume met 29–30 March 1995 at the School of Oriental and African Studies, University of London. Our collective task was to consider China's transitional economy in the perspective of the post-communist economies of Eastern Europe and the Soviet Union, and to critically evaluate claims made about China in recent international discussions about transitional economies. At the same time, we hoped to address directly the long-standing but recently sharpening divergence of opinion among China specialists about the degree of progress China has made, and the future prospects for its reforms. What is distinctive about China's reforms from an international perspective? How successful have they been in transforming the central processes of economic decision-making and behaviour? What lessons, if any, does China's experience hold for other transitional economies? And how serious are various claimed threats to China's ability to sustain its recent record? The essays collected here take stock of opinion and evidence on these questions, stake out positions, and in so doing inform both the international debate and the dialogue among China specialists about the significance of China's economic transformation under Deng Xiaoping.

ANDREW G. WALDER

Hong Kong
November 1995

Contents

x   Contents

CONCLUSIONS

Contributors

ROBERT F. ASH teaches in the Department of Economics at SOAS. Between 1986 and 1995 he was Director of the Contemporary China Institute and he has had a long association with *The China Quarterly*, both as a contributor of articles and compiler of the "Quarterly Chronicle." Dr Ash has published a wide variety of articles on various aspects of the Chinese Economy. His most recent book is *The Chinese Economy Under Deng Xiaoping* (edited with Y. Y. Kueh).

STEVEN M. GOLDSTEIN is Professor of Government at Smith College and Associate in Research at the John K. Fairbank Center for East Asian Research at Harvard University. He has written widely on questions related to Chinese foreign policy, domestic policies and revolutionary history. In 1989 he was part of the press corps covering Mikhail Gorbachev's trip to China and the demonstrations at Tiananmen, where he broadcast for CNN television. His most recent book is *China at the Crossroads: Reform after Tiananmen*. Professor Goldstein is currently working on a study of the domestic politics of Taiwan's relations with the mainland.

NICHOLAS R. LARDY is a Senior Fellow in the Foreign Policy Studies program at the Brookings Institution. He has written numerous articles and several books on the Chinese economy, including *China in the World Economy* and *Foreign Trade and Economic Reform in China, 1978–1990*. Lardy serves on the Board of Directors and the Executive Committee of the National Committee on United States–China Relations, is a member of the Board of Trustees of the Blakemore Foundation, and is a member of the Editorial Board of *The China Quarterly*, the *Journal of Asian Business*, and the *China Economic Review*.

BARRY NAUGHTON is Associate Professor at the Institute of International Relations and Pacific Studies, University of California–San Diego. An economist, he holds a B.A. in Chinese language and literature from the University of Washington, and a Ph.D. in economics from Yale University. He is the author of *Growing Out of the Plan: Chinese Economic Reform, 1978–1993*, as well as numerous articles on the Chinese economy. He is also co-editor and contributor to *Reforming Asian Socialism: The Growth of Market Institutions* and *Urban Spaces in Contemporary China*. His research interests include problems of economic transition, and China's industrialization and industrial management, macroeconomic policies and stability.

PETER NOLAN is Fellow and Director of Studies in Economics at Jesus College, Cambridge, and Chair of Development Studies, Cambridge University. His most recent book is *China's Rise, Russia's Fall*. He is the editor, with Doug Fureng, of the series "Studies on the Chinese Economy" (Macmillan). He is currently researching the emergence of big business in China.

JEAN C. OI is Associate Professor of Political Science, Stanford University, having previously taught at Harvard and Lehigh universities. She is the author of *State and Peasant in Contemporary China: The Political Economy of Village Government*, of *Rural China Takes Off: Incentives for Industrialization*, and of recent articles in *World Politics* and *Journal of Development Studies*. During the 1995–96 academic year, she was Visiting Associate Professor of Social Science, Hong Kong University of Science and Technology.

LOUIS PUTTERMAN is Professor of Economics at Brown University in Providence, Rhode Island. Since receiving his Ph.D. at Yale University in 1980, he has researched and written on a number of topics, including incentives, property rights, and the organization of production at firm and farm level; labour-managed firms and collective farms; agricultural policy and outcomes in Tanzania; agriculture and industrial reform in China; and the theory of market socialism and egalitarianism in market economies. He is the author of numerous scholarly articles and author, co-author, or editor of six books, including *Continuity and Change in China's Rural Development: Collective and Reform Eras in Perspective*.

THOMAS G. RAWSKI is Professor of Economics and History at the University of Pittsburgh. His research focuses on the economy of China, including studies of historical as well as contemporary issues. His recent publications oriented towards contemporary issues include a series of papers, many written in collaboration with Gary Jefferson and Yuxin Zheng, that use studies of industrial productivity change as a springboard for elaborating the dynamics of China's economic reforms. On the historical side, his works include books on *Economic Growth in Prewar China*, *Chinese History in Economic Perspective* (co-edited with Lillian M. Li), and *Economics and the Historian* (with several co-authors).

TERRY SICULAR is Associate Professor of Economics at the University of Western Ontario. She has formerly held positions at Harvard and Stanford universities. Her research has examined such topics as planning and markets, agricultural reforms, rural incomes and inequality, state-owned enterprises, and public finance in China.

ANDREW G. WALDER is Professor of Sociology and Senior Fellow, Institute of International Studies, Stanford University. He has previously taught at Harvard and Columbia universities. He is the author of *Communist Neo-Traditionalism: Work and Authority in Chinese Industry*, editor of *The Waning of the Communist State: Economic Origins of Political Decline in China and Hungary*, and of recent articles in *American Sociological Review*, *American Journal of Sociology*, *Theory and Society*, and other journals. During the 1995–96 academic year, he was Visiting Professor of Social Science, Hong Kong University of Science and Technology.

MARTIN KING WHYTE is Professor of Sociology and International Relations at George Washington University. He received his B.A. degree in physics from Cornell University, an M.A. in Russian Area Studies from Harvard University, and a Ph.D. in Sociology, also from Harvard. He taught for 25 years at the University of

Michigan before assuming his current position. He has written widely on many aspects of social life in contemporary China, including two books co-authored with William Parish, *Village and Family in Contemporary China* and *Urban Life in Contemporary China*. He has also published works dealing with family life elsewhere, including *The Status of Women in Preindustrial Societies* and *Dating, Mating, and Marriage*. Since 1987 he has been engaged in survey research projects in the PRC dealing with continuities and changes in urban family life, with the most recent survey, carried out in 1994 in Baoding, Hebei, focusing on aging and intergenerational relations.

China's Transitional Economy: Interpreting its Significance

Andrew G. Walder

China's post-Mao economic reforms have generated rapid and sustained economic growth, unprecedented rises in real income and living standards, and have transformed what was once one of the world's most insular economies into a major trading nation. The contrast between China's transitional economy and those in Eastern Europe and the former Soviet Union could not be more striking. Where the latter struggle with severe recessions and pronounced declines in real income, China has looked more like a sprinting East Asian "tiger" than a plodding Soviet-style dinosaur mired in the swamps of transition. The realization that reform measures and energetic growth continue even after the political crisis of 1989 has made China a subject of intense interest far outside the customary confines of the China field. Understood increasingly as a genuine success story, it is moving to the centre of international policy debates about what is to be done to transform the stagnating economies of Eastern Europe, and various aspects of its case now figure prominently in academic analyses ranging from theories of the firm and property rights to the political foundations of economic growth.

For many, China's transitional economy is an intriguing anomaly: a transition heralded as difficult and painful has sparked an economic boom. As a gradual rather than abrupt transition to the market, with public industry protected rather than subject to privatization, China's reform path has confounded the widespread and deeply held belief that gradual reform and public ownership simply cannot work, not even as a transitional strategy.[1] Indeed, some have pointed to the apparent irony that China has succeeded precisely by ignoring the advice widely offered to East European nations by many prominent economic advisors.[2]

---

1. See Olivier Blanchard, Rudiger Dornbusch, Paul Krugman, Richard Layard and Lawrence Summers, *Reform in Eastern Europe* (Cambridge, MA: MIT Press, 1992); Olivier Blanchard, Maxim Boycko, Marek Dabrowski, Rudiger Dornbusch, Richard Layard and Andrei Shleifer, *Post-Communist Reform: Pain and Progress* (Cambridge, MA: MIT Press, 1993); János Kornai, *The Road to a Free Economy: Shifting from a Socialist System, The Example of Hungary* (New York: Norton, 1990); and Merton J. Peck and Thomas J. Richardson, *What is to be Done? Proposals for the Soviet Transition to the Market* (New Haven: Yale University Press, 1992). Peck and Richardson (p. 20) write, "the solution lies in abandoning the search for halfway houses, in abandoning the dream of a regulated market economy," while Kornai (p. 58) argues "it is futile to expect that the state unit will behave as if it were privately owned and will spontaneously act as if it were a market-oriented agent. It is time to let go of this vain hope once and for all...state ownership permanently recreates bureaucracy."

2. See Peter Nolan, "China's post-Mao political economy: a puzzle," *Contributions to Political Economy*, Vol. 12 (1993), pp. 71–87, and "The China puzzle: 'touching stones to cross the river'," *Challenge*, Vol. 37 (January–February 1994), pp. 25–31; Thomas G. Rawski, "Chinese industrial reform: accomplishments, prospects, and implications," *American Economic Review* Vol. 84, No. 2 (May 1994), pp. 271–275, and "Progress without

This contrast with the former Soviet bloc would suggest that China's transitional economy has important policy and theoretical implications. But what are they? This depends on how one characterizes China's main reform measures and how successful one judges them to be; what factors one sees as responsible for this economic dynamism and how unique they are to China; and judgments about the sustainability of this growth, which are connected also with judgments about China's political institutions and *their* probable future. Opinions vary widely about all of these questions.

What is notable about China's reform path? Some see China's gradual and cautious approach towards liberalization and privatization as the antithesis of the "big bang" and "shock therapy" approaches advocated so often in Eastern Europe. Others emphasize to the contrary that China's reforms started with an early "big bang" of privatization and liberalization in agriculture, and that in industry the reforms have worked well only in the partially private "non-state" sectors of the economy.

How successful are China's reforms? Some see steady improvements in output, incomes, productivity and export capability throughout the economy, beginning in agriculture and spreading to collective and eventually even to the much-maligned state industry. Others see China as a half-reformed economy in which the relative success of the rural sector contrasts markedly with an urban industrial base chronically losing money and still stuck in the inefficiencies of the past.

Does China yield lessons for other transitional economies? Some see China as an alternative model of gradual reform, in which the steady introduction of competition and market mechanisms alters incentives and behaviour of actors throughout the economy, making unnecessary the hardships of shock therapy and rapid privatization and allowing a transitional economy to "grow out of the plan." Others see its rapid growth as due not to gradualism but to a daring abandonment of collective agriculture under uniquely favourable conditions: a largely agrarian economy with a socialist welfare system that covered only the urban population.

Can China's successes be sustained, or do serious problems cloud the horizon? Some see China's reforms as firmly rooted and sustainable, following an East Asian pattern of industrialization under authoritarian rule earlier taken in South Korea and Taiwan. In the most optimistic scenario, China will continue its recent pace of growth and emerge from authoritarianism early in the 21st century as the world's largest economy. Others, however, see a future fraught with risk and instability, of which the political and economic shocks of the late 1980s were but a foretaste. In this view, an uncertain leadership transition, growing potential for social instability, and continuing problems of inflation, unemployment, uprooted rural populations, deepening political corruption and declining

footnote continued
privatization: the reform of China's state industries," in Vedat Milor (ed.), *Changing Political Economies: Privatization in Post-Communist and Reforming Communist States* (Boulder: Lynne Rienner, 1994), pp. 27–52.

central power all predict a hazardous road ahead.

The essays collected here seek to give clearer answers to these four questions and put China's transitional economy more firmly into international perspective.

What is Distinctive About China's Reform Path?

Those who argue that China's reforms hold important lessons about transitional economies emphasize two features. First, the approach is gradual and flexible, involving evolutionary changes in institutions and policies. There is no rapid leap to free prices, currency convertibility or cutting of state subsidies. Secondly, privatization of government enterprise has not played a significant role, although a new but small private sector has emerged. Viewed from this perspective, China contradicts rather strikingly the advice of those who counsel a "big bang" – rapid or immediate release of price controls and subsidies and restrictions of foreign competition and investment – and the "mass privatization" through sale or direct distribution of state assets.[3]

This view has been challenged by proponents of rapid reform who argue that China bears out the wisdom of their advice. Their first counter-argument is that China's leaders, while timid about privatization and price reform, in fact implemented a bold and unprecedented "big bang" in agriculture early on, dismantling all forms of collective agriculture in favour of a system of family smallholding. This led rapidly to a doubling of agricultural output, and then to a release of labour and entrepreneurial energies into non-staple sidelines and non-agricultural pursuits. This rural "big bang," not China's gradualism, is what gave the economy a burst of growth at the outset.[4] Their second argument is that privatization *has* played a key role. The rural economy, they argue, is a form of private family farming; and in industry nearly half of industrial output was produced *outside* the state sector by the early 1990s. Therefore despite claims to the contrary, China's economy has already moved decisively toward privatization and it is precisely in the non-state sectors that economic dynamism has been most pronounced.[5]

3. See, for example, John McMillan and Barry Naughton, "How to reform a planned economy: lessons from China," *Oxford Review of Economic Policy*, Vol. 8, No. 1 (1993), pp 130–143; Barry Naughton, "What is distinctive about China's economic transition? State enterprise reform and overall system transformation," *Journal of Comparative Economics*, Vol. 18 (June 1994), pp. 470–490; Peter Nolan, "Transforming Stalinist systems: China's reforms in the light of Russian and East European experience," Discussion Papers on Economic Transition, Department of Applied Economics, University of Cambridge, August 1992; Rawski, "Progress without privatization," Ping Chen, "China's challenge to economic orthodoxy: Asian reforms as an evolutionary, self-organizing process." *China Economic Review*, Vol. 4, No. 2 (1994), pp. 137–142.

4. Jeffrey D. Sachs and Wing Thye Woo, "Structural factors in the economic reforms of China, Eastern Europe, and the former Soviet Union," *Economic Policy*, Vol. 18, No. 1 (1994), pp. 102–145.

5. *Ibid.* and Jeffrey Sachs, *Poland's Jump to the Market Economy* (Cambridge, MA: MIT Press, 1993), pp. 81–82, where in the midst of a spirited argument in favour of rapid privatization, we read, "But what about China? Hasn't China maintained state ownership and

These arguments are generally viewed sceptically by China specialists, even those who disagree with one another about other aspects of the reforms. While the commune system was rapidly dismantled in the early 1980s, peasants remained obliged to raise and sell quotas of staple crops at low state procurement prices for over a decade, almost all agricultural products and inputs remained predominantly under state pricing and distribution for many years, and to this day government commercial agencies dominate the marketing of output.[6] This gradual retreat from planned agriculture is exactly what the proponents of rapid and decisive change counsel against. It is not at all clear, moreover, that family farming *per se* is the key to rising grain output: while some analysts argue that productivity increases were directly attributable to the incentive effects of *de facto* family land ownership, others argue that the planned rise in state procurement prices and greater flexibility in cropping decisions are responsible for large portions of productivity increases.[7] The land ownership argument supports proponents of privatization, while the latter argument emphasizes incremental policy change.

The claim that most industrial output is now in a vaguely privatized "non-state" sector also meets with deep scepticism. Over 70 per cent of output in this sector is under a form of public ownership by local governments.[8] While township and village enterprises have been referred to occasionally as "semi-private," "*de facto* private" or as a "hybrid" property form,[9] most agree that they are nevertheless largely government

---

footnote continued
yet succeeded in growing rapidly? The answer is yes, but the Chinese policymakers themselves know that state ownership has been a hindrance, not a help, to their economic growth since the start of the reforms. It is estimated that two thirds or more of state-owned enterprises are losing money in China. This has been a serious threat to macroeconomic stability. Moreover, the great dynamism of the country has come in the nonstate sector, including township and village enterprises and joint ventures."

6. See Terry Sicular, "Grain pricing: a key link in Chinese economic policy," *Modern China*, Vol. 14 (October 1988), pp. 451–486, "Plan and market in China's agricultural commerce," *Journal of Political Economy*, Vol. 96 (1988), pp. 283–307, and "China's agricultural policy during the reform period," in Joint Economic Committee, Congress of the United States, *China's Economic Dilemmas in the 1990s*, Vol. 1 (Washington D.C.: U.S. Government Printing Office, 1991), pp. 304–364.

7. See Louis Putterman, "Dualism and reform In China," *Economic Development and Cultural Change*, Vol. 40 (April 1992), pp. 467–493, p. 475; John McMillan, John Whalley and Li Jing Zhu, "The impact of China's economic reforms on agricultural productivity growth," *Journal of Political Economy*, Vol. 97 (August 1989), pp. 781–807; Louis Putterman, "Does poor supervisability undermine teamwork? Evidence from an unexpected source," *American Economic Review*, Vol. 81 (September 1991), pp. 996–1001; and Scott Rozelle, "Decision-making in China's rural economy: the linkages between village leaders and farm households," *The China Quarterly*, No. 137 (March 1994), pp. 99–124.

8. See Barry Naughton, "Chinese institutional innovation and privatization from below," *American Economic Review*, Vol. 84, No. 2 (May 1994), pp. 266–270, Jean C. Oi, "Fiscal reform and the economic foundations of local state corporatism in China," *World Politics*, Vol. 45 (October 1992), pp. 99–126; Andrew G. Walder, "Local governments as industrial firms: an organizational analysis of China's transitional economy," *American Journal of Sociology*, Vol. 101, No. 2 (September 1995), pp. 263–301.

9. See Victor Nee, "Organizational dynamics of market transition: hybrid forms, property rights, and mixed economy in China," *Administrative Science Quarterly*, No. 37 (March 1992), pp. 1–27; Victor Nee and Su Sijin, "Local corporatism and informal privatization in China's market transition," Working Papers on Transitions from State Socialism No. 93-2,

owned and operated.[10] The common finding that private enterprises sometimes register as public, and that some rural officials appropriate public revenues as private income, qualifies but does not alter this observation.[11]

Beneath these disputes lies a deeper question about China's reform path. Those who see in China vindication of arguments for rapid marketization and privatization contend that successes have been limited to areas where these changes have been most pronounced. In this relatively critical view, China remains stuck in the contradictions of partial reform, and has only postponed the difficult tasks of final price and ownership reform. This view finds more support from China specialists, and raises the second question.

How Enviable is China's Record of Reform?

Views of China's economic reforms come in many subtle shadings, but it is possible to identify two which are opposed: one emphasizing their limits and the difficult tasks postponed, and another emphasizing their cumulative breakthroughs. The first dominated the 1980s, especially outside the discipline of economics, and reached its greatest influence in the aftermath of the Tiananmen protests. The second gained adherents rapidly during the 1990s, especially among economists in academia and in international organizations.

The view that China exhibits the classic pathologies of partial reform has been persistent and popular. This reflects in part the influence of such critics of earlier partial reform in Eastern Europe as János Kornai, whose writings about Hungary suggested the incompatibility of market allocation with state ownership. Kornai's works became widely available in English-speaking countries just as China's reforms began, and they popularized the view that market reforms in a socialist economy create new problems (such as inflation and liquidity crises) without curing the underlying defects of central planning.[12]

---

footnote continued

Einaudi Center for International Studies, Cornell; and Yusheng Peng, "Wage determination in rural and urban China: a comparison of public and private industrial sectors," *American Sociological Review*, No. 57 (April 1992), pp. 198–213.

10. See e.g. William A. Byrd, "Entrepreneurship, capital, and ownership," in William A. Byrd and Qingsong Lin (eds.), *China's Rural Industry: Structure, Development, and Reform* (New York: Oxford University Press, 1990), pp. 189–218; Jean C. Oi, "Commercializing China's rural cadres," *Problems of Communism*, No. 35 (September–October, 1986), pp. 1–15, and "The fate of the collective after the commune," in Deborah Davis and Ezra Vogel (eds.), *Chinese Society on the Eve of Tiananmen: The Impact of Reform* (Cambridge, MA: Harvard University Press, 1990), pp. 15–36; and Christine P. W. Wong, "Interpreting rural industrial growth in the post-Mao period," *Modern China*, No. 14 (January 1988), pp. 3–30.

11. See Nee and Su, "Local corporatism and informal privatization," Yialing Liu, "Reform from below: the private economy and local politics in the rural industrialization of Wenzhou," *The China Quarterly*, No. 130 (1992), pp. 293–316; Ole Odgaard, "Inadequate and inaccurate Chinese statistics: the case of private rural enterprises," *China Information*, Vol. 5 (Winter 1990), pp. 29–38.

12. See, for example, Christine P. W. Wong, "The economics of shortage and problems of reform in Chinese industry," *Journal of Comparative Economics*, No. 10 (December 1986),

Near the end of the 1980s, it was possible to see China's economy as bogged down in the contradictions of partial reform. Agriculture, which responded rapidly to reform measures in the early 1980s, met deepening difficulties. Grain prices could not rise to market clearing levels because of their impact on the urban cost of living, and grain output stagnated. Subsequent restoration of compulsory sales for staple crops led peasants to flee agriculture and shift to more lucrative sidelines and non-agricultural pursuits.[13] Compensating wage rises for urban workers would only make urban industry – the overwhelming source of the state budget – less profitable, while urban grain price subsidies could only lead to large state budget deficits – as they did in the early to mid-1980s. Meanwhile, urban state industry remained protected from competitive pressures and seemingly impervious to change. As Kornai predicted, enterprise managers bargained with bureaucratic superiors for more supplies of inputs at low state prices, permission to sell more output at high market prices, tax breaks and investment subsidies, in ways that might soften their budget constraint.[14] Moreover, as in Hungary years before, state managers consented to wage rises and better housing and benefits as a strategy to motivate their workers, feeding inflation.[15] The profitability of state firms deteriorated, requiring ever-larger subsidies.[16] Even the success story of township and village industry is seen by some observers as a wasteful

footnote continued

pp. 363–387; Andrew G. Walder, "The informal dimension of enterprise financial reforms," in Joint Economic Committee, Congress of the United States, *China's Economy Looks Towards the Year 2000*, Vol. 1 (Washington, D.C.: U.S. Government Printing Office, 1986), pp. 134–149; Barry Naughton, "Hierarchy and the bargaining economy: government and enterprise in the reform process," in Kenneth G. Lieberthal and David M. Lampton (eds.), *Bureaucracy, Politics and Decision-Making in Post-Mao China* (Berkeley: University of California Press, 1992), pp. 245–279; and Andrew G. Walder, "Local bargaining relationships and urban industrial finance," in *ibid.* pp. 308–333. Kornai would later synthesize his arguments in *The Socialist System: The Political Economy of Communism* (Princeton: Princeton University Press, 1991).

13. Putterman, "Dualism and reform in China," p. 478; James Kaising Kung, "Food and agriculture in post-reform China: the marketed surplus problem revisited," *Modern China*, Vol. 18 (April 1992), pp. 138–170, and Calla Weimer, "Price reform and structural change: distributional impediments to allocational gains," *Modern China*, Vol. 18 (April 1992), pp. 171–196.

14. Putterman, "Dualism and reform in China," p. 478. See also Andrew G. Walder, "Wage reform and the web of factory interests," *The China Quarterly*, No. 109 (March 1987), pp. 22–41, and "Factory and manager in an era of reform," *The China Quarterly*, No. 118 (June 1989), pp. 242–264.

15. Putterman, "Dualism and reform in China," p. 478. See also Walder, "Wage reform," and "Factory and manager"; Terry Sicular "Public finance and China's economic reforms," Discussion Paper No. 1618, Harvard Institute of Economic Research, November 1992, and "Going on the dole: why China's state enterprises choose to lose," unpublished paper, University of Western Ontario, May 1994. Sicular finds evidence of a managerial orientation to the maximization of retained funds rather than profits, and a propensity to spend these funds disproportionately on consumption and benefits for employees. However, she disputes the view that the profitability of state enterprises has suffered major declines.

16. Sachs and Woo write, "The results of attempts to reform the state sector have been extremely disappointing. On almost all fronts, the state-enterprise sector in China has continued to perform poorly. It is heavily loss-making; lagging in total factor productivity growth behind the non-state sector; dependent on state subsidies; and apparently suffused with economic corruption. China's growth has come despite the lack of discernible progress in establishing satisfactory performance of state industrial enterprises, with a heavy macroeconomic burden resulting from state enterprise losses" (p. 18).

duplication of investment activities that fails to take advantage of economies of scale, and whose uncontrolled growth generates inflation, material shortages, larger budgetary deficits and other symptoms of macroeconomic instability.[17] According to this view, China's growth masks serious structural problems.[18]

A second view acknowledges remaining problems, but emphasizes cumulative changes in the mechanisms by which the Chinese economy operates and evidence that the economy is responding to "partial" reform measures in ways thought improbable.[19] While state industry is changing more slowly than other areas of the economy, there are increasing signs that it too is responding to reform. Naughton finds that variation in profit rates across industrial sectors, an artifact of state pricing policy, has declined steadily, showing the increased exposure of state firms to market forces. As the state sector's monopoly position has been challenged by the entry of new firms operated by rural governments, overall profit rates in all industrial sectors decline and converge. The declining profitability of state industry reflects not the failure of reform, but its *success* in exposing this formerly protected sector to genuine competitive pressures.[20]

The centrepiece of this interpretation is that declining profits coexist with – and indeed may cause – increasing productivity in both state and rural collective sectors. Some researchers find that the declining trend of total factor productivity of the late Mao era has been reversed. While rural collective enterprises have improved their total factor productivity at more than double the rate of state industry, state industry itself began to respond to reform efforts in the mid-1980s, and its response then accelerated.[21] If these estimates are valid, they provide strong evidence of

17. Christine P. W. Wong, "Interpreting rural industrial growth," "Fiscal reform and local industrialization: the problematic sequencing of reform in post-Mao China," *Modern China*, No. 18 (April 1992), pp. 197–227, and "Central–local relations in an era of fiscal decline: the paradox of fiscal decentralization in post-Mao China," *The China Quarterly*, No. 128 (December 1991), pp. 691–715.

18. For a recent overview of China's reforms that emphasizes their limits, see Christine Wong, "China's economy: the limits of gradualist reform," in William A. Joseph (ed.), *China Briefing, 1994* (Boulder: Westview, 1994), pp. 33–54.

19. See especially Barry Naughton, *Growing Out of the Plan: Chinese Economic Reform. 1978–1993* (New York: Cambridge University Press, 1995), and Rawski, "Progress without privatization."

20. Barry Naughton, "Implications of the state monopoly over industry and its relaxation," *Modern China*, No. 18 (January 1992), pp. 14–41. Sicular, "Public finance and China's economic reforms," however, argues that Naughton overstates the extent of the decline of profitability in state enterprises and also the declines in government revenue.

21. See the following series of publications, which lay out the evidence: Kuan Chen, Gary H. Jefferson, Thomas G. Rawski, H. C. Wang and Y. X. Zheng, "Productivity change in Chinese industry: 1953–85," *Journal of Comparative Economics*, No. 12 (1988), pp. 570–591, Gary H. Jefferson, Thomas G. Rawski and Yuxin Zheng, "Growth, efficiency, and convergence in China's state and collective industry," *Economic Development and Cultural Change*, No. 40 (1992), pp. 239–266, Gary H. Jefferson and Wenyi Xu, "The impact of reform on socialist enterprises in transition: structure, conduct, and performance in Chinese industry," *Journal of Comparative Economics*, No. 15 (1991), pp. 45–64. More accessible summaries of the evidence are provided in Rawski, "Progress without privatization"; Gary H. Jefferson and Thomas G. Rawski, "Enterprise reform in Chinese industry," *Journal of Economic Perspectives*, No. 8 (Spring 1994), pp. 47–70; and Thomas G. Rawski, "Chinese industrial

"progress without privatization" – that the reputed limits of partial reform have already been surmounted.

Others have developed estimates fully consistent with the "limits" interpretation: impressive productivity growth in rural industry, none in the state sector. They criticize alleged bias and error in the methodology used to develop more favourable estimates.[22] The first exchange about these estimates centred on methodological issues: how to deflate prices for intermediate inputs, and the characteristics of the enterprise samples.[23] The dispute so far appears inconclusive, especially given the small productivity increases under dispute.

This debate is important for judgments about the success of China's reforms: if there is convincing evidence that the state sector is turning round, then budget constraints are hardening for state firms despite all the theory to the contrary. The question would then become whether the rates of improvement in factor productivity seen in China are large enough, given the comparatively low productivity of state industry at the outset of reform, to make the reform strategy worth emulating. If gradual reform *does* work in state industry, this undercuts one of the central claims of those who advocate a "big bang" and mass privatization in other transitional economies. However, the question of China's relevance abroad hinges on much more than the debate about factor productivity in industry.

Is China Relevant to Other Transitional Economies?

There is a logical equivalence between the tasks of reform in China and Eastern Europe. All these economies are struggling with legacies of a Soviet-style command economy, even though that model was not implemented identically in all regimes. All the command economies faced the same basic problems at the outset of reform: investment capital given as a grant, administered prices that did not reflect relative scarcities, domestic economies insulated from foreign competition and world prices, poor export performance, lack of competition on product markets, poor distribution networks, and so forth. All face the same initial dilemmas:

---

footnote continued
reform: accomplishments, prospects, and implications," *American Economic Review*, Vol. 84, No. 2 (May 1994), pp. 271–275. The work of a second group who also find evidence of changes in the behaviour of state enterprises has recently begun to appear: Theodore Groves, Yongmiao Hong, John McMillan and Barry Naughton, "Autonomy and incentives in Chinese state enterprises," *Quarterly Journal of Economics*, Vol. 109, No. 1 (1994), pp. 183–209.

22. See Wing Thye Woo, Wen Hai, Yibiao Jin and Gang Fan, "How successful has Chinese enterprise reform been? Pitfalls in opposite biases and focus," *Journal of Comparative Economics*, Vol. 18, No. 3 (1993), pp. 410–437, and Wing Thye Woo, Gang Fan, Wen Hai and Yibiao Jin, "The efficiency and macroeconomic consequences of Chinese enterprise reform," *China Economic Review*, Vol. 14, No. 2 (1993), pp. 153–168.

23. See Gary H. Jefferson, Thomas G. Rawski and Yuxin Zheng, "Productivity change in Chinese industry: a comment," *China Economic Review*, Vol. 5, No. 2 (Fall 1994), pp. 235–241, and Wing Thye Woo, Gang Fan, Wen Hai and Yibiao Jin, "Reply to comment by Jefferson, Rawski and Zheng," *China Economic Review*, Vol. 5, No. 2 (Fall 1994), pp. 243–248.

the dangers of inflation arising from state subsidies and uncontrolled wage growth, the potential dangers of social unrest because of employment cutbacks in bloated state industry, how to make a credible commitment not to bail out loss-making firms. It makes sense to treat the transitional economies of Poland and China as variants of a single intellectual and policy problem.

However, the economies of Poland (or Russia) and China are at the same time very different, complicating the lessons to be drawn. One oft-mentioned difference is in sectoral composition: at the outset of reforms, employment in China was 75 per cent agricultural; in the USSR, 75 per cent in industry. The USSR was already an urbanized industrial society. One could therefore argue that China had yet to exhaust the "extensive" phase of its growth potential – the sources of growth in early industrialization accomplished via capital investment. The economies of Eastern Europe had long since done so, and were struggling with stagnation resulting from a failure to induce "intensive" growth – for which increased productivity due to organizational and technical innovation are the sources. China, in other words, could still achieve rapid growth rates by taking labour out of agriculture and increasing its productivity by putting it to work in industry.[24]

Such differences, moreover, may have made reform inherently more difficult for Russia and easier for China. Two decades ago the Soviet Union extended its social safety net – health insurance, job security, state pensions, and subsidies of living standards through places of work and residence – to the entire urban and rural labour force. In China, it covers only some 20 per cent, primarily in the urban state sector.[25] China's reformers have trodden lightly upon the security and benefits of its urban workers, but one can imagine how much more difficult reform would be if *all* Chinese citizens had these rights, and reform meant taking them away.[26]

Another potentially important difference is China's East Asian location and associated legacies. China is ringed by a number of vigorously expanding market economies that can serve as important markets and sources of investment. But more importantly, Hong Kong, Taiwan, Singapore and the Chinese diaspora in South-East Asia and North America are filled with ethnic Chinese entrepreneurs who have proved to be valuable sources of knowledge and investment and who have served as important bridges to the world economy. Hong Kong itself has played a major role in this respect for Guangdong province and much of the rapidly growing South China region.[27] And the swift development of rural

24. Sachs and Woo, "Structural factors." See also Wing Thye Woo, "The art of reforming centrally planned economies: comparing China, Poland, and Russia," *Journal of Comparative Economics*, Vol. 18 (June 1994), pp. 276–308.
25. Andrew G. Walder, *Communist Neo-Traditionalism: Work and Authority in Chinese Industry* (Berkeley: University of California Press, 1986), ch. 2.
26. Sachs and Woo, "Structural factors."
27. Ezra F. Vogel, *One Step Ahead in China: Guangdong Under Reform* (Cambridge, MA: Harvard University Press, 1989).

coastal regions appears to be building upon the foundations of a highly commercial past, on the traditional features of the Chinese family as an economic unit, and perhaps also upon the legacies of corporate property in single-surname villages. Russia and the other former Communist regimes enjoy no similar advantages.

China's Maoist legacies are also increasingly seen as a foundation for post-Mao success. Maoism introduced a much greater degree of regional decentralization of planning, investment and materials allocation than in the Soviet Union or any of the smaller countries of Eastern Europe,[28] a trend extended further in the rural industrialization programmes of the 1960s and 1970s.[29] China began its reforms with a more geographically dispersed industrial base, and with ownership and control distributed more evenly across the entire hierarchy of government.[30] This left local officials with the experience and the capacity to respond in an entrepreneurial way to subsequent reform policies.[31] Some see the decentralization of the Chinese economy as a structural factor that allowed China's reform strategy to work.[32] Such an historically path-dependent advantage is not transferable to other countries.

Finally, one fundamental difference between China and the former Soviet bloc is that Communist rule has collapsed elsewhere, while it survives in China. Economic reform has explicitly political objectives in all of these countries. Where in Eastern Europe shock therapy and mass privatization are designed in part to dismantle Communism and strip former Communists of power and privilege, in China gradual reform is intended to allow the Party to survive as an instrument of economic development. Proponents of rapid change have defended shock therapy and mass privatization as *political* programmes,[33] and authors of economic proposals for *post*-Communist regimes emphasize the fundamental difference between reforming a socialist economy and creating a *free*

28. See, for example, H. Franz Schurmann, *Ideology and Organization in Communist China* (Berkeley: University of California Press, 1968), Carl Riskin, *China's Political Economy*. (New York: Oxford University Press, 1987), and Christine P. W. Wong, "Material allocation and decentralization: impact of the local sector on industrial reform," in Elizabeth J. Perry and Christine P. W. Wong (eds.), *The Political Economy of Reform in Post-Mao China* (Cambridge, MA: Harvard University Press, 1985).

29. See Carl Riskin, "Small industry and the Chinese model of development," *The China Quarterly*, No. 46 (April/June 1971), pp. 245–273, and Dwight Perkins (ed.), *Rural Small-Scale Industry in the People's Republic of China* (Berkeley: University of California Press, 1977).

30. See Christine P. W. Wong, "Ownership and control in Chinese industry: the Maoist legacy and prospects for the 1980s," in Joint Economic Committee, Congress of the United States, *China's Economy Looks Towards the Year 2000*, Vol. 1; and David Granick, *Chinese State Enterprises: A Regional Property Rights Analysis* (Chicago: University of Chicago Press, 1990).

31. See, for example, Byrd, "Entrepreneurship, capital, and ownership,"; Oi, "Commercializing China's rural cadres," and 'Fiscal reform"; Christine P. W. Wong, "Between plan and market: the role of the local sector in post-Mao China," *Journal of Comparative Economics*, No. 11 (1987), pp. 385–398, and "Interpreting rural industrial growth."

32. Qian Yingyi and Chenggang Xu, "Why China's economic reforms differ: the M-form hierarchy and entry/expansion of the non-state sector," *Economics of Transition*, No. 1 (1993), pp. 135–170.

33. Sachs, *Poland's Jump to the Market Economy*, esp. pp. xiii and 43.

economy as the foundation for a *free* society – a liberal political vision reviled by China's leaders.[34] China's reform is inspired not by the impulses that drive what Sachs calls "Poland's return to Europe"; it is instead tailored to the vision of earlier East Asian developmental dictatorships that laid the foundations of a modern economy before eventual political liberalization and a shift to multi-party competition.

These considerations greatly complicate the drawing of lessons from China in two distinct ways. First, they raise questions about whether a similar approach to reform would be as successful outside China, given the special circumstances and legacies that its reform policies have enjoyed. Secondly, they raise deeper questions about whether it is China's specific strategy of reform, or some underlying legacy or historical advantage, that is behind its relative success.

Is China's Growth Sustainable?

Judgments about the relevance of China's reforms often hinge on the question of whether the advances of the past 15 years will soon reach a point of diminishing returns. Some view partial reform as introducing inflation, fear of unemployment, liquidity crises and drops in state revenue that are bound to have serious economic and political consequences. Others view these transitional problems as manageable, and see the Chinese regime as better able to withstand popular pressures to curtail reform than the fragile new parliamentary democracies of Eastern Europe. Ultimately, views about the sustainability of China's reforms are based both on the analysis of the economy and on judgments about the interaction of economic and political change.

A relatively pessimistic strain has long been linked to the view that China's reforms are limited in scope and success. In this view, with the most difficult tasks of reform still lying ahead (such as the transformation of the urban state sector), China has already suffered serious bouts of macroeconomic instability and political unrest, and the prospect of serious reform of state industry creates the likelihood of rising urban unemployment. In addition, there is already a massive army of workers who migrate from the countryside in search of work, and who are thrown out of work during periodic economic downturns. And while inflation diminishes the real wages of officials, partial reform creates new opportunities for enrichment through corruption, because it permits officials to control vast productive resources.[35]

This troubling scenario found its fullest expression in May and June 1989. Easily the largest unrest faced by any Communist regime during that tumultuous year, Tiananmen appeared to be the climactic act in the pessimist's script for partial reform. Rapid inflation, popular disgust over

34. Kornai, *The Road to a Free Economy*, esp. pp. 17 and 22–23.

35. An excellent statement of this interpretation is Kathleen Hartford, "The political economy behind Beijing Spring, 1989," in Tony Saich (ed.), *The Chinese People's Movement: Perspectives on Spring 1989* (Armonk, N.Y.: M. E. Sharpe, 1990), pp. 50–82.

official corruption and fear of looming unemployment spilled over into dissatisfaction about the slow pace of political liberalization. Many writing in the aftermath of Tiananmen thought the episode marked a dead end for the strategy of limited reform.[36]

From this perspective, the Chinese path appeared to reach its end. Reform created new sources of instability and dynamism, and weakened the political order as a result of a corruption that threatened the organizational integrity of the state and caused the legitimacy of the regime to sink to one of its lowest points. Infighting among the political elite triggered by student protests underlined how fragile were the relations among top leaders, and how insecure were arrangements for political succession. Some concluded that only serious political reform could ensure an orderly transfer of power and recoup the kind of popular support necessary to carry out the more painful urban reforms. While Eastern Europe was laying a foundation for pluralistic political institutions suited to a market economy, China postponed the difficult problems to an uncertain future.

Others subscribe to an optimism fuelled by the resumption of market reform and rapid growth in the 1990s, and by the stagnating economies and unstable polities that have emerged in much of Eastern Europe. This view does not deny problems of inflation, financial instability, corruption and so forth, but interprets them as transitional diseases rather than terminal illnesses.[37] One important corollary of this optimism is the view that deep structural changes have already occurred in the economy. Central industrial planning is now a shadow of its former self, as market forces and competition have penetrated key sectors of the economy, and China has become deeply involved in international trade and finance.[38] These changes are seen as irreversible: any attempt to turn back would involve heavy economic and political costs, and spirited resistance from the population and from within the government itself.[39]

36. See e.g. *ibid.*, and Andrew G. Walder, "Workers, managers and the state: the reform era and the political crisis of 1989," *The China Quarterly*, No. 127 (September 1991), pp. 491–92.

37. Nicholas Lardy argues persuasively that reports of the death of China's reforms in 1989 were greatly exaggerated in "Is China different? The fate of its economic reforms," in Daniel Chirot (ed.), *The Crisis of Leninism and the Decline of the Left: The Revolutions of 1989* (Seattle: University of Washington Press, 1991), pp. 147–162. China's record of macroeconomic stability in fact has been quite positive when compared to other transitional economies. See Ronald I. MacKinnon, "Financial growth and macroeconomic stability in China, 1978–1992: implications for Russia and other transitional economies," *Journal of Comparative Economics*, Vol. 18 (June 1994), pp. 438–469.

38. See, for example, William A. Byrd, *The Market Mechanism and Economic Reforms in China* (Armonk, N.Y.: M. E. Sharpe, 1991), Naughton, *Growing Out of the Plan*, and Nicholas Lardy, *Foreign Trade and Economic Reform in China, 1978–1990* (Cambridge: Cambridge University Press, 1992), all of which document the gradual but fundamental changes in the principles by which China's economic system operates.

39. See Andrew G. Walder, "The quiet revolution from within: economic reform as a source of political decline," in Andrew G. Walder (ed.), *The Waning of the Communist State: Economic Origins of Political Decline in China and Hungary* (Berkeley: University of California Press, 1995), pp. 1–24.

Moreover, in retrospect China's strategy of pursuing economic reform without political change appears to have been a wise choice.[40] For China faces only one major transition: from a command to a market economy. Post-Communist regimes face a daunting "dual transition," attempting an historic transformation of the economy while at the same time trying to build stable and effective democracies out of the ruins of a single-party dictatorship. Some of these new democracies face problems of legitimacy as deep as China's regime at the end of the 1980s. The fragility of parliamentary coalitions in Eastern Europe makes the formulation and implementation of economic reforms difficult.[41] Elections as a constraint upon government make it much more difficult to carry out policies that create unemployment and reduce incomes in the short term.[42] Therefore it is possible to view China's continuing dictatorship as a form of government well-suited to the implementation of economic policies that an electorate would not choose for itself, or that an unstable democracy could not successfully undertake.

But how stable will China's "developmental dictatorship" be? Many observers have commented on the erosion of central state power.[43] The balance of control over total revenues in the wake of tax reform, for example, has shifted decisively in favour of the provinces and localities. In addition, the rise of revenue and income generating opportunities outside the planned economy has been seen to reorient local officials towards market opportunities rather than to their bureaucratic superiors for their personal advancement.[44] Some observers see in this erosion of central dominance a cause for alarm: a serious decline in China's central state capacity that threatens macroeconomic stability, the organizational integrity of the state and potentially even national unity.[45] Others see it as

40. See Susan L. Shirk, *The Political Logic of Economic Reform in China* (Berkeley: University of California Press, 1993); Marshall I. Goldman and Merle Goldman, "Soviet and Chinese economic reform," *Foreign Affairs*, Vol. 66, No. 3 (1988), pp. 551–573; and Marshall I. Goldman, *Lost Opportunity: Why Economic Reforms in Russia Have Not Worked* (New York: Norton, 1994).

41. See, for example, Sachs' discussion of privatization in *Poland's Jump to the Market Economy*, and the discussion of stalled reforms in Russia in Olivier Blanchard *et al.*, *Post-Communist Reform: Pain and Progress* (Cambridge, MA: MIT Press, 1993), chs. 2–4, and Goldman, *Lost Opportunity*.

42. Mancur Olson argues that the greater openness of democracy to the influence of special interest groups has so far made the problems of soft budget constraints worse. See his "From communism to market democracy: why is economic performance even worse after communism is abandoned?" unpublished paper, University of Maryland, n.d.

43. See Wong, "Fiscal reform and local industrialization,"' and Shaoguang Wang, "The rise of the regions: fiscal reform and decline of central state capacity in China," in Andrew G. Walder (ed.), *The Waning of the Communist State: Economic Origins of Political Decline in China and Hungary* (Berkeley: University of California Press, 1995), pp. 87–113.

44. See Walder, "The quiet revolution from within," and "The decline of Communist power: elements of a theory of institutional change," *Theory and Society*, Vol. 23 (April 1994), pp. 297–323.

45. See Shaoguang Wang, "The rise of the regions," and Wang Shaoguang and Hu Angang, *Zhongguo guojia nengli baogao (A Report on China's State Capacity)* (Shenyang: Liaoning renmin chubanshe, 1993).

a positive sign: as a "market preserving federalism" in which economic competition among provincial and local governments serves to deter any single locality from arbitrary and unproductive intervention in the realm of marketing and taxation, because investors and customers could flee to more favourable jurisdictions.[46] These same observers argue that the eventual codification of this informal "federalism" into legally defined powers and rights of central and regional government could provide a path towards institutionalized political competition[47] – one not usually considered by those who herald the rise of "civil society" as *the* way in which democracy shall evolve.

Gauging the sustainability of China's progress therefore draws attention to the interaction of economic and political institutions. On the one hand, economic reforms have had a discernible impact on politics either through their effects on ordinary citizens and the creation of social unrest or by directly affecting state structures themselves. On the other hand, economic progress depends on the stability and coherence of political institutions. The ultimate question is whether China's can serve this purpose for a sufficient period of time, or whether they will become so weakened that growth will stall amidst corruption and political strife. The answer lies far beyond the boundaries of economic inquiry.

Conclusions

The articles collected here all grapple with one or more of these questions. Some offer forceful answers, while others seek to correct widespread misconceptions or redefine the questions. The first two articles ask whether China enjoyed advantages that may have made its reform path easier. Peter Nolan and Robert Ash question the common assumption that China's lower level of industrial development gave it obvious advantages over the Soviet Union. They argue that the *ex ante* wisdom is specious: if one had examined the economic prospects of the USSR and China at the outset of reform one would not necessarily have predicted that China's advantages were so clear as they are now seen to be. Martin Whyte, focusing on the potential entrepreneurial role of the family, finds that the Chinese family emerged from Maoism strong, while the Russian family disintegrated under the impact of urbanization and economic change.

The next four articles examine various dimensions of China's economy: agricultural commerce, property rights, foreign trade and macroeconomic stability. Terry Sicular argues that China's agrarian reforms were far from a "big bang"; instead, they gradually released control over prices

46. See Gabriella Montinola, Yingyi Qian and Barry R. Weingast, "Federalism, Chinese style: the political basis for economic success in China," *World Politics*, Vol. 48 (October 1995), pp. 50–81; and Ronald I. McKinnon, "Market-preserving fiscal federalism: notes on the American and Chinese models," unpublished paper, Stanford University, August 1993. See also McKinnon's "Spontaneous order on the road back from socialism: an Asian perspective," *American Economic Review*, No. 80 (May 1992), pp. 31–36.
47. Montinola, Qian and Weingast, "Federalism, Chinese style."

and marketing outlets, a process managed throughout by state commercial agencies, who remain deeply involved to this day. Louis Putterman adjudicates the competing claims of those who argue that China has undertaken extensive *de facto* privatization and those who argue that China has maintained public ownership, and suggests that there has been extensive change in the allocation of property rights in China, though the dichotomous public/private distinction helps little to understand them. Nicholas Lardy finds that net foreign investment is almost a negligible factor in China's overall growth rate, although it has proved crucial in generating exports, as the traditional state sector has so far lagged a long way behind the foreign invested firms. Barry Naughton takes on conventional wisdom about macroeconomic instability in China and argues provocatively that investment, not subsidies, are the problem. Net subsidies to loss-making state firms are a tiny fraction of the state budget, and budgetary subsidies for living standards have fallen steadily. Naughton replaces the image of a weak central state struggling to cover state enterprise debts with one of a strong state pushing forward investment, but still without sophisticated instruments to modulate an economy now largely driven by market mechanisms.

Two subsequent articles examine the role of political institutions. Steven Goldstein reviews arguments of political scientists about the connection between political and economic reform in Soviet-style regimes, and argues that variations in the structures of Communist polities and economies have allowed China to defy the predictions of those who see party dictatorship as incompatible with market reform. Looking ahead, however, Goldstein wonders whether China's escape from this oft-emphasized connection will prove to be temporary. Jean Oi sees in China the emergence of a distinctive new variant of the East Asian developmental state. Unlike the other interventionist states of the region in which the central government is the only actor of interest, local governments play a crucial role – not solely through "industrial policy" but through direct ownership and entrepreneurship in the promotion of local industry.

Thomas Rawski's concluding synthesis of the lessons of China's reforms critiques the dogmatism of some economic analysis and calls for greater institutional and historical realism. At the same time, he emphasizes what an open mind may learn from studying China – both about the process of institutional change in *any* transitional economy and about the assumptions of mainstream economic theory.

These articles do not present a unified argument about China's transitional economy, but I detect three overriding conclusions about which there is consensus. The first is that history and institutions matter, and China has indeed enjoyed legacies that have assisted its path from a command economy. Nolan and Ash dispose of the idea that China's low level of industrialization was advantageous, but others identify legacies that do appear to have assisted the progress of reform. Whyte shows how the Chinese family emerged from the period of collectivism with a much higher capacity to sustain small-scale entrepreneurship than the Russian family. Lardy notes that Maoist austerity allowed China to begin its engagement in the world economy without severe international debt and poor credit ratings. Putterman and Rawski both point out that the dispersal of industrial ownership across local jurisdictions served to heighten the interest and experience of local cadres in industry, while Oi argues explicitly that the Mao era left a strong political infrastructure which, combined with new tax incentives, laid the foundation for rural China's rapid industrialization. All these essays favourably distinguish China's starting point from other transitional economies.

The second conclusion is that despite its historical and institutional distinctiveness, China nevertheless holds important lessons for all transitional economies. These lessons do not involve imitation of any specific Chinese policy, and "gradualism" is now a moot point, because the pace of change in Eastern Europe has in the end been no faster than in China. Perhaps the most important lesson is that economics (and nearby disciplines) has as much to learn from transitional economies as it has to teach them. Rawski makes very clear the weakness of much economic analysis when applied to transitional economies; Nolan and Ash find that China's refusal to heed the advice of Western economists, and Russia's effort to implement it, assisted China's rise and Russia's fall. Sicular argues explicitly that the distinction between "plan" and "market" no longer helps one understand China's agricultural commerce; Putterman questions the categorical conception of property rights that underlies the macroeconomist's faith in privatization; Oi questions the commonplace assumption that public bureaucrats cannot behave as if they were private entrepreneurs. While all these authors share the view that there are no authoritative answers, and that persistent pragmatic experimentation through time can work, they also share a deeper assumption: successful reform involves the relentless introduction of choice, alternatives and competition into the environment of all actors in the economy, regardless of who they are.

This last point leads to the third and final conclusion, which I find to be the most important of all. A transitional economy must alter incentives not merely for individuals and firms but for government agencies and government officials themselves, for the behaviour of the latter can have enormous economic consequences. Conventional economic analysis, upon which much policy advice has been based, is remarkable for the degree to which it is blind to the analysis of government agencies and officials. Yet the articles collected here are all about the shifting opportunities and constraints facing them. Sicular emphasizes the strong market incentives to which state commercial organs now must respond. Naughton shows the market-driven processes with which the central state must increasingly grapple. Oi analyses the incentives that turn rural bureaucrats into market-oriented entrepreneurs. Rawski argues that competition for resources affects the behaviour of all actors, be they state finance officials, managers of large state factories or petty entrepreneurs. A transitional economy is defined as one undergoing profound institutional change, and institutional change involves changing incentives and

constraints facing all actors whose behaviour has economic consequences. This, then, is the final lesson of China's reforms: the task is not
to revile state involvement but to change it.

China's Economy on the Eve of Reform

Peter Nolan and Robert F. Ash

Pressures for change are inherent in leadership succession under any political system. In China, because of his longevity and close involvement in major strategic initiatives, Mao Zedong's passing was bound to intensify such pressures. When he died in September 1976, Mao had held supreme power, largely unchallenged, for four decades. Since 1949, China's economic development had been uniquely, if not consistently, influenced by his personal prejudices and idiosyncratic view of how best to realize the country's development potential.

To argue that post-1978 Dengist reforms were shaped by the Maoist economic legacy is not to suggest that they were its *inevitable* outcome. Analysis of the recent comparative experience of China and the former Soviet Union shows the fallacy of such simplistic logic. But the origins of those reforms lie in the prior accumulation of experience. It is with these origins and this experience – judged in their own terms, as well as from the comparative perspective of conditions in the former USSR – that this article is concerned. It seeks to determine whether, as of the late 1970s, China's prior pattern of development or existing economic structure gave it inherent advantages in implementing reforms. Contrary to what others have argued, we find that such advantages were by no means self-evident and in some respects China was *disadvantaged* vis-à-vis the former Soviet Union.

The three core sections which follow have separate but related goals. The first analyses the Maoist economic legacy, inherited by the new government in 1976. The second examines the impact of this legacy on economic policy and perceptions of reform in the aftermath of Mao's death. The final section investigates China's capacity for accelerated economic and social development on the eve of reform, compared with that of the other Communist giant, the former Soviet Union.

The Maoist Legacy

Behind the Maoist economic system lay a highly centralized bureaucratic apparatus, which facilitated an unprecedented degree of socio-economic control by the Chinese Communist Party.[1] The basic framework of the command economy was set up, under Soviet tutelage, during the First Five-Year Plan (1FYP) (1953–57) and thereafter remained largely intact.

---

1. Such control generated powerful negative economic consequences. Decisions were frequently taken by Party members, who lacked appropriate training and skills. Ideological orthodoxy constrained economic debate – for example, insisting that "planning" provided a framework in which resource allocation could take place without reference to such fundamental economic concepts as price, cost and profit. The centralized system also contained the potential for major errors, the most outstanding examples of which (in the Chinese case) were the Great Leap Forward (1958–59) and Cultural Revolution (1966–76).

At the heart of the system was a comprehensive material balances supply matrix, which controlled the allocation of many major products. Most output and investment decisions were determined in accordance with plan instructions. Almost all profits were remitted to planning bodies.

Planning was intended to substitute for the supposed "anarchy" of competitive capitalism. Instead, it generated problems of its own. The inherent complexity of constructing a material balance plan generated in-built, permanent imbalance between supply and demand. A pervasive atmosphere of shortage gave rise to a seller's market, while the specification of production targets in physical terms resulted in a narrowing of product variety towards goods which were easy to produce, without regard for their quality.

Thus, instead of eliminating the shortcomings of the capitalist system, planning exhibited many of the same deficiencies in an even more acute form. Far from abolishing waste, it generated waste on a grand scale. It abolished production for profit, but failed to replace it with production for use. It eliminated the short-termism of competitive capitalism only to substitute the short-termism of current plan fulfilment. It steered economic activity in socially undesirable directions, but was unable to alter the underlying pattern of economic behaviour.

The origin of China's post-1978 reforms lies in the economy's disappointing growth record since the end of the 1FYP and in the structural problems which stemmed from it. To speak of a "disappointing performance" demands qualification. Between 1960 and 1981 China's average growth of per capita GNP (5 per cent p.a.) was one of the highest among developing countries.[2] It is in terms of China's own development aspirations and against the background of a declining growth trend since 1957 that a more pessimistic assessment seemed justified.

The figures in Table 1 highlight the distinct deceleration of growth, which characterized China's economic performance after 1957. They also indicate that the growth momentum was significantly slower during the second half of the Cultural Revolution decade (1966–76),[3] even though the campaign's most disruptive phase is usually thought to have occurred before 1970.

Agriculture is the basis of a poor country's economy, not only because food is such a large share of consumption, but also because light industry depends critically on raw materials from the farm sector. In the 1FYP, the agricultural growth rate was 3.7 per cent p.a. – significantly higher than the population growth rate; by the Cultural Revolution decade, it had

2. See World Bank, *World Development Report* (*WDR*), 1983 (New York: Oxford University Press, 1983), pp. 148–49. The corresponding figure for low-income countries (excluding India and China) was 0.88%; for India – in many ways, the most relevant comparator country – it was 1.4% p.a.

3. An exception is the performance of China's merchandise trade, whose annual growth accelerated from 1.54% (1965–70) to 17.89% (1970–76) (State Statistical Bureau (SSB), *Zhongguo tongji nianjian* (*TJNJ*) (*Chinese Statistical Yearbook*), 1993 (Beijing: Zhongguo tongji chubanshe, 1993), p. 633). Even so, by the end of the 1970s, the export earnings of the "four Asian dragons" – whose combined population was about the same as that of Guangdong province – was more than four times larger than that of the whole of China!

Table 1: **China's Historical Growth Record** (average rate of growth, % p.a.)

	1952–57	1957–76	of which: 1957–65	1965–70	1970–76	1976–78
NMP	8.88	4.82	3.24	8.34	4.08	10.03
NVAO	3.73	1.49	0.29	2.61	2.18	0.66
NVIO	19.60	8.96	8.73	12.56	6.36	15.94
GVIO	17.98	9.47	8.91	12.01	8.12	14.08
GVIO (light)	12.88	8.00	8.21	8.70	7.16	12.68
GVIO (heavy)	25.45	10.78	9.68	15.02	8.80	15.14

Notes:
   Data given in comparable prices. NMP: net material product; NVAO: agricultural net value output; NVIO: industrial net value output; GVIO: industrial gross value output.
Source:
   State Statistical Bureau (SSB), *Zhongguo tongj nianjian* (*TJNJ*) (*Chinese Statistical Yearbook*), 1993 (Beijing: Zhongguo tongji chubanshe, 1993), pp. 33 and 55.

fallen to 2.6 per cent – hardly above the rate of natural increase. Table 1 shows that after 1957, the industrial growth also declined sharply.

Judged by these macro indicators, as well as by those for key industries (grain, steel and coal are the most notable examples),[4] post-Mao economic assessments were understandably informed by an underlying concern. Per capita estimates suggested an even more discouraging picture, for apart from the abnormal demographic impact of the "great famine" of 1959–61, the rate of natural increase of population remained high throughout the Maoist period.[5] There is evidence too that the effectiveness with which resources were used declined over the long term. Official figures show that the incremental output–capital ratio[6] was halved between the First and Fourth FYPs. Studies of state industry's performance show a similar long-run deterioration in capital productivity.[7]

The estimates in Table 1 show the lagging performance of agriculture and light industry vis-à-vis that of heavy industry. Concealed in such varying sectoral rates of growth were marked changes in China's

4. Previous peak levels of steel and coal production (1960) were not re-attained until 1971–72. The growth of total grain output between 1965 and 1976 was almost identical to that of the 1FYP, although it too demonstrated a declining trend (*TJNJ*, 1993, pp. 364 and 446–47).

5. Some 30 million "excess deaths" may have resulted from mainly policy-induced errors during the Great Leap Forward (J. Banister, *China's Changing Population* (Stanford, CA: Stanford University Press, 1987), p. 85. The average rate of natural increase during the 4FYP (1965–70) was 2.33% p.a. – virtually identical to that of the 1FYP years (2.35%) (*TJNJ*, 1993, p. 81).

6. That is, the increase in national income per 100 *yuan* of accumulation.

7. See Kuan Chen *et al.*, "New estimates of fixed investment and capital stock for Chinese state industry," *The China Quarterly* (*CQ*), No. 114 (June 1988), pp. 243–266.

Table 2: **Structural Characteristics of China's and Other Economies (1980)**

	China	USSR	LIEs	MIEs	IMEs
As percentage of GDP					
Agriculture	31	16	45	15	4
Industry	47	62	17	40	37
Services	22	22	38	45	62
As percentage of employment					
Agriculture	71	14	73	44	6
Industry	17	45	11	22	38
Services	12	41	19	34	56

Notes:
  LIE = low-income economies (excl. China and India); MIE = middle-income economies; IME = industrial market economies.
Source:
  WDR, 1982.

economic structure. Agriculture's share in GDP declined steadily at the expense of that of industry during the Maoist period.[8] Meanwhile, the Stalinist strategy of forced industrialization was reflected in the growing weight of heavy industry in the industrial sector's overall expansion.[9] The outcome of these developments is summarized in Table 2, which shows the relative output and employment contributions of the three main sectors[10] (including some comparative indicators) at the beginning of the reform period.

So far as changes in living standards and welfare during the Maoist periods are concerned, estimates of per capita income suggest that after a quarter of a century of planned development China remained a poor country.[11] Raising income is admittedly more difficult than improving social indicators and there is clear evidence of a major reduction in poverty, measured by levels of infant mortality and life expectancy.[12] But high and rising rates of accumulation and the bias towards heavy

8. This process was interrupted between 1962 and 1968 in the wake of a strategy which temporarily afforded a higher investment priority to agriculture. See *TJNJ*, 1993, p. 60.

9. To what extent the two economies can be described as having been "over-industrialized" is considered at length below.

10. The relative size of the service sector was probably greater than Table 2 suggests. Many services, which might otherwise have been generated by specialist suppliers, were provided directly by agricultural and industrial enterprises.

11. Useful international comparisons can be found in World Bank, *China: Socialist Development* (Washington, D.C.: The World Bank, 1981), Annex A. By the late 1970s, the incomes of over a quarter of China's total population (some 270 million people) fell below a poverty line roughly comparable with that used by the World Bank to analyse poverty in developing countries (World Bank, *China: Strategies for Reducing Poverty in the 1990s* (Washington, D.C.: The World Bank, 1992), p. ix.

12. By the early reform period, the infant mortality rate had fallen to 71 per thousand, compared with 124 in LIEs (excluding India and China), and may even have been lower than in MIEs. Life expectancy at birth had risen from 35 (pre-1949) to 71 years (1981) (*WDR*, 1983, pp. 192–93).

industrial investment were reflected in low rates of non-productive investment. The rate of growth of consumption also slowed markedly, from 4.2 per cent p.a. (1FYP) to 2.1 per cent (4FYP, 1971–75).[13]

Transforming the Maoist Economy: Perspectives on Economic Policy and Performance on the Eve of Reform

The new orthodoxy which emerged after Mao's death[14] was openly critical of the economic damage caused by earlier, supposedly "Leftist" policies. Disproportions and imbalance – between major economic sectors, between production relations and productive forces, between consumption and accumulation – were the generic factors which defined an emerging structuralist critique. They were reflected in the differential sectoral growth performance of the economy under Mao (see Table 1), as well as in the absence of any significant improvement in mass consumption standards for more than two decades. As it evolved, the critique also made reference to deeply-rooted systemic problems and the need to reform economic management methods in order to reverse declining levels of efficiency and productivity.

The emerging view of the Maoist legacy was not uniformly negative.[15] But it did suggest that the most notable economic achievements since 1949 had occurred when policies had *least* embodied Mao's own developmental vision. To endorse the "healthy" development of economic structural relations during the Stalinist 1FYP period[16] was implicitly to condemn the subsequent decision to adopt a more expressly indigenous (Maoist) developmental strategy – the Great Leap Forward. From the perspective of the 1980s, approval of the readjustment policies of 1962–65 is less surprising,[17] for they bore a striking resemblance to the pragmatic measures adopted in the countryside in the early years of post-1978 reform. But the recovery which they facilitated derived from an economic approach towards development that was the antithesis of Mao's.

The urgency with which the immediate post-Mao economic situation was viewed is evident from measures which Hua Guofeng's government introduced as early as the last quarter of 1976. They included a cutback

13. In 1978, only 52% of rural households possessed a clock, 27% a wristwatch, 31% a bicycle, 20% a sewing machine and 17% a radio (*TJNJ*, 1988, p. 835).

14. The critical re-appraisal of Mao's legacy began during the interregnum of his chosen successor, Hua Guofeng, although it was left to Deng Xiaoping to complete the revisionist process.

15. The economic legacy was not devoid of positive features. The centralized system bequeathed a strong organizational framework, as well as a large task-force of people who were capable of mobilizing popular energies, who thought in strategic terms and who viewed themselves as members of a team rather than individuals.

16. E.g. see Ma Hong and Sun Shangqing (eds.), *Zhongguo jingji jiegou wenti yanjiu* (*Research on Problems Relating to China's Economic Structure*) (Beijing: Renmin chubanshe, 1981), p. 23.

17. A characteristically positive assessment is given in Cao Bi-jun and Lin Mu-xi (eds.), *Xin Zhongguo jingji shi, 1949–1989* (*A New Economic History of China, 1949–1989*) (Beijing: Jingji ribao chubanshe, 1990), part 4, pp. 170–224.

in basic construction investment, the freezing of institutional bank deposits and the readjustment of economic plans for 1977.[18] They were supplemented by efforts to bring inflation under tighter control and the granting of wage increases to some 60 per cent of industrial employees. Further initiatives were introduced in 1977 and 1978, the most important of which was explicit official encouragement of foreign capital inflows and imports of advanced technology.

Such measures no doubt helped facilitate rapid recovery during 1976–78 (see Table 1). Even if natural disasters left the 1977 agricultural plan unfulfilled, GVAO registered positive growth (by 1.6 per cent), which accelerated to 11.9 per cent the following year. The total output of grain and oil crops meanwhile rose to record levels. Industrial recovery was also in evidence, GVIO rising by more than 13 per cent in both 1977 and 1978. Modest expansion of foreign trade in 1977 (by 10 per cent) was the prelude to a spectacular rise (by almost 40 per cent) during 1978.[19]

The post-1976 initiatives were, however, far from constituting fundamental system reform and although they facilitated short-term recovery, they did not solve the more deeply-rooted structural problems. Indeed, in order to lend proper perspective to developments during Hua Guofeng's interregnum, the pragmatism of some aspects of economic strategy must be weighed against its more conservative features. Riskin has referred to the "hybrid ideological atmosphere" which prevailed after Mao's death,[20] and there is certainly evidence of backward as well as forward-looking policies during this period.[21]

Hua Guofeng's recognition of the urgent need for economic rehabilitation made possible the first critical reassessment of Mao's legacy. But it was Deng Xiaoping's belief in the pre-eminent role of economic construction which encouraged a more radical reappraisal to take place and thereby paved the way for economic reforms. The true significance of the Third Plenum of the 11th CCP Central Committee (December 1978) lay in its endorsement of the very "economistic" philosophy which Mao had condemned and for which Deng and his supporters had come under attack.[22]

The absence of clear objectives, let alone a visionary blueprint, is thought by many to have worked to China's advantage by encouraging a

18. Note too that a rapid rise of state financial revenues during 1977 generated a sizeable budget surplus – the first in four years. For details of all these measures, see *ibid*. pp. 290 and 298.

19. Significant in this regard was the transformation of a small surplus in China's balance of merchandise trade (US$0.38 billion, 1977) into a record deficit (US$1.14 billion, 1978).

20. C. Riskin, *China's Political Economy: The Quest for Development Since 1949* (Oxford: Oxford University Press, 1987), p. 259.

21. E.g. in agriculture there was advocacy of replacing the production team by the brigade as the basic accounting unit, while private plots and household sideline activities were condemned for exhibiting "capitalist tendencies."

22. Thus, the Third Plenum communiqué: "… the emphasis in the work of the whole Party should … shift towards the task of socialist modernization" (Documentary Research Department of the CCP Central Committee (ed.), *Sanzhong quanhui yilai – zhongyao wenxian xuanbian* (*Selected Important Documents Since the Third Plenary Session of the 11th CCP Central Committee*) (Beijing: Renmin chubanshe, 1982), Vol. 1, p. 1.

gradual, evolutionary approach towards economic reforms.[23] Caution and gradualism certainly came to characterize that approach, although it is likely that their advocacy followed, rather than preceded, the earliest reforms.[24] There was no shortage of arguments in favour of espousing a gradualist reform programme in China. Recent direct experience of the potential disastrous consequences of policy "leaps," the perennial Chinese fear of policy-induced "chaos" (*luan*), the benefits of compromise for securing a pro-reform consensus – all underlined the advantages of caution. But evidence that such arguments were used to advocate a strategy of explicit gradualism and caution from the outset is lacking.[25] In the wake of the Third Plenum, consensus embraced economic objectives; much greater uncertainty surrounded the economic strategy and tactics needed to secure such objectives.

In short, the fundamental ideas of the reformers at the end of the 1970s were simple. They arose logically from their perception of the shortcomings of the inherited economy. Premised on the fundamental need for political stability, policy pronouncements extended no further than advocacy of a greater (but supplementary) role for the market mechanism, less emphasis on egalitarianism, the pursuit of proportionate and balanced growth, the decentralization of economic decision-making, and the closer integration of China in the world economy.

The Potential for Accelerated Economic Growth: China and the Soviet Union on the Eve of Reform

Systematic comparison of the reform experiences of the Chinese and Russian economies remains limited.[26] The most influential proposition to have emerged from this literature argues that the different outcomes of reform in the two countries derives not from choice of policy but from contrasting initial conditions. Thus:

It was neither gradualism nor experimentation, but rather China's economic structure, that proved so felicitous to reform. China began reform as a peasant agricultural

23. E.g. see Barry Naughton, "Deng Xiaoping: the economist," *CQ*, No. 135 (1993), pp. 491–92.

24. The earliest institutional reforms in the countryside seem to have reflected a spontaneous peasant response, which only later received official – and grudging – endorsement.

25. One of the most interesting early comments against the adoption of rapid, comprehensive system reform and in favour of an incremental and experimental approach was made by Liu Guoguang and Wang Ruisun. See their "Restructuring of the economy," in Yu Guangyuan (ed.), *China's Socialist Modernization* (Beijing: Foreign Languages Press, 1984), esp. pp. 119–120.

26. E.g. see A. Aslund, *Gorbachev's Struggle for Economic Reform* (London: Pinter, 1991); M. Goldman, *What Went Wrong with Perestroika?* (New York: Norton, 1992); Jeffrey Sachs and Wing Tye Woo, "Structural factors in the economic reforms of China, Eastern Europe and the former Soviet Union," *Economic Policy*, Vol. 9, No. 18 (April 1994); and Peter Nolan, *China's Rise, Russia's Fall: Politics, Economics and Planning in the Transition from Stalinism* (Basingstoke: Macmillan, 1995).

society, EEFSU[27] as urban and overindustrialized ... . In Gerschenkron's famous phrase [China] had the "advantage of backwardness."[28]

Implicit in Gerschenkron's "advantage of backwardness" is the belief that a country coming late to development enjoys the potential for faster growth than its predecessors. Not only does a latecomer have access to a larger pool of advanced technology than early industrializers, but new fixed asset formation promises to confer a more efficient vintage profile on its capital stock. The large size of its farm sector may be another advantage, agriculture often being considered more susceptible to reform than industry. Further, a large surplus of rural labour may be the source of rapid growth in labour-intensive industries, where gestation lags are shorter and technological coefficients more flexible than in large-scale industry. Finally, latecomers may also benefit from an increasing pool of international capital.

The validity of such arguments to conditions in pre-reform China and the USSR is questionable. Although more than 70 per cent of China's workforce were employed in agriculture, compared with only 14 per cent in the USSR, the Soviet share remained significantly higher than in advanced capitalist countries (Table 2). Soviet agriculture contained the potential to release large numbers of surplus workers for productive work elsewhere in the economy. But the implicit assumption that a large share of agriculture in national output and employment is necessarily an advantage is not self-evident. In a densely populated country like China, the capital requirements of agricultural expansion are large. It is not coincidental that the economic success of the East Asian NIEs derived from accelerated growth in economies which had *small* farm sectors.[29]

But what of the industrial sector? In 1980, it accounted for 62 per cent of Soviet GDP – a higher share even than in advanced market economies (Table 2). Interestingly, industry in China also contributed a larger share of GDP (47 per cent) than in such economies. As discussed below, there were serious inefficiencies in both Chinese and Soviet industry, but "over-industrialization" may have been a greater burden in China, where lower incomes generated less savings with which to finance investment (especially in heavy industry).[30]

The accelerated globalization of capital during and after the late 1970s offered a major catch-up opportunity to reforming Communist countries.

27. Eastern Europe and the former Soviet Union.
28. Sachs and Woo, "Structural factors," pp. 102–104.
29. "It is very rare for agriculture to grow faster than 5% in any country where agriculture is an important part of the economy. Therefore, the less important is agriculture, the easier it is to strike up very high growth rates of GDP. This is what people have in mind when they dismiss Hong Kong and Singapore as irrelevant" (I. Little, "An economic reconnaissance" in Walter Galenson (ed.), *Taiwan* (Cornell: Cornell University Press, 1979), p. 450).
30. "Over-industrialization" was more evident in the USSR in terms of its employment share (45%). But if labour hoarding and high levels of job security generated over-manning in Soviet industry, such practices were not absent in China. In both countries, appropriate institutional reform promised to raise labour productivity and encourage state enterprise managers to release labour for productive work elsewhere in the economy (not least, in the service sector).

Mere availability of such capital is not sufficient to guarantee access to it, nor does access to it ensure sustained growth. But the formulation of appropriate policies of structural transformation in developing countries can encourage inflows of overseas capital and, as China's own recent experience shows, be the source of accelerated growth. Foreign direct investment (FDI) is especially attractive in this regard, giving the investor a direct and lasting interest in improving efficiency in the firm where investment is taking place.

China also enjoyed the unique potential advantage of having access to enormous volumes of capital controlled by overseas Chinese, especially in their east and south-east Asian diaspora. Significantly too, it was located in the most dynamic region of the world economy, embracing Japan and the Asian NIEs – countries which experienced acute labour shortages, large trade surpluses and appreciating exchange rates just as China was embarking on its economic reforms. As a result, China became a major beneficiary of its neighbours' search for overseas investment opportunities, notably in less technologically demanding lines of manufacturing, where labour costs were lower.

But the USSR too had the potential to become an attractive foreign investment destination. Notwithstanding the inhospitable nature of much of its Central Asian and Far East regions, the core of the Russian economy west of the Urals was essentially part of Europe. Its labour force was more educated and skilful than China's,[31] but its workers were prepared to work hard for much lower wages than people of comparable training in the West. It also possessed a vastly more developed pool of scientific and technical personnel, even if its record in utilizing such expertise to promote technical progress had been disappointing. Its infrastructure too was more developed than that of China. Yet far from attracting significant levels of foreign investment, the appeal of FSU (later, Russia) as an investment environment steadily deteriorated.[32]

Institutional and economic factors were largely responsible for the disappointing return, in terms of *civilian* technical progress, from scientific investment in both China and the USSR prior to reform.[33] The emphasis indicates the major share of scientific expertise absorbed by the military sector in the two countries. The inference is that the end of the

31. PPP estimates for the mid-1970s suggest that the USSR was ahead of all Western countries, except the USA, in its per capita consumption of educational services (G. Schroeder, "Consumption" in A. Bergson and D. Levine, *The Soviet Economy: Towards the Year 2000* (London: Allen and Unwin, 1983), p. 319).

32. This was the outcome of disastrous political and economic policy choices. Based on conditions at the beginning of 1993, an estimate of credit risk by the Economist Intelligence Unit showed Russia to be the second most risky country in the world, next to Iraq. Despite some downgrading because of its overheated economy, China ranked high – between Malaysia and Thailand (*The Economist*, 21 August 1993, p. 88).

33. Most scientific research personnel had no direct contact with economic activities, technical progress being regarded as a public good. In the absence of competition and profit seeking, enterprise managers also had little incentive to pursue technical progress. Pervasive shortages were reflected in the existence of a seller's marker so that in the production of both capital and consumption goods there was little encouragement to use scientific skills to improve product quality.

Table 3: **Educational Attainments: Some Comparative Indicators, 1978** (enrolments as a percentage of appropriate age group)

	Primary school	*Secondary school*	*Higher education**	*Adult literacy rate*
LIES	74	20	2	43
MIEs	95	41	11	72
IMEs	100	89	37	99
China	93	51	1	66
USSR	97	72	22	100
India	79	28	8	36
USA	98	97	56	99

Note:
*The appropriate age group comprises those between the ages of 20 and 24.
Source:
   WDR, 1981.

Cold War promised to release a substantial peace dividend by reallocating scientific and material resources to civilian use. The potential gain from technology imports was also considerable,[34] if only adequate foreign exchange could be secured. Overall, however, the potential benefits from technological catch-up were probably greater for the USSR than for China.

In order to understand this last statement, social capability levels in the two countries must be considered.[35] Table 3 presents comparative data relating to educational attainments in 1978. On the eve of reform, China's level of school education was highly advanced by the standards of low-income countries, and in some respects comparable with those of middle-income countries. The data may, however, conceal lower educational attainments among those already working. One source suggests, for example, that in the early 1980s 63 per cent of the labour force had an educational level no higher than that of elementary schooling (including

34. In the mid-1970s, the value of the USSR's equipment imports was equivalent to a mere 2% of total domestic equipment investment (P. Hanson, "The import of Western technology" in A. Brown and M. Kaser (eds.), *The Soviet Union Since the Fall of Khrushchev* (London: Macmillan, 1978), p. 31). In China's machine-building industry, "the stock of Soviet equipment was rapidly becoming obsolete and domestically produced equipment was primitive" (Jack Craig, Jim Lewek and Gordon Cole, "A survey of China's machine-building industry" in U.S. Congress, Joint Economic Committee, *Chinese Economy Post-Mao* (Washington, D.C.: U.S. Government Printing Office, 1978), p. 311).
35. "A country's potential for rapid growth is strong not when it is backward without qualification, but rather when it is technologically backward but socially advanced" (M. Abramowitz, "Catching up, forging ahead, falling behind," *Journal of Economic History*, Vol. 46, No. 2 (1986), p. 38; see also S. Gomulka, *The Theory of Technological Change and Economic Growth* (London: Routledge, 1991)).

more than a quarter who were illiterate).[36] School enrolment levels were even higher in the USSR, comparing favourably with advanced capitalist countries. But the Soviet Union was also more highly urbanized than China and did not have the same problem of a large semi-literate peasantry.

In any case, China's record in the provision of higher education was much less successful. In 1978 a mere one per cent of the relevant age group (20–24) was enrolled in higher educational institutions (HEIs), compared with 2 per cent in LIEs and 8 per cent in India. The cost of the Cultural Revolution in this regard was especially high, HEIs having been closed for much longer than schools.[37] By the late 1970s, the ratio of scientific and technical personnel to total manpower was low – for example, a mere 4.5 per cent in the chemical and machine-building industries. The educational disruption and isolation of China during the Cultural Revolution had also had an adverse effect on the *quality* of technical expertise.

A corollary of the poor record of the USSR in utilizing scientific skills in order to generate technical progress was its allocation of sizeable resources in order to strengthen its manpower base in this area. As a result, the USSR had a much greater pool of scientific and technical personnel than did China. In the mid-1970s, there were 66 scientists and engineers per thousand population, compared with 62 in the United States.[38]

If the general quality of labour in both China and the USSR was high, its motivation under a command system was more questionable. A variety of factors kept the workforce operating well within its capacity. In agriculture, familiar problems associated with large-scale production units (collectives or state farms) arose. In the non-farm sector, the inability to dismiss workers greatly reduced the pressure which enterprise managers could exert upon the workforce. Indeed, the material balances system encouraged managers to hoard labour (and capital) in an effort to ensure fulfilment of key planning targets. Nor did the administrative planning system succeed in maintaining timely deliveries of inputs to keep production processes running smoothly at full capacity. The outcome was an uneven work pace throughout each production period.

Such phenomena constitute an indictment of the planning system as it operated in China and the Soviet Union. But they were not fixed parameters of economic activity. Rather, the slow work pace and low work effort, reflecting stagnating living standards during years of high

36. K. C. Yeh, "Macroeconomic changes in the Chinese economy during the readjustment," *CQ*, No. 100 (1984), p. 693. Remember too that primary and secondary education had been hugely disrupted by the Cultural Revolution, when schools were closed for long periods.

37. "The Cultural Revolution is estimated to have cost China 2 million middle level technicians and one million university graduates ..." (World Bank, *China: Socialist Development*, p. 106).

38. In addition, the low effectiveness of Soviet scientific research was reflected in the high ratio of ancillary personnel per scientist and engineer (5.0 in 1970, compared with 1.3 in the USA) (U.S. Congress, Joint Economic Committee, *Soviet Economy in a Time of Change* (Washington, D.C.: U.S. Government Printing Office, 1979), p. 745).

savings and investment rates, signalled potential windfall gains that were available from existing resources if only appropriate incentive schemes could be found to motivate workers.

The nature of the relationship between China's Confucian heritage and its economic development remains a controversial issue and is beyond the scope of this article.[39] But a factor which does deserve mention is China's powerful entrepreneurial tradition. By the 11th century AD, its economy exhibited well-developed markets and a large urban sector. Despite China's failure to institute its own modern Industrial Revolution, in those areas where there was a semblance of political order, rapid progress in the development of modern industry did occur in the first three decades of the 20th century. If this owed much to foreign influences, it also reflected the emergence of a thriving indigenous bourgeoisie.[40]

Early studies highlighted the supposed absence in Russia of a similar entrepreneurial spirit and degree of capitalist development.[41] Subsequent analysis suggests a more complex reality, indicating that by the late 19th century capitalism was well advanced in European Russia.[42] In short, it is not self-evident that China's reforms were destined to be more successful than those of the USSR because of an inherently greater capacity for entrepreneurial activity in the former.[43]

Overall, there is a strong case for arguing that, through the introduction of competition and the profit motive, considerable potential for large increases in output existed in both countries. It is possible that in terms of availability of education and skill levels, as well as scientific and technical expertise, such potential may have been greater in the Soviet Union than in China. Finally, it is notable that on the eve of reform, China's demographic factors continued to generate large annual incremental increases in total population – a situation which contrasted with that of the USSR. In particular, the Soviet farm population had stabilized and although both economies embarked on reform with large backlogs of surplus labour, demographic pressures gave China a greater problem in absorbing such workers.

The industrial sector. The extreme inefficiency with which the Stalinist economies used investment resources meant that both China and Russia required a large input of intermediate goods to generate a unit of final

39. See Martin Whyte's article in this issue.
40. See Marie-Claire Bergère, *The Golden Age of the Chinese Bourgeoisie* (Cambridge: Cambridge University Press, 1989). On the dynamism of the modern sector in pre-war China, see also Thomas G. Rawski, *Economic Growth in Prewar China* (Berkeley: University of California Press, 1989).
41. E.g. see Maurice Dobb, who argued that by 1914 capitalism had "... as yet touched little more than the hem of Russia's economic system" (*Studies in the Development of Capitalism* (London: Routledge and Kegan Paul, 1966), pp. 35–36).
42. See W. Blackwell, "The Russian entrepreneur in the Tsarist period," in G. Guroff and F. V. Kasteson (eds.), *Entrepreneurship in Imperial Russia and the Soviet Union* (Princeton, N.J.: Princeton University Press, 1983); also P. Gatrell, *The Tsarist Economy, 1850–1917* (London: Batsford, 1986).
43. Nor is it self-evident that almost 60 years of "anti-capitalist" Stalinist planning in the USSR had had a greater inhibiting effect than 30 years of similar experience in China. A large

Table 4: **Intermediate Input Levels Per Dollar of GNP (1979–80)**

	Steel (grams)	Sulphuric acid (grams)	Cement (grams)	Energy (kilograms of coal equivalent)
China	146	31	319	3.21
USSR	136	21	116	1.49
USA	42	17	27	1.16
Japan	109	7	87	0.48
FDR	61	7	47	0.56

Source:
   World Bank, *China: Socialist Development*

output. Selected comparative indicators are presented in Table 4. China was even more profligate than the USSR in its use of inputs. In both cases, the quality of much heavy industrial output, especially machinery, was below that required to compete in world markets. The potential ability of enhanced competition to reduce input utilization per unit of output and to raise the quality of capital goods was therefore considerable.

A striking feature of the industrial structures of China and the Soviet Union was the pre-eminent role played by large plants. In the early 1980s, in both countries around 1,000 very large plants (over 5,000 employees) employed 12–14 million workers, accounted for between one-third and a half of the total value of industrial fixed assets, and produced one-fifth to one-third of GVIO. Large plants (over 1,000 employees) accounted for 64 per cent of the total value of industrial fixed assets and 48 per cent of GVIO in China; and 81 and 75 per cent in the USSR.[44]

Consideration of the functioning of the large enterprise in former Communist countries is essential to an understanding of the structural demands of reform. Large plants were characterized by a high degree of vertical integration, stemming from the complexity of material balances planning. Taut planning tended to generate attempts to maximize self-sufficiency within enterprises in order to obviate shortages of materials and fuel inherent in the command system.[45] In addition, many spare parts

---

footnote continued
"second economy" developed in both countries and private-sector activity characterized their agricultural sectors.

44. Relevant data can be found in Liu Nanchuan, Chen Yichu and Zhang Chu, *Sulian guomin jingji fazhan qishi nian* (*70 Years of Soviet Economic Development*) (Beijing: Jijie chubanshe, 1988), pp. 120 and 145; and SSB, *Zhongguo gongye jingji tongji nianjian* (*Statistical Yearbook of China's Industrial Economy*), 1988 (Beijing: Zhongguo tongji chubanshe, 1988), pp. 7 and 293.

45. In 1978 some 80% of the 6,057 engineering factories produced their own iron castings (Ma Hong, *Xiandai Zhongguo jingji shidan* (*The Contemporary Chinese Economy: A Compendium*) (Beijing: Zhongguo shehui kexue chubanshe, 1982), p. 231). In the USSR, less

and machinery requirements were produced within large plants, where general-purpose machine tools were used at low utilization rates to produce a wide variety of inputs in small quantities. Far from benefiting from large-scale specialized production, large-scale plants in China and the USSR often produced small-batch output at below-optimal scale.

Ironically, the Chinese and Soviet structural problem was not that of there being too few specialist producers, with large monopolistic propensities. Rather, many areas of industrial activity were characterized by the existence of too many small-scale producers. The task of reform was to construct out of the non-competitive environment of a command economy industrial giants, which would benefit from economies of scale associated with multi-plant operation and be able to compete in world markets. Small-scale, in-house plants, each producing at below-optimal scale, demanded re-organization into large multi-plant companies – a process involving horizontal mergers within the shell of existing enterprises. Further policy implications included the need to select managers on merit, introduce profit-orientated goals and implement gradual price de-control.

The underlying structural problems were common to both China and the USSR, but in China's case they were exacerbated by difficulties associated with the idiosyncrasies of indigenous economic strategies. If China's huge size and poor infrastructure favoured a self-reliant pattern of industrial development, the strategic imperatives of the "Third Front" policy gave it an added impetus. The outcome was a significant increase in the industrial weight of inland provinces at the expense of the coastal region.[46]

But a high cost attached to siting new industrial facilities in the interior. The remoteness of many new factories meant that economic returns to inland industrial investment were often low, and infrastructural – especially transport – costs were extremely high.[47] Out of the emphasis on "self-reliance" came also a rapid increase in the number of small-scale industrial plants, although the urgent need for modern farm inputs in the aftermath of the Great Leap Forward was also a powerful stimulus to their appearance in the countryside. By the mid-1970s some 45 per cent of nitrogen output, half of cement production and much of China's farm machinery was being supplied by such plants.[48] Many of these units were tiny in scale: in 1979, for example, there existed 580,000

---

footnote continued

than 20% of cast iron and steel was purchased from specialist suppliers, compared with more than 80% in the USA (D. Granick, *Soviet Metal-Fabricating* (Madison, Milwaukee: University of Wisconsin Press, 1967)).

46. Relevant data can be found in SSB, *Zhongguo gongye jingji tongji ziliao* (*Statistical Materials on China's Industrial Economy*) (Beijing: Zhongguo tongji chubanshe, 1985), p. 137.

47. New railways built to the west of the main north–south coastal axis accounted for 84% of total investment in railway construction between 1963 and 1978 (Yu Guangyuan, *China's Socialist Modernization*, p. 168).

48. *Ibid.* p. 156; D. H. Perkins (ed.), *China: Small-Scale Industry in the People's Republic of China* (London: University of California Press, 1977), pp. 156 and 178.

enterprises (62 per cent of all industrial enterprises) at brigade or team level, employing an average of only 17 workers per plant and producing just 3.4 per cent of GVIO.[49]

High costs attached to the industrial strategies pursued by China and the Soviet Union. Large-scale industry failed to benefit from economies of scale, nor did it derive the advantages of specialization and exchange. Material consumption was high and much of the output it produced was of low quality. In China's case, costs of production were also high in many small-scale factories, not only because of their inherent inefficiency[50] but also because they frequently produced capital goods which should have gained from economies of scale in large plants. In consequence, industrial reform in China had to address both the familiar problems of restructuring its large-scale enterprises and the task of reorganizing its small-scale facilities.[51]

The agricultural sector. The two countries' farm sectors differed fundamentally by virtue of climatic conditions and resource endowments. The Soviet Union's harsh climate and relatively low man–land ratio dictated overwhelming reliance on extensive farm practices, as well as a different balance of grain and meat production. By contrast, in China population pressure caused a steady decline in the per capita availability of farmland to a level that was amongst the lowest in the world.[52] This gave rise to a system of intensive farming, which placed a premium on the use of large farm machinery. China's production brigades were about the same size as Soviet collective farms. But whereas in the pre-reform USSR each collective possessed an average of 20 tractors, 14 combine harvesters and 44 trucks, Chinese brigades' access to such facilities was negligible.[53]

In the USSR, agriculture's share of total state investment rose to more than 20 per cent by the 1970s, compared with 5 per cent in the United States.[54] In China, the corresponding figure was around 10 per cent,[55] although this underestimates the true share by ignoring the contribution of

49. World Bank, *China: Socialist Development*, Annex D, pp. 20–21.

50. Perkins has argued that high fuel and other costs in small plants contributed significantly to China's heavy consumption of power and other material inputs (*China: Small-Scale Industry*, pp. 72–76).

51. Cf. Yu Qiuli (January 1978) on the need to restructure small-scale industry and to "convert most small- and medium-sized [machine-building] plants from general equipment producers to producers of specialized components under contract to large plants ..." (Craig *et al.*, "China's machine-building industry," pp. 297–98).

52. In 1979, average arable area per head in China was 0.1 ha., but with significant regional variations. Comparative international indicators include Japan (0.04 ha.), India (0.26 ha.), USA (0.86 ha.) and USSR (0.89 ha.).

53. Detailed data for the USSR can be found in Liu Nanchuan *et al.*, *70 Years of Soviet Economic Growth*, pp. 287, 289 and 303. Figures for China show that in 1980, on average, each production brigade had 1.1 large or medium tractors, and 2.6 walking tractors (SSB, *Zhongguo nongcun tongji nianjian* (*Chinese Rural Statistical Yearbook*), 1989 (Beijing: Zhongguo tongji chubanshe 1989), pp. 232–33 and 244).

54. *Soviet Economy in a Time of Change*, p. 40.

55. See Robert F. Ash, "The peasant and the state," *CQ*, No. 127 (1991), p. 498.

the collective sector.[56] An area in which agricultural fixed investment assumed particular importance in China was that of drainage and irrigation. By the late 1950s, more than a quarter of the total arable area was already under effective irrigation and by 1978 that figure had reached 45 per cent.[57]

China's advanced irrigation ratio, high labour input per unit arable area and rapid increases in the use of working inputs (especially chemical fertilizers)[58] generated high yields per arable and sown hectare.[59] However, the growing scarcity of arable land and the attainment of such high yields pointed to the need for continuing investment in the farm sector – a need which would become even more urgent when post-1978 reforms generated rises in income and demands for a better diet.[60]

Agricultural policies in all socialist countries have been based on the erroneous belief that farming, like industry, should seek to realize economies of scale in all its activities. It was on this basis that the decision to collectivize was premised. China and the USSR shared the same institutional framework of agriculture, although the basic level of daily work organization and income distribution differed.[61]

Methods of organization under collectives and state farms were the source of serious inefficiencies.[62] The peculiar difficulty of labour supervision in agriculture, as well as the role of natural factors, gave rise to large managerial diseconomies of scale in most aspects of direct cultivation. Yet there remained considerable scope for co-operation and the realization of scale economies in many ancillary farm activities, such as research, irrigation, crop spraying, processing marketing and the dissemination of technical information. Indeed, advocacy of a two-tier system, embracing household-based cultivation and higher-level co-operation, was ultimately to define the major thrust of institutional reform in China's agricultural sector.

In general, similarities in the institutional settings of the two countries'

---

56. E.g. the World Bank estimated that agriculture was receiving around 20% of total national investment in the late 1970s (*China: Socialist Development*, p. 49).

57. *TJNJ*, 1993, p. 349.

58. Chemical fertilizer use rose from 0.4 to 8.8 million tonnes between 1957 and 1978 (*TJNJ*, 1993, p. 349).

59. The distinction reflects the extent of multiple cropping. By 1980, China's multiple cropping index had reached 152 (K. R. Walker, "Trends in crop production," in Y. Y. Kueh and Robert F. Ash (eds.), *Economic Trends in Chinese Agriculture: The Impact of Post-Mao Reforms* (Oxford: Clarendon Press, 1993) p. 166).

60. On the eve of reform, the level and quality of food (especially high-quality food) intake in China lagged well behind those of the USSR, let alone Taiwan and the USA. Remember too that total population in the Soviet Union was growing slowly. It follows that whereas the major thrust of reform in the USSR was to improve efficiency, in China it embraced the twin goals of improved efficiency and higher output.

61. In China, the basic unit was the production team, which on average embraced 56 farm workers and 26 hectares of sown area; in the USSR, it was the collective, with 488 workers and 3,485 ha. (Liu Nanchuan et al., *70 Years of Soviet Economic Development*, p. 287; *TJNJ*, 1981, p. 132). Chinese production brigades contained 449 workers, but only 206 ha. of sown area (1980). Another difference with potentially important implications was the much higher average educational and technical level of the Soviet rural workforce.

62. See Peter Nolan, *The Political Economy of Collective Farms* (Cambridge: Polity Press, 1988).

agricultural sectors pointed to the potential benefits, in terms of labour and capital productivity, of similar institutional reform policies. Above all, the delegation of decision-making power to individual households promised to generate significant gains.[63] But contrasting baseline conditions in China and the USSR highlighted the desirability of different policies, whether of kind or degree, in other areas. Providing continued access to lumpy inputs was one example. Their more important role in Soviet farming suggested the need for reforms which would guarantee secure individual access to large inputs that were beyond the resources of a single household. With hindsight, however, the pre-eminent role of irrigation and drainage facilities defined a similar problem of access and a similar challenge to institutional reform in China.

Conclusion

This article has reviewed the economic legacy bequeathed to the Chinese leadership at the end of the 1970s. It has examined in detail economic conditions in China on the eve of reform and sought to capture comparable conditions in the former Soviet Union at a similar point in its history.

At the end of 1978, China's Maoist economic legacy remained largely intact. Ambivalent initiatives introduced during the brief interregnum of Mao's successor, Hua Guofeng, had done little to alter the basic characteristics of the economic system. Structural defects inherent in the former planning system, as well as features more closely associated with indigenous economic strategies, were reflected in sectoral and regional imbalances, and low levels of productivity and efficiency.

A comparative analysis of China and the former USSR indicates that the two countries shared important similarities at the start of their reform programmes. The history of both pointed to the existence of large reservoirs of entrepreneurial skills. The basic framework of planning within a command system was the same, as were key features of collective farming and industrial enterprises. Both countries had large amounts of capital and technical expertise locked up in their military sectors. The economic system of each was massively under-performing relative to the productive potential of existing stocks of physical and human capital.

But there were also important differences. They included China's more severe shortage of arable land, its educational deficiencies and lack of scientific and technical expertise, as well as its lower levels of per capita income, industrialization and urbanization. The greater role of small-scale industrial enterprises and the location of a much higher proportion of its industrial assets in remote areas were characteristic features of China's Maoist developmental model. Its population growth was more rapid,

---

63. China's experience during the recovery from the Great Leap Forward provided clear evidence of the effectiveness of establishing contractual arrangements with individual farm households.

although national minorities significantly constituted a far smaller percentage of total population than in the USSR. Under appropriate conditions, China also had access to much larger concentrations of capital held by its overseas citizens.

Some of these characteristics worked to the advantage of both countries. Others favoured one of them more than the other. An inference common to both is that conditions were the source of considerable catch-up potential. Relatively simple changes promised to generate immediate improvements in performance, which in turn might promote further reform. It is certainly not apparent to us that inherited economic or systemic differences made it more likely that well-chosen policies would generate faster growth in China than in the USSR.

In reality, however, from the perspective of the mid-1990s there is no doubt which of the two countries has achieved the greater economic success. If our analysis is correct, the main source of the contrasting outcome under system reform in China and Russia must be differences in policy choice. It is beyond the scope of this article to analyse the complex historical factors which generated fundamentally different approaches towards the task of transforming the Stalinist system.[64] Suffice to say that the contrast in policy choice applies not only to narrowly economic considerations but also to the broader relationship between economic and political reform. Under the impact of early reform, hopes of fundamental political reform may have been more widespread in the Soviet Union than in China. The policy decisions of Mikhail Gorbachev, given expression through the implementation of *glasnost* and *perestroika*, transformed such hopes into real expectations. This contrasted sharply with the situation in China, where the central authorities seem to have reached a near consensus that political democratization would not accompany economic modernization.[65]

In sum, the Soviet failure stems primarily from the wholehearted embrace of the "transition orthodoxy" policies of political reform (*perestroika* and *glasnost*) and subsequent economic change ("shock therapy") advocated by foreign advisers and commentators,[66] as well as their domestic counterparts in the USSR and Russian Federation.[67] By contrast, China's reform success stems primarily from its refusal to implement the "transition orthodoxy" policies, which were also urged upon its leaders

64. For detailed consideration of these historical determinants, see Nolan, *China's Rise, Russia's Fall*.

65. This was self-evidently so after the "Tiananmen massacre." But well before that climacteric, a series of campaigns against "bourgeois-liberalization" sought to reduce expectations of political reform.

66. Cf. J. Kornai, *The Road to a Free Economy* (New York: Norton Books, 1990); D. Kennett and M. Lieberman (eds.), *The Road to Capitalism* (Orlando: Dryden Press, 1992) (especially the chapters by D. Lipton and J. Sachs); J. Prybyla, "The road from socialism: Why, where, what and how," *Problems of Communism*, Vol. XL (January–April 1991); and A. Aslund, "Gorbachev, perestroika and economic crisis," *Problems of Communism* (January–April 1990), pp. 13–41 and *Gorbachev's Struggle for Economic Reform*.

67. E.g. the authors of the "500 day plan" for transforming the Soviet economy; also, subsequently, Chubais and Sobchak.

during the 1980s.[68] The outcome for China was to release the potential concealed within the Stalinist system. Meanwhile, the maintenance of an authoritarian political system allowed the gradual development of market forces, helped facilitate fiscal stability, provided a stable environment for large-scale foreign capital inflows and provided a means of intervention in areas of market failure.

Implicit in this analysis are two counter-factual propositions. The implementation of different policies in Russia could have produced rapid growth of output and a significant improvement in popular living standards. By the same token, the selection of different policies in China could have precipitated political and economic disaster, reflected in a major decline in popular living standards.

---

68. Cf. Liu Guoguang and Wang Ruisun, "Restructuring of the economy" in Yu Guangyuan, *China's Socialist Modernization*.

The Social Roots of China's Economic Development

Martin King Whyte

Why has China been so much more successful than the former Soviet Union and its East European satellites in making the transition away from a centrally planned economy? While other articles address a wide range of explanations of China's success, this one explores the possible contribution of China's grass roots social organization, and particularly its family and kinship structures. Attention is drawn to social factors by the obvious fact that China, through its spectacular recent growth, has taken its place among other Chinese (and Chinese cultural orbit) populations in East Asia, reinforcing the position of this region as the most dynamic portion of the world economy. Could China share with other Chinese populations, despite more than 30 years of collectivist socialism, grass roots social structures that are conducive to economic growth under the proper conditions – social structures that are different in strategically important ways from those in the former Soviet Union and Eastern Europe?

If the claim of a favourable influence of grass roots social patterns, and of family patterns in particular, has merit, this could be from a combination of several different possibilities[1]:

- Pre-revolutionary family patterns in China were more favourable to economic dynamism than were the "traditional" family patterns in Russia and the various countries of Eastern Europe.
- The elements of China's family patterns that were favourable to economic dynamism survived the experience of revolution and collectivism better than did their counterparts in the Soviet Union and Eastern Europe.
- Socialism in China altered family patterns in ways that would eventually help foster economic development to a greater extent than in the Soviet Union and Eastern Europe.
- The recent Chinese market reforms and other policies reinforce the potential contribution of Chinese family patterns to economic dynamism more so than do the institutional forms adopted in the former Soviet Union and Eastern Europe.
- Changes in the global economy in recent years release and reinforce

---

1. For the sake of simplicity and because it is my primary focus, these statements are framed in terms of the family. However, it will become obvious that broader kinship relations and community arrangements are involved, and not simply "the family" defined narrowly. In order to present the broad comparisons required for this article it will be necessary to oversimplify reality. For the most part I ignore important variations within China and other societies in order to focus on the modal or dominant tendencies. This oversimplification does not mean that I believe that in any society, family patterns are universals that affect everyone in the same fashion.

the economic potential of families in China more so than in the former Soviet Union and Eastern Europe.

There is likely to be some degree of truth in all these statements. This article briefly considers each one, with a primary focus on contrasts between China and the Soviet Union/Russia. While most discussions of this sort concentrate on the role of China's traditional culture in fostering economic development, the focus here is on the role of specific social structures, and particularly family patterns. This approach explains the use of the phrase "social roots" in the title, rather than "cultural roots."[2]

Changing Views on the Chinese Family and Development

What was Chinese family life like prior to 1949, and what impact did this institution have on the economy? Consideration of what has been written about the influence of Chinese family patterns on development prospects immediately reveals the nearly total reversal in accepted views. A generation ago it was widely agreed that the Chinese family constituted an obstacle to economic development. Even earlier, Max Weber described the negative role played in China by the "sib fetters of the economy," encouraging a picture of family bonds as grasping tentacles, preventing the economy from growing. Weber and later scholars argued that the nature of the Chinese family helped to explain why the industrial revolution did not happen first in China and also why it responded less well to the 19th-century Western challenge than did Japan.[3] In recent times the obvious economic dynamism of the various Chinese populations in East Asia has given rise to the reverse view – that the Chinese family is a veritable engine of economic growth. As a first step, it is necessary to review this controversy briefly and see what sense can be made out of these contrary claims.[4]

The dominant view of a generation ago – that Chinese family patterns constituted an obstacle to economic development – was based on a series of claims. The most central was a set of arguments about the supposed defects of family-run firms. Given the strong family loyalties stressed in Chinese culture and the existing patterns of economic life, it was

2. I recognize that culture and social structure are intimately intertwined. However, cultural explanations tend to assume that cultural forces are unchanging; social structures, in contrast, can and do change, and may reinforce or obstruct the expression of particular cultural values. The dramatic shifts in popular values and economic behaviour in China require an explanation that is dynamic, rather than one that assumes a constant role of enduring cultural forces.

3. Some of the most important works detailing the way in which Chinese family firms impeded economic development were Albert Feuerwerker, *China's Early Industrialization: Sheng Hsuan-huai and Mandarin Enterprise* (Cambridge, MA: Harvard University Press, 1958); Marion Levy, *The Family Revolution in Modern China* (Cambridge, MA: Harvard University Press, 1949). Feuerwerker and Levy were, of course, following the intellectual lead of Max Weber. See Weber's books, *The Protestant Ethic and the Spirit of Capitalism* (London: G. Allen & Unwin, 1930 [originally 1904–05]) and *The Religion of China* (Glencoe, IL: The Free Press, 1951 [originally 1916]).

4. I deal with this controversy more extensively in a related paper, "The Chinese family and economic development: obstacle or engine?" under submission. Only an abbreviated version of the ideas covered in that paper is presented here.

acknowledged that most new economic activity would take the form of family firms rather than large, impersonal corporations. In an era dominated by modernization theory, family-run firms were seen as an outmoded organizational form, suited to an agrarian society but not a modern industrial one. In the words of a widely read book by Clark Kerr and colleagues, "[The family] provides shelter and food for all its members, regardless of their individual contributions, so that the indigent and indolent alike are cared for. ... Working members are expected to pool their earnings for the benefit of everyone; individual saving is discouraged. ... Family loyalty and obligations take precedence over other loyalties and obligations. Thus, the extended family tends to dilute individual incentives to work, save, and invest."[5] Among the specific tendencies embedded in family firms, it was claimed, were the following:

- Family obligations and the need to make positions in the firm correspond to roles in the family hierarchy prevented such firms from hiring, promoting, demoting and firing individuals according to their skills and efforts.
- Family members working in the firm, as the quotation above indicates, had their incentives dulled by the redistribution of resources according to need or family position.
- The stress on filial piety and the strong emphasis in Chinese culture on maintaining traditional customs and rituals ran directly contrary to the entrepreneurship, risk-taking and innovation that are required for success in a modern industrial society. As a result, Chinese family firms were too conservative and cautious to compete with entrepreneurial non-family firms.
- Demands for family loyalty inhibited or prevented talented junior members from taking advantage of new opportunities elsewhere. As a result, talents were not fully utilized, and geographic mobility and the spread of ideas and technology were inhibited.
- Non-relatives might be employed in a family-run firm, but the monopoly of top managerial roles by family members and the pervasive desire of talented individuals to be their own bosses created frictions and early departures of such individuals. As a result, it was very difficult for family-run firms to grow beyond a modest scale or retain the services of talented technical and managerial personnel who were not relatives.
- The joint-family ideal and the customary rule that each son receives an equal share of the family property limited not only the size but also the longevity of Chinese family firms. As a result, one recent study observes, "it was almost impossible to build up over many generations a business that could be secured against a future family quarrel and the

5. Clark Kerr et al., Industrialism and Industrial Man (Harmondsworth: Pelican Books, 1977), p. 94 [originally published by Harvard University Press in 1960], quoted in S. L. Wong, "The applicability of Asian family values to other sociocultural settings," in Peter Berger and H. H. Michael Hsiao (eds.), In Search of an East Asian Development Model (New Brunswick, NJ: Transaction Books, 1988), p. 134.

consequent splitting up of assets."[6] It was very difficult for such firms to create significant economies of scale and mobilize resources for the long-term research and development effort that would be needed to compete with modern, non-family corporations.

The strong preference of most Chinese to do business through people with whom personal relationships had been established was also seen as a weakness. Despite the skill of Chinese in cultivating *guanxi*, the time, effort, and resources required to do so diverted Chinese firms from their primary tasks and generated corruption. In addition, the importance of such networks for business success worked to the disadvantage of start-up firms, since they had not had a chance to develop extensive *guanxi* networks.

In addition to such traits built into the very nature of Chinese family-run firms, other negative characteristics were described. For example, the pro-natalist essence of Confucianism was seen as leading families to bear too many children. As a result, any surplus generated by family economic success was diverted to feeding more mouths, rather than reserved for reinvestment in the firm. In addition, women were seen as more harshly discriminated against than in Western cultures, with pervasive female illiteracy and footbinding stark indicators of this fact. As a result of the greater exclusion of Chinese women from productive economic activity, the family system contributed once again to China's inability to compete in the modern world. A final trait concerned the social mobility to which Chinese aspired. Merchants were traditionally held in low esteem, and families that prospered tended to try to escape from merchant status by buying land and training their sons for official careers. The "open class" nature of late Imperial China meant that it was difficult to develop family business traditions and nourish the development of an entrepreneurial class.[7]

The conventional wisdom of a generation ago noted that family-run firms had been dominant in the West in pre-industrial times, but that these had receded in importance with the rise of bureaucratic corporations run by professional managers.[8] This new organizational form was as much responsible for the triumph of industrialism as were particular technological innovations. It seemed logical to conclude that a similar fate was in store for China. Only if individuals could be "liberated" from the

6. William Jenner, *The Tyranny of History* (London: Penguin, 1992), p. 80. Sociologist S. L. Wong, drawing upon his research on textile firms in Hong Kong, argues that there is a natural "life cycle" of Chinese family firms with four phases: emergent, centralized, segmented and disintegrative. See his article, "The Chinese family firm: a model," *British Journal of Sociology*, Vol. 36 (1985), pp. 58–72.

7. This argument involving social mobility was stressed by Marion Levy in his article, "Contrasting factors in the modernization of China and Japan," in S. Kuznets, W. Moore and J. Spengler (eds.), *Economic Growth: Brazil, India, Japan* (Durham, NC: Duke University Press, 1955).

8. See Alfred D. Chandler, "The emergence of managerial capitalism," *Business History Review*, Vol. 58 (1984), pp. 473–503, reprinted in M. Granovetter and R. Swedberg (eds.), *The Sociology of Economic Life* (Boulder: Westview, 1992).

constraints of family obligations and employed in rational, bureaucratic firms could China hope to compete with the established powers.

In recent years, in contrast, a diametrically opposite set of arguments has become the conventional wisdom. Once predatory and irrational policies of political authorities and other external constraints are removed, sociologist S. L. Wong tells us, "Chinese familism will fuel the motor of development."[9] At the centre of this positive view is the claim that the unusually strong loyalties of Chinese families are a potent source of motivation and performance. A number of related points derive from this central claim:

- For the sake of their families, young Chinese study hard, pursue advanced education and training, and maximize their qualifications. Once on the job, they work very hard, put in extremely long hours, and labour for less than non-family members would, all more for the sake of the family than for personal benefit. These motivations are also important in non-family work settings. Many Chinese who work in large, non-family corporations far removed from the parental home remain powerfully motivated to live frugally so they can send cash remittances home, help other family members find similar employment, and learn new skills so that they can leave and start a new, family-run firm.[10]
- Family members are likely to stay with the firm even when better paying opportunities arise elsewhere, contributing to continuity in firm management. (Note that here a supposedly "bad" feature of family firms is reinterpreted as a "good" feature.)
- The use of family position as a basis for firm authority provides a secure cultural grounding for that authority, reducing conflict with the "boss" and helping to maintain secrecy about firm operations.[11]
- The obligation to provide for not only the entire family and multiple heirs but also for a family or even lineage estate and generations to come provides a powerful incentive for the firm head/entrepreneur.
- Chinese family firms do not operate through pooling all funds and retaining all decision-making power in the hands of the family patriarch. Rather, they tend to diversify, spawning a number of subsidiaries, with family members (most often sons) in charge of each subordinate unit. Only a portion of the profits generated is pooled for redistribution to other branches of the firm as needed. Through salaries and retained profits, the managers of each subsidiary are rewarded for their success. Sons who succeed gain control over such funds, which they can invest on their own without parental or family approval. These arrangements, combined with the normally intense rivalry among brothers, provide

9. Wong, "The applicability of Asian family values," p. 146.

10. See, for example, the discussion in Janet Salaff, *Working Daughters of Hong Kong* (Cambridge: Cambridge University Press, 1981); James L. Watson, *Emigration and the Chinese Lineage* (Berkeley: University of California Press, 1975).

11. See the discussion in Josephine Smart and Alan Smart, "Obligation and control: employment of kin in capitalist labour management in China," *Critique of Anthropology*, Vol. 13 (1993), pp. 7–31.

what Susan Greenhalgh calls "a package of individual incentives and group insurance against failure that encourages the emergence of highly motivated, risk-taking entrepreneurs."[12]

- Chinese family firms are not obliged to hire and give responsible positions to any and all relatives. Rather, strict competence and performance criteria are used in deciding whether to employ or retain cousins, uncles or other relatives outside the *jia*. Even within the *jia*, a son who does not perform satisfactorily may be eased out of his position and replaced by another son or other family member, although accomplishing such a change almost always creates family conflict.[13]

- The size limits on family firms are often an advantage. Because of their small size start-up costs are minimized and rapid responses to changing market conditions are made easier. The dominance in many sectors of the economy of small firms, rather than large corporations, helps to keep the markets involved highly competitive and to stimulate firm establishment. The splitting up or collapse of established family firms is not a serious problem if dozens of newly founded firms are ready to fill the gaps.[14]

- Reliance on personal connection networks is also more advantageous than problematic. Such networks help to overcome the limited size of family groups and enable family firms to operate in an increasingly far-flung way. *Guanxi* networks provide trustworthy access to opportunities and resources in unstable political and economic environments and when bank loans are not readily available. Reliance on personal connections also lowers the likelihood of commercial and legal disputes. These networks provide flexibility that allows family firms to

12. Susan Greenhalgh, "Land reform and family entrepreneurialism in East Asia," in G. McNicoll and Mead Cain (eds.), *Rural Development and Population: Institutions and Policies* (New York: Oxford University Press, 1990), p. 90. See also Susan Greenhalgh, "Families and networks in Taiwan's economic development," in E. Winckler and S. Greenhalgh (eds.), *Contending Approaches to the Political Economy of Taiwan* (Armonk, NY: M.E. Sharpe, 1988); Stevan Harrell, "Why do the Chinese work so hard? Reflections on an entrepreneurial ethic," *Modern China*, Vol. 11 (1985), pp. 203–226; and S. Gordon Redding, *The Spirit of Chinese Capitalism* (Berlin: de Gruyter, 1990). Case studies of the operation of Chinese firms include John Omohundro, *Chinese Merchant Families in Iloilo: Commerce and Kin in a Central Philippine City* (Athens: Ohio University Press, 1981); Robert Silin, *Leadership and Values: The Organization of Large-Scale Taiwanese Enterprises* (Cambridge, MA: Harvard University Press, 1976); Justin Niehoff, "The villager as industrialist: ideologies of household manufacturing in rural Taiwan," *Modern China*, Vol. 13 (1987), pp. 278–309; and Ellen Oxfeld, *Blood, Sweat, and Mahjong* (Ithaca: Cornell University Press, 1993).

13. One study in Hong Kong found that there was no correlation between the rate of growth of industrial firms and the extent to which kin were employed in them. See J. L. Espy, "The strategy of Chinese industrial enterprise in Hong Kong," unpublished DBA dissertation, Harvard University, 1970, cited in Wong, "The applicabililty of Asian family values," p. 139.

14. Research dealing with Taiwan and Korea during the 1960s found that small firms were as efficient or more efficient as larger firms in many sectors of those economies. See Yhi-min Ho, "The production structure of the manufacturing sector and its distribution implications," *Economic Development and Cultural Change*, Vol. 28 (1980), pp. 321–343; Samuel P. Ho, "Small scale industries in two rapidly growing less developed economies: Korea and Taiwan – a study of their characteristics, competitive bases, and productivity," *Studies in Employment and Rural Development*, No. 53 (Washington, D.C.: The World Bank, 1978) (studies discussed in Greenhalgh, "Families and networks in Taiwan's economic development," p. 229).

meet changing market demands through subcontracting and similar arrangements without incurring high fixed costs.

- When modern social mobility opportunities arise which require lengthy educational investment, Chinese populations have shown an ability to reduce their fertility rates extremely rapidly, even in the absence of government pressure to do so.[15] When business careers are sufficiently attractive, and careers as officials, landlords and so on sufficiently unattractive, Chinese have no difficulty developing strong family business traditions.[16]

These purported positive implications of Chinese families contrast sharply with the negative implications listed earlier. How are such dramatically divergent views to be reconciled? Sociologist Peter Berger reports imagining Max Weber returning to life and being installed in a Taipei high-rise office building, looking out of the window and confessing, "Well, I was wrong."[17] However, I suggest that this is not a simple case in which one set of arguments is right and the other is wrong. Rather, Chinese families exist in great variety, and most contain a mixture of tendencies, some favourable and others unfavourable to development. Whether the positive or negative tendencies predominate in practice depends crucially on the nature of the outside forces and institutions confronting Chinese families. Those forces and institutions have changed markedly over time, as shown below.

The Chinese Family and Development prior to 1949

What was the institutional context in late Imperial China, and how did this influence the economic potential of Chinese families? My thinking on these issues has been influenced by the work of Susan Greenhalgh, and particularly by her thoughtful article, "Land reform and family entrepreneurship in East Asia."[18] Oversimplifying her discussion, the centuries of existence in China of a highly commercialized and competitive system of markets and an open class system, with easy and frequent geographic and social mobility, in combination with recurring dynastic

15. The reduction in fertility rates in Taiwan after 1960 was almost as rapid as in the PRC in the 1970s, even though the coerciveness of the PRC family planning system was not present in the ROC. See the discussion in Susan Greenhalgh, "Fertility as mobility: sinic transitions," *Population and Development Review*, Vol. 14 (1988), pp. 629–674; D. Gale Johnson, "Effects of institutional policies on rural population growth: the case of China," *Population and Development Review*, Vol. 20 (1994), pp. 503–531.

16. The widespread success of émigré Chinese in South-East Asian countries provided evidence for this phenomenon and an apparent exception already visible a generation ago to the claim that Chinese families inhibited entrepreneurship.

17. Peter Berger, "An East Asian development model?" in Berger and Hsiao, *In Search of an East Asian Development Model*, p. 7.

18. We have also exchanged communications and drafts of papers related to these issues. She is, of course, not responsible for my interpretation of her ideas in the present article. See also Victor Nee and Frank Young, "Peasant entrepreneurs in China's 'second economy': an institutional analysis," *Economic Development and Cultural Change*, Vol. 39 (1991), pp. 293–310; Thomas Rawski, "Social foundations of East Asian economic dynamism," unpublished paper, 1994.

and market cycles, produced an environment encouraging families to develop effective mobility strategies stressing property accumulation, economic diversification, worker dispersal and family expansion. However, severe population pressure and inequalities in the ownership of the most crucial type of property, land, left many Chinese unable to pursue these mobility strategies fully or, indeed, left them locked in a struggle for survival and security, without even a full complement of family members to join in the struggle.

The dynastic decline of the late 19th century and the military and political chaos and corruption of the first half of the 20th century produced conditions that tipped the balance further in favour of security and against entrepreneurship even among complete, landholding families. In Greenhalgh's view, in order for the entrepreneurial potential possessed by Chinese families to be fully manifested, they have to possess adequate security of property ownership and an ability to manage their own economic affairs, combined with full freedom to pursue multiple upward mobility strategies. These conditions were not generally present in China during the century prior to 1949, and as a result the kinds of behaviour noted by Weber and other critics of Chinese familism were more often manifested than bold entrepreneurship.

Despite these problems, in many ways the institutional context faced by Chinese families before 1949 was more favourable to an entrepreneurial ethic and behaviour than was the case for Russian families prior to 1917. There are various superficial similarities between traditional Russian and Chinese family systems. Both are patrilineal and patriarchal systems stressing the joint family ideal and division of the family property among sons. However, the surrounding historical and institutional setting differed in important ways. For the bulk of the Russian population, the peasants, serfdom had only been abolished in the 1860s. The system that superseded it was not much better, from the standpoint of encouraging entrepreneurial sentiments. The rural *mir* system locked villagers into a collective obligation to repay the redemption payments that had been the price for freeing them from serfdom, making migration elsewhere difficult until the Stolypin reforms of 1906. In most areas the *mir* periodically redistributed land among village families to compensate for differential births and deaths. The result may have provided a feeling of security, but the lack of firm property rights did little to encourage Russian families to develop upward mobility strategies – a fact that the break-up of the *mir* system in the Stolypin reforms belatedly tried to correct. China prior to 1949 may be seen as "a society brimming with entrepreneurial potential,"[19] but this could not be said of pre-revolutionary Russia.[20] However, this potential in China was displayed primarily in

19. Greenhalgh, "Land reform and family entrepreneurship in East Asia," p. 86.

20. See David Ransel (ed.), *The Family in Imperial Russian* (Urbana, IL: University of Illinois Press, 1978); Naum Jasny, *The Socialized Agriculture of the USSR* (Stanford: Stanford University Press, 1949), pp. 134–146. The available literature suggests that, while entrepreneurship was not totally absent in Imperial Russia, a large proportion of the entrepreneurs in that society were either foreigners or members of ethnic minorities, rather

Overseas Chinese communities, because conditions within China tended to reinforce aspects of family dynamics that were less favourable to economic growth.

The Impact of Socialism on Chinese Families in the PRC

The literature reviewed earlier suggests that in order to play an important and positive role in economic development, families must retain strong loyalties that can be used to mobilize the full efforts of family members and an ability to use those efforts in productive ways. Did the experience of Chinese families under socialism reinforce these loyalties and obligations or undermine them? Was the Chinese experience in this regard different in significant ways from the experience of Russians and East Europeans? The general argument of this article is that while the socialist era in China contained a mix of experiences that both threatened and reinforced family obligations, on balance and for most families powerful family obligations survived, but with a significant softening of the power of the senior generation. The continued strength of family loyalties provided a resource that could be used to mobilize family economic efforts under changed conditions, while the softening of parental authority helped to ensure that these efforts would take innovative and productive directions.[21] In the Soviet Union, in contrast, the socialist era produced more substantial erosion of familial obligations and the emergence of something closer to the individualistic family orientation of Western societies.[22]

The first and most obvious point is that for China (and for Eastern Europe), the socialist phase was briefer than for the Soviet Union. Since family change in part involves a succession of generations, this simple fact means that there are many more people still alive who were socialized in, and had personal experience with, a petty capitalist environment. In the case of China's rural population, the "socialist detour" was less than 25 years, roughly from 1956 to 1980 or thereabouts. Even some capitalists who were not so petty survived to operate and make deals another day – witness the return to prominence of Rong Yiren, one of China's "red capitalists" from the 1950s who is now president of China

---

footnote continued

than Russians. See the discussion in Gregory Guroff and Fred Carstensen (eds.), *Entrepreneurship in Imperial Russia and the Soviet Union* (Princeton: Princeton University Press, 1983).

21. The claim here is that softening the family hierarchy helped to reduce one of the main problems the earlier literature saw in Chinese family firms – the tendency of patriarchs to monopolize all decisions, ignoring the ideas and advice of their better educated and potentially more innovative children.

22. See the discussion in David Olson and Mikhail Matskovsky, "Soviet and American families: a comparative overview," in J. Maddock *et al.* (eds.), *Families Before and After Perestroika* (New York: Guilford, 1994). This is a gross generalization which applies much less to the national minority populations of the Soviet Union than it does to the Russians, Ukrainians and Belorussians, not to mention people in the Baltic republics. Throughout the Soviet period and still today, Georgians and other non-Russians have displayed family loyalties and commercial predilections much stronger than those of the dominant Russians.

International Trust and Investment Corporation (CITIC, assets 80 billion *yuan*) and a vice-president of the PRC.[23]

However, time is not the only important factor, and the actual impact of post-1949 experiences on Chinese families must be considered. The picture is clearly mixed, and many images of the PRC concern threats to family solidarity: children denouncing parents in recurring campaigns, couples assigned to work in different locations, young people sent down to live in the countryside, family members dying in officially induced famines and political campaigns, and official propaganda stressing that loyalty to the Party and Chairman Mao should come before loyalty to one's own family. In addition, the nature of bureaucratic socialism and the volatility of Chinese politics meant that families had great difficulty formulating mobility strategies or planning how to realize family goals. The powerlessness of families to protect their own members, plan their lives or even to decide how many children to bear generated great anxiety and stress. However, these experiences are not the whole story, nor do they distinguish China significantly from the Soviet Union, where similar assaults on families occurred.[24]

On the other side of the coin, a variety of policies and institutions reinforced family obligations and solidarity in socialist China. To begin with, supporting ageing parents was made a legal obligation in the 1950 Marriage Law of the PRC, and in the socialist era this obligation was reinforced, if necessary, through automatic deductions from the wages of unfilial children. This and other policies, combined with improved health care and decreased infant mortality, meant that China's elderly were more likely than before 1949 to live with a grown child and have some degree of economic security.[25]

When evaluating what happened under socialism to other family relationships, it is necessary to consider rural and urban China separately. In rural China the socialist system quite directly and in multiple ways reinforced family solidarity and obligations. To begin with, China's collectivized agricultural organizations (APCs, later people's communes) were constructed on the basis of existing residential arrangements, which to a considerable extent reflected kinship ties.[26] The strong migration restrictions enforced from the end of the 1950s then ensured that even

23. See the earlier account of Rong Yiren offered in Edgar Snow, *The Other Side of the River* (New York: Random House, 1961), p. 198. At the time Rong, the eldest son of a Shanghai textile magnate, was deputy mayor of Shanghai and a vice-minister of the Textile Ministry. Compare his current situation, described in *Beijing Review*, No. 35 (1994), pp. 22–23.

24. Some of the details of these experiences differ, of course. The Soviet Union had no counterpart to China's coercive birth control campaigns but instead a mild pro-natalist policy. The rupture of families as a result of deaths (particularly in the mass purges and during the Second World War) was at least proportionally much greater in the Soviet Union.

25. See the discussion in Deborah Davis-Freedman, *Long Lives* (Cambridge, MA: Harvard University Press, 1983); Hai'ou Yang, "Population and kinship dynamics of the elderly in China: a microsimulation study," *Journal of Cross-Cultural Gerontology*, Vol. 7 (1992), pp. 135–150.

26. See William Parish, "China – team, brigade, or commune?" *Problems of Communism*, Vol. 25 (1976), pp. 51–65.

most ambitious and educated rural young people remained on the farm, rather than escaping elsewhere. Indeed, in most cases traditional practices continued, with sons marrying and bringing their new brides to live with them and their parents.[27] The work point system used to compensate for collective labour also reinforced the rural family. Work points were accumulated by individual team members, but then they were totalled and used for distribution of grain and cash on the basis of family units. This practice meant that many adult members of the community had no direct control over their own earnings, since that control rested with the heads of their families. Housing was financed and constructed almost everywhere by families, rather than by the collective or the state, a pattern which once again reinforced the need to rely on the larger family unit.

It is true that, while engaged in collective labour, people were not operating as a family unit but as individuals assigned to varying tasks by their team heads. However in most periods and localities a residual family production unit remained in the form of a private plot and household sidelines. Increased demands for participation in collective labour combined with the fact that many peasant families depended on their private plot and sideline activities for 25 per cent or more of their total income (and most of their cash income) meant that families had to plan their private economic activities carefully. Even though sideline activities were attacked when the political atmosphere shifted to the left, they provided a mechanism through which some degree of family pursuit of joint economic success survived through the socialist period.[28]

In some respects peasant families in the USSR had similar experiences. In fact, after 1936 there were fewer threats to Soviet private plots and free market activities than in China. However, in other ways official policies and practices eroded family solidarity. The Soviet five-year plans produced massive recruitment of labour power from the countryside, rather than an effort to keep peasants down on the farm. As a result, many of the younger generation left for the cities.[29] By the 1960s, strong trends toward the ageing and feminization of the rural labour force were clearly visible in the USSR. In a number of respects Soviet collective farming was more bureaucratic and less kinship based than was the case in China – such as in the reliance until 1958 on external Machine Tractor Stations and the 1950s effort to consolidate the dwindling rural population in new apartments in consolidated *agrogorods*.[30] Another critical

27. See Martin K. Whyte, "Revolutionary change and patrilocal residence in China," *Ethnology*, Vol. 18 (1979), pp. 211–227.

28. For a personal account of repeated efforts to augment family income from private sidelines and marketing despite official threats and sanctions, see He Liyi, *Mr China's Son* (Boulder: Westview, 1993).

29. Until the 1960s adult collective farmers did not possess internal passports and therefore could not migrate to urban areas without special permission. However, there were massive rural recruitment drives connected to major new industrial projects, and rural young people could use education, military service and other means to escape the farms and receive an internal passport. In the Khrushchev era the internal passport system was abolished.

30. Such efforts to uproot villages took place on an even greater and more disruptive scale in Ceaucescu's Romania. In a few locales in the PRC experiments were made with building

difference was that the peasant family was phased out as the recipient of payments for labour in Soviet agriculture. By the end of the Khrushchev era, many collective farms had been converted into state farms, and even on the remaining collective farms, the labour day system of payment to *kokhozniki* (the equivalent of China's work point system) had been phased out in favour of money wages paid to individuals.[31] Through such changes, collective farmers became rural proletarians. Even without considering the much more wrenching nature of the collectivization drive in the Soviet Union, it is clear that there was much less operating in the Soviet system to keep individuals bound to their families and kin groups.[32]

In China's cities the situation is qualitatively different. After 1957 urbanites lacked a residual set of private, family economic activities, and most were assigned to work in bureaucratic state and collective enterprises. Wages in such enterprises were paid to individuals rather than to family heads, although family members might agree to turn over a portion of their wages to a common family pot (or to send some to parents living elsewhere). Housing was also increasingly supplied bureaucratically by work units and city agencies rather than by families, although some people were able to hold on to at least a share of the private housing they had owned prior to 1949. In most respects, then, the forces that acted to reinforce family solidarity in the Chinese countryside were weak or absent in the cities.

However, again this is not the complete picture. The system of assignment of jobs and housing, while sometimes splitting families apart, on balance tended to keep them together. Young people could not freely relocate to other cities and hope to obtain jobs or housing there. One 1992 survey conducted in cities in 12 provinces found that 97 per cent of the people over age 60 surveyed who had non-coresident children had at least one such child living in the same city.[33] Toward the end of the Mao era the *dingti* system was formalized, allowing retiring parents to secure employment for one of their children in their work unit. The de-emphasis on housing construction after the 1950s also meant that urban housing became increasingly cramped, with long waiting lists for any newly

---

footnote continued

apartment complexes to replace villagers' scattered private homes, but such experiments were not part of a national policy, as in the Soviet Union and Romania.

31. See the discussion in Stephen Dunn, "Structure and functions of the Soviet rural family," in James Millar (ed.), *The Soviet Rural Community* (Urbana, IL: University of Illinois Press, 1971), pp. 234–35.

32. The wrenching experiences for Chinese peasants came not with collectivization but with the collapse of the Great Leap Forward a few years later, when an estimated 30 million excess deaths occurred, overwhelmingly in rural areas. Unlike the Soviet collectivization drive, however, this episode did not involve mobilized class struggle and forced deportation of parts of kin groups, and the survivors of the Chinese famine were probably driven closer together, for reasons discussed below. Large numbers of excess deaths were caused by Soviet collectivization and the famine it induced, as detailed in Robert Conquest, *Harvest of Sorrow: Soviet Collectivization and the Terror-Famine* (New York: Oxford University Press, 1986).

33. China Research Centre on Ageing, *A Data Compilation of the Survey on China's Support Systems for the Elderly* (Beijing: Hualin Press, 1994), p. 95.

assigned apartments. As a consequence, after the 1950s it became less likely that newly marrying children would be able to set up an independent household, and more likely once again that they would live with parents, most often those of the groom.[34]

In addition to these phenomena, the impact on urban families of two other experiences of the 1960s and 1970s – the Cultural Revolution and the increasing shortages of consumer goods – must be considered. The Cultural Revolution, as noted earlier, is usually seen as tearing families apart through political strife. What is less often appreciated is how for most families – those not affected by pressures on one family member to denounce another – the effect was the opposite.[35] What was involved was a particular instance of a more general phenomenon in any society: in times of crisis, when the social environment becomes more dangerous and unpredictable, people are thrown back on their closest bonds in order to survive, and particularly on their families. As factional chaos broke out and the bureaucratic rules of the game ceased to apply, relying on workmates, friends and past patrons became increasingly risky. Even after factional strife ended, it continued to be necessary to rely on family members in multiple ways: to help a child return from the countryside, to gain special medical treatment for a sick parent, or even to obtain a proper funeral for a loved one. The increasing consumer goods shortages and tight rationing system of these years had a similar effect, although in this case *guanxi* relations stretching far beyond kin were cultivated by families struggling with unmet needs.

In the cities of the former Soviet Union the political dangers of the Stalin period had a similar potential to drive families inward, and shortages of housing also produced a tendency for couples to start out married life with one or the other set of parents. However, the cessation of mass terror and the major housing drives of the post-Stalin years eased these situations, and in most other respects centrifugal tendencies within families were reinforced throughout the Soviet era. There was nothing comparable in the Soviet Union to the *dingti* system of inheriting jobs in parental work units, and through education and other bureaucratic means young Soviet urbanites generally found their own place in life. Indeed,

34. See my paper, "Changes in mate choice in Chengdu," in D. Davis and E. Vogel (eds.), *Chinese Society on the Eve of Tiananmen* (Cambridge, MA: Harvard University Press, 1990), p. 197; Jonathan Unger, "Urban families in the eighties: an analysis of Chinese surveys," in D. Davis and S. Harrell (eds), *Chinese Families in the Post-Mao Era* (Berkeley: University of California Press, 1993), p. 28. The *dingti* system of job inheritance was formally abolished in 1983.

35. Even for Red Guards who denounced a parent, family rupture was often followed by eventual reconciliation and closer bonds. See the account in Gao Yuan, *Born Red* (Stanford: Stanford University Press, 1987). One of the most important stories of the immediate post-Mao period was Lu Xinhua's "The Scar," the short story which gave its name to a new genre of critical works on the Cultural Revolution era. The story concerns the emotional turmoil of a young woman who had broken all ties with her mother when the latter was branded a traitor in 1969. The young woman learns in 1978 that her mother has been exonerated and is in failing health. The daughter tries to return in time to apologize and be reconciled with her dying mother, but arrives too late. The story is translated in Liu Xinwu, Wang Meng *et al.*, *Prize-Winning Stories from China. 1978–1979* (Beijing: Foreign Languages Press, 1981).

the USSR, unlike China, had a functioning labour market, and individuals could readily obtain jobs and housing elsewhere.[36] Battling consumer shortages did require some degree of family co-ordinated effort in the USSR, although this was more a matter of finding members willing to stand in queues than of juggling ration coupons and finding a personal connection who could supply a good that was not available to the public.

On balance this discussion indicates that in both rural and urban China, as compared with the former Soviet Union, there were more forces at work that tended to strengthen family solidarity, although the contrast is sharper in the countryside than in the cities. This is not meant to imply that the socialist experience preserved Chinese family patterns unchanged. Despite considerable continuities, the families that were reinforced by Chinese socialism were also being changed in significant ways, such as by the increasing involvement in paid employment and access to education of women and, after 1970, by sharp declines in fertility.[37] One additional change is less often noted – the changing balance of power between the older and younger generations. The elimination for a generation of meaningful family property, combined with rising education of the young and other trends, significantly softened the power of the senior generation in Chinese families. This was particularly the case in urban China, but to some degree also in the countryside.

One clear indicator of the shift is the decline in the ability of parents to control whom their children marry. The result to date is still not the degree of youth autonomy that is visible in the West or in the former Soviet Union, but it is a marked change from the days when many brides and grooms didn't even meet until the day of the wedding. By the 1970s in the Chinese countryside the most common pattern was for young people to meet via an introduction, often still provided by the parents or other kin, but then to have substantial freedom to decide whether to marry or not. In the cities by the 1970s the most common pattern involved slightly more freedom of choice for the young: couples generally met on their own, or through introductions from friends, but then sought advice from their parents about whether to marry or not, and might or might not listen to parental views.[38]

For the purposes of this article what is important is not how young people find spouses but what this increasing autonomy means for the economic potential of Chinese families. Parents now cannot automati-

36. There were restrictions on moving into the largest Soviet cities, although these did not restrict urban migration as sharply as in China during the Mao period. Individuals were forbidden to move to or register in such cities without a job. However, the existence of a labour market and the perennial labour shortages of the Soviet system meant that individuals could obtain urban jobs and use those to move legally into large cities.

37. The variety of changes, as well as continuities, in Chinese family patterns during the socialist period are discussed in detail in my two books co-authored with William Parish and published by the University of Chicago Press: *Village and Family in Contemporary China* (1978) and *Urban Life in Contemporary China* (1984).

38. See the discussion in my paper, "Changes in mate choice in Chengdu." See also Yunxiang Yan, "Socialist transformation and family relations: the rise of conjugality and individuality in a Chinese village," unpublished paper for the American Anthropological Association meeting, 1992.

cally require obedience from their grown children. Rather, they have to provide inducements so their children will continue to contribute to the larger family unit. In many cases this adaptation involves respecting the partial autonomy and the ideas and efforts of the children. By the 1980s in rural areas the practice spread of expecting parents to provide a new home for each son as he married. In this fashion sons and their nuclear families could continue to engage in joint economic efforts with the parents while maintaining some autonomy.[39] The recent ability of rural young people to join the "floating population" in the cities also means that parents need to be flexible if they want the family to benefit from the loyalty (and remittances), education and ideas of their children.

In sum, the socialist era produced a complex set of pressures and strains on Chinese families. While experiences varied a great deal, the most general pattern was one which reinforced the solidarity of families, even while it changed them significantly. On balance the changes that occurred, particularly the softening of the power of the senior generation, modified or eliminated some of the main "obstacles" to development of the Chinese family described in the earlier scholarly literature. However, the softening of parental power did not weaken substantially the feeling of individuals of all ages that they had to rely on their families in order to survive. By reinforcing the tendency of Chinese to rely heavily on their families, the socialist era also sustained the positive potential of Chinese families to contribute to economic growth through a pattern of family mobilization of efforts – a potential similar to that displayed in Taiwan, Hong Kong and Singapore. However, this occurred to a greater degree in the countryside than in China's cities. That potential for family-mobilized economic dynamism – less to begin with in Russia and Eastern Europe – was not reinforced by experiences under socialism to the same extent in those countries. For this economic potential of Chinese families to be realized, however, required a wide range of changes in the policies and institutions of the PRC as well as in the global economic system.

The Economic Role of Chinese Families in the Reform Era

As decollectivization swept the Chinese countryside in the early 1980s, the rural family farm re-emerged as the primary unit of agricultural production. The reforms stopped short of providing full private ownership of agricultural land, but by 1984 central documents reassured China's villagers that they would have substantial security of tenure (15 years or more) and some ability to engage in transactions normal with private ownership (such as inheritance, rent, transfer). Other major changes in policy and institutions were critical to the release of peasant entrepreneurial efforts. In particular, the removal of restrictions on private enterprise and the eventual contracting out of management rights and quasi-

---

39. See the discussion in Yunxiang Yan, "Socialist transformation and family relations"; Myron Cohen, "Family management and family division in contemporary rural China," *The China Quarterly*, No. 130 (1992), p. 371.

privatization of many rural collective enterprises and facilities provided routes for rural families to get involved in non-agricultural activities. The open door policy and the ability of foreign firms to make direct investments and form joint ventures in China were also critical. Initially much of the investment capital came from Hong Kong and overseas Chinese sources, and these funds again tended to foster small to medium scale firms located in towns and villages, firms usually embedded in the local kinship system.[40]

As other articles in this issue illustrate, there is considerable debate about the nature of rural enterprises in the 1990s (see in particular the articles by Jean Oi, Louis Putterman and Thomas Rawski).[41] Are many of the township and village enterprises (TVEs) which have contributed so much to China's economic dynamism really disguised or quasi-private firms, despite their "collective" label, firms in which family-based entrepreneurship is an important element? Or is the dominant pattern one of genuinely collective firms run by hired, professional managers, with entrepreneurial drive supplied primarily from the outside, particularly by local officials?[42] The evidence suggests that stating the question in this "either-or" form is misleading, since a wide range of organizational types are hidden under the "collective" and TVE labels, with the mixture varying from place to place. Even in "pure" managerial enterprises family concerns are a source of employee performance and productivity, as noted earlier. In hybrid and private firms and the rest of the rural economy, including not simply agriculture but commerce, transportation, construction and sidelines, the dynamics of Chinese families are absolutely central.

Turning to other aspects of the reforms, the partial relaxation of restrictions on urban migration and the urban hiring of non-residents provided additional new outlets for family mobility strategies. By the early 1990s it was estimated that at any time up to 100 million villagers were off in China's large cities as members of the "floating population." Initially most of these newly footloose villagers came as individuals and often only for a short time. However, in recent years China's major cities have seen the rise of an increasing number of inns, shops and other enterprises financed and run by villagers, and the re-emergence of residential areas based on rural places of origin, as in the pre-1949 period, such as Beijing's Zhejiang village, Henan village and so on.[43] In addition, a substantial portion of migration in recent years has involved movement

40. See the discussion in Ezra Vogel, *One Step Ahead in China* (Cambridge, MA: Harvard University Press, 1989). See also Smart and Smart, "Obligation and control: employment of kin in capitalist labour management in China."

41. For alternative views, see Ole Odgaard, *Private Enterprises in Rural China* (Aldershot: Avebury, 1992); Elisabeth Croll, *From Heaven to Earth: Images and Experiences of Development in China* (London: Routledge, 1994); Kate Xiao Zhou, *How the Farmers Changed China* (Boulder: Westview Press, forthcoming).

42. These alternatives can be stated in a different form: is the analogy with Taiwan's development experience, with family-run firms a dominant feature, appropriate or inappropriate in understanding the dynamism of rural industry in the PRC in recent years?

43. See the discussion in Yan Yunxiang, "Dislocation, reposition and restratification: structural changes in Chinese society," in M. Brosseau and Lo Chi Kin (eds.), *China Review 1994* (Hong Kong: Chinese University Press, 1994).

among rural areas. as villagers seek their fortunes through peddling and providing hired labour in richer villages and regions.

In the framework developed by Susan Greenhalgh, these changes, China's "second land reform," have provided major institutional supports for the entrepreneurial efforts of rural families, although not quite as full a set of supports as Taiwan rural families received after that island's 1949–53 land reform. Increased security of rights to land and other productive assets and increased freedom for families to control their own economic affairs exist, but with continuing restrictions and interference from rural officials. Rural mobility strategies involving diversification of economic activity, dispersal of family members and accumulation of assets have been encouraged, but the ability to control family size and membership is still sharply limited by official birth control policy. Despite the limitations on family mobility strategies in the PRC, Green-halgh argues that the pent-up demand for family autonomy and mobility that existed in Chinese villages prior to 1978 resulted in a major upsurge of entrepreneurial efforts.[44]

In China's cities the response to market reforms has been less dramatic. The urban reforms lagged behind those in rural areas, and when they occurred they mostly took the form of changes around the edges, rather than a total transformation. Many of the urban changes involved efforts to provide market incentives for existing state and collective enterprises, rather than for individuals and families directly. Eventually a growing number of urban private enterprises began to spring up, and an increasing number of urbanites found ways to moonlight and supplement their income with other private initiatives. However, broadly speaking the great bulk of China's urban residents – more than 90 per cent – remain predominantly workers and employees, rather than petty capitalists. The obstacles to gaining access to the resources needed for operating a private or family-run firm in an urban economy dominated by state and collective enterprises remain daunting, although the situation is improving slowly.

When viewed in terms of Susan Greenhalgh's framework, the conditions required in order for the entrepreneurial potential of Chinese families to be displayed are still absent or relatively weak in China's cities. A substantial amount of the new, small-scale and family-run business activity visible there is provided by rural migrants, rather than by urbanites themselves.[45] If this article's discussion of the socialist era in China is correct, this situation does not indicate that urban families have no potential for family-based entrepreneurship, but simply that the conditions are not yet such as to allow much expression of that potential.

Indirect confirmation of the notion that both experiences in the collec-

44. Greenhalgh, "Land reform and family entrepreneurship in East Asia," pp. 105–106. One 1989 survey conducted in eight provinces found that an average of one in every seven rural households surveyed was involved in non-agricultural businesses, and that the distribution of such activity was surprisingly even, rather than concentrated in coastal regions or near cities. See Barbara Entwisle *et al.*, "Gender and family businesses in rural China," *American Sociological Review*, Vol. 60 (1995), pp. 36–57.
45. See the discussion in Zhou, *How the Farmers Changed China.*

tive era and the institutional changes of the reform era promote family-based entrepreneurial inclinations in China's countryside much more than in the cities comes from a recent survey of individual attitudes in the Tianjin area directed by Alex Inkeles and colleagues. The goal of the survey was to measure the extent to which individuals possess a complex of "modern" attitudes, a syndrome which overlaps substantially, although not perfectly, with entrepreneurial attitudes.[46] In every other country in which comparable surveys had been carried out, including one state socialist society (Bulgaria in 1988), urbanites were significantly more "modern" in their attitudes than rural residents. In the Tianjin survey, surprisingly, residents of the surrounding rural areas were significantly more "modern" in their attitudes than residents of the city itself, a pattern that Inkeles and his colleagues explain in a manner that parallels the argument in the preceding pages. China's urban residents, through their experience with a highly bureaucratized pattern of daily life (a pattern that persists to a considerable extent despite the post-1978 reforms) are less inclined than rural residents to assume that individual and family efforts to get ahead will be rewarded. Even though fairly high levels of family solidarity may persist among urbanites, the conditions of urban life still do not help convert that resource into family-based entrepreneurship.[47]

Comparisons with the post-socialist era in Russia and Eastern Europe are difficult because the experiences in those countries have varied quite widely. In general there appears to have been much less institutional support or even possibility for drawing on the entrepreneurial potential of families. Although in the Russian countryside and elsewhere there have been limited experiments with allowing the emergence of family farms, in most cases the former collective farms persist in some form.[48] Ideological opposition to the re-emergence of private landholding is only one source of the resistance to such a change. Family farming appears much less feasible than in China, since agriculture has been more bureaucratized and mechanized, and many rural families have few young and vigorous members. Where substantial tracts of land have been farmed for decades by bureaucratic units employing individuals as tractor drivers, milkmaids, agronomists and so on, finding families with the labour power and broad skills needed to operate viable family farms is not easy. In urban areas of Russia and Eastern Europe the situation is more compar-

46. Alex Inkeles, C. Montgomery Broaded and Zhongde Cao, "Causes and consequences of individual modernity in mainland China," unpublished paper. Common elements in Inkeles's syndrome of individual modernity and entrepreneurship include conceptions of personal efficacy, the ability to get ahead through diligent effort, and rational planning. However, the notion of strong loyalty to the family is somewhat discordant with Inkeles's conception of individual modernity. For a more general discussion of the concept of attitudinal modernity as a cross-national phenomenon, see Alex Inkeles and David Smith, *Becoming Modern* (Cambridge, MA: Harvard University Press, 1979).

47. The family-based firms that have been established by Chinese urbanites tend to be small-scale efforts in the service sector, such as family-run restaurants, rather than the full range of industrial, construction and other firms that their rural counterparts are establishing.

48. In Poland, of course, private farming was allowed to persist from the 1950s onwards, as was the case in the former Yugoslavia.

able to that in China's cities, but is perhaps even less favourable to the re-emergence of family-run firms. Some privatization, of course, has taken the form of the selling of former state firms to foreign companies. In addition, new private firms are often run by individuals or partnerships, rather than by families. In short, neither the previous experience of families in these countries nor the current institutional structures are encouraging the emergence of family-run firms to anywhere near the same extent as in China.

There is one final, important point of difference between China and the former Soviet Union and Eastern Europe. China's economic boom has been fuelled in no small part by Hong Kong, Taiwan and overseas Chinese capital, as noted earlier. The existence of millions of émigrés in organized communities outside China has provided a powerful resource for China's post-1978 development, although Nicholas Lardy's article indicates that this resource was less important as a source of net capital flows than for access to technology and overseas markets.[49] The situation with regard to Russia and Eastern Europe is quite different. There are a few examples of individual émigrés returning home to resume business activity in their native lands. There is the exceptional case of the "foreign aid" being doled out in these countries by billionaire Hungarian émigré George Soros. However, for the most part these countries have not benefited from anything like the major infusions of funds and skills that China has received from ethnic Chinese living beyond its national borders.

The evidence reviewed in this article suggests that the entrepreneurial instincts and strong loyalties of families survived the socialist era in the PRC and found an encouraging set of institutional supports during the reform era, particularly in China's rural areas. However, for the positive economic potential of Chinese families and kinship relations to be unleashed, another set of conditions also had to be favourable – those operating in the world economy. By the 1980s conditions here had changed compared with a generation earlier in ways that played to the strengths of Chinese families and family-run firms.

The changes involved are complex, and there is not space to go into them in detail.[50] However, in general they are ones that helped make family-run firms so successful earlier in Taiwan, Hong Kong and the other "mini-dragons." The development of global competition using advanced technology and communications in relatively open markets, combined with rising labour costs in the more advanced countries, placed a premium on relatively small and medium-sized firms with well educated and highly motivated and disciplined (but modestly paid) workers, firms that could respond rapidly to changing market conditions and

---

49. A recent study produced an estimate that in 1990 there were 37 million overseas Chinese, with more than 32 million of these residing in Asia. See Dudley Poston, Michael Mao and Mei-yu Yu, "The global distribution of the overseas Chinese around 1990," *Population and Development Review*, Vol. 20 (1994), pp. 631–645.

50. For further discussion see my paper, "The Chinese family and development: obstacle or engine?"

produce high quality products for low cost. Relatively secure legal, financial, transportation and other institutional frameworks in industrialized economies provided a more secure and profitable set of opportunities than many such firms could find in their own domestic markets. Some analysts argue that in this changed environment, "Fordist" firms (the kind of large, hierarchical corporations once assumed to be the most efficient) have great difficulties competing and holding on to their markets, unless they enter into joint venture, subcontracting or other arrangements with more nimble firms employing cheaper but high quality labour.[51] China's large state factories are prototypical "Fordist" enterprises in this sense, and they have had considerable difficulty competing with newer and smaller rivals for the opportunities flowing from China's post-1978 open door policy. In the former Soviet Union and Eastern Europe, where capital intensive industrial giants were the general rule, it has also proved difficult to take advantage of the niches the global economy of the 1980s and 1990s provided for small firms staffed by diligent employees.

Conclusions

If the impressionistic evidence reviewed in this article is correct, the family and kinship patterns at the base of Chinese society have played a positive role in China's recent economic surge. By the same token these grass roots social patterns help explain why China has been much more successful than the countries of Eastern Europe and the former Soviet Union in making the transition away from a centrally planned economy. Whereas the conventional wisdom in earlier decades was that individuals and firms had to be "liberated" from strong family obligations in order to operate efficiently, the Chinese experience (both inside and outside the PRC) suggests an alternative approach, with strong family loyalties mobilized to produce economic dynamism. However, these positive contributions are not due to the fact that the Chinese family is an "engine of development" under any and all circumstances. A variety of historical influences and institutional supports were necessary in order for this potential to be displayed. A large number of such influences and supports have been suggested by the present analysis, including: a cultural legacy of family mobility strategizing; the fact that the era of full socialism in China lasted only a generation; an experience of Chinese families under socialism that preserved and may even have enhanced family loyalties for most, while softening the power of the older generation; the fact that large numbers of Chinese émigrés with entrepreneurial inclinations and access to capital stood ready to invest in operations in the PRC under suitable conditions; a set of post-1978 reforms that met many of the basic conditions needed to unleash family entrepreneurial efforts; and a global

51. See the discussion in Michael Piore and Charles Sabel, *The Second Industrial Divide: Possibilities for Prosperity* (New York: Basic Books, 1984); Martin Kenney and Richard Florida, *Beyond Mass Production* (New York: Oxford University Press, 1993); Paul Hirst and Jonathan Zeitlin, "Flexible specialization versus post-Fordism: theory, evidence, and policy implications," *Economy and Society*, Vol. 20 (1991), pp. 1–56.

economic situation that allowed small and medium-scale PRC firms, many of them with family links, to surge into the economic niches that had been occupied by similar firms in places like Hong Kong and Taiwan. Without such a favourable set of conditions, the contribution of Chinese "entrepreneurial familism" would have been much less. Furthermore, to date these contributions are much more evident in China's rural areas than in the cities.

Given the evidence reviewed here, it is still difficult to say just how important the "social roots" found in Chinese families have been for China's recent economic success. It now seems difficult to give credence to the earlier claim that China's family system is an obstacle to economic development, but it is less clear whether the family's positive role mattered a little or a lot. As other articles indicate, there are many historical, institutional, geopolitical, policy and other factors that have differentiated China from the former Soviet Union and East European countries and help to explain its superior economic performance in recent years. In this sense China's better record is "overdetermined," and it is difficult to assess the relative importance of any single factor. There is also debate, as noted earlier, about how important family-based entrepreneurship has been in explaining the success of China's township and village enterprises, the most dynamic sector of the economy in recent years. Given these uncertainties, the best I can do is conclude that the contributions of China's family system are part of the explanation for China's recent economic success, but not the primary factor. An explanation that attributes China's superior economic performance mainly to Confucian family values would be much too simple, but so would an explanation that left Chinese families out of the picture entirely.

If the conclusion that China's family system has played some role in China's recent economic dynamism is accepted, then a more provocative set of questions is raised. The PRC has had the most rapidly growing economy in the world in the last few years, despite significant restrictions on the ability of families to make their own economic decisions and plan mobility strategies. Most urban families are still dependent upon only partially reformed state and collective enterprises and are confronted with a situation in which markets in several areas (such as labour and housing) are not fully operative.[52] Rural families are better off in these respects, but still constrained in several ways – by controls over their fertility, by lack of full property rights in land, by weaknesses in the legal system that make them vulnerable to the predatory behaviour of rural cadres, and by significant remaining barriers to their ability to diversify into urban occupations. If the PRC is able to reform its institutional structure in ways that reduce or remove such constraints, will the released family-based entrepreneurship make China's economy even more dynamic? Is it possible that China could grow even more rapidly, and if so, what would the world be like?

52. Urbanites also have their fertility limited even more sharply than do rural residents. In China's largest cities there is a high degree of compliance with the one child policy, whereas in the countryside the norm is closer to two children.

Redefining State, Plan and Market: China's Reforms in Agricultural Commerce*

Terry Sicular

Since the late 1970s the Chinese government has taken major steps to open up domestic markets and promote the development of commerce. Policies during the reform period have included reducing the scope of commercial planning, eliminating state commercial monopolies, and permitting individuals, collectives and enterprises to buy and sell at mutually acceptable, market-based prices. The effects of such measures are evident in the busy retail districts of China's cities and in the lively market fairs in the countryside.

The depth and nature of this commercial development are not well understood. In particular, questions exist concerning the extent to which China's commercial reforms have promoted the development of competitive, efficient and widely accessible markets. Although the government has lifted restrictions on trade, simply announcing the removal of restrictions does not ensure that well-functioning markets will emerge. The infrastructure, institutions and economic attitudes necessary for competitive, efficient markets may require time to develop and need active nurture. While planning has been reduced, the government continues to set prices and plan the procurement and sale of key products. The procurement quotas and ration programmes that remain could still heavily influence production, commercial participation and market outcomes. Although state monopolies have been lifted for most products, the pre-existent system of state commercial enterprises and agencies largely remains in place. New market entrants may therefore be at a competitive disadvantage, and the reforms could lead to the development of monopolistic markets.

This article examines the reforms in commerce for agricultural products with an eye towards shedding light on these questions. Four broad conclusions emerge. First, commerce has grown substantially and has penetrated deeply in rural areas. Secondly, the reforms have led to the development of increasingly complex commercial activities and relationships. In this context, familiar terms like "state," "plan" and "market" must be re-evaluated. These terms are examined below and definitions appropriate for the current environment are suggested.

Thirdly, the state continues to play an important role in the commercial sphere. State commercial agencies still handle a significant share of

* I thank Richard Garbaccio and Scott Rozelle for their generous help with data and sources, and Peter Nolan, Andrew Walder and other participants at the *China Quarterly* workshop for their comments. This research received financial support from the National Science Foundation under grant number SES-8908438, the Committee on Scholarly Communications with China with funds from the U.S. Information Agency, and the University of Western Ontario.

commercial transactions, and for certain products they dominate the market.[1] Nevertheless, a large market share does not always translate into market power. In markets where the state dominates, the extent to which the state can exercise market power is limited by indirect competition from products in other markets and by growing competition among state agencies. Finally, although the government continues to set planned procurement quotas for grain and cotton, the presence of quotas does not necessarily imply the existence of truly "planned" trade. In the case of cotton, underfulfilment of quotas is so widespread that farmers are apparently no longer constrained, or perhaps only weakly constrained, by the plan.

While these conclusions are based on analysis of the commercial reforms for agricultural products, they have broader relevance. Reforms in the domestic trade of consumer manufactures and of producer goods have followed similar paths.[2] While differences exist in the depth and extent of commercial liberalization, in all spheres commercial relationships have become increasingly complex, necessitating reconsideration of terms like "state" and "plan." In all spheres, moreover, the reforms have to a greater or lesser extent allowed the entry of new commercial actors and encouraged competition among agencies in the formerly monolithic state commercial system.

An Overview of Commercial Reforms in Agriculture[3]

Before 1978 state commerce dominated the exchange of major farm products in China. Cotton, grain and vegetable oils were subject to unified procurement (*tongyi shougou*), under which the government set plans for procurement and maintained a monopoly or near-monopoly on domestic trade. For cotton, farmers could sell only to state procurement stations run by the Cotton and Hemp Bureau, which was administratively under the National Federation of Supply and Marketing Co-ops. The government prohibited other organizations and individuals from engaging in cotton trade. Farm sales of grains and oilseeds went primarily to state

1. Here and below state commerce includes trade by the National Federation of Supply and Marketing Co-ops, which, despite being nominally collective, has effectively been a branch of the state commercial system.

2. For discussion of commercial reforms in these spheres, see William A. Byrd, "The impact of the two-tier plan/market system in Chinese industry," *Journal of Comparative Economics*, Vol. 11, No. 3 (1987), pp. 295–308, Athar Hussain, "The Chinese enterprise reforms," London School of Economics China Programme Working Paper No. 5 (June 1990), Richard H. Holton and Terry Sicular, "Economic reform of the distribution sector in China," *American Economic Review*, Vol. 81, No. 2 (1991), pp. 212–17, and the World Bank, *China: Internal Market Development and Regulation* (Washington, D.C.: The World Bank, 1994).

3. This section summarizes the 1980s reforms and gives more detail on the 1990s. For in-depth discussion of the 1980s, see Jean Oi, *State and Peasant in Contemporary China: The Political Economy of Village Government* (Berkeley: University of California Press, 1989), Andrew Watson, "The reform of agricultural marketing in China since 1978," *The China Quarterly*, No. 113 (1988), pp. 1–28, and Terry Sicular, "China's agricultural policy during the reform period," in Joint Economic Committee of the U.S. Congress, *China's Economic Dilemma in the 1990s: The Problems of Reforms, Modernization, and Interdependence* (Washington, D.C.: U.S. Government Printing Office, 1991), pp. 340–364.

procurement stations under the Ministry of Grain (later the Bureau of Grain).[4] After local delivery quotas had been met, farmers could sell additional amounts to the state at higher, above-quota prices. Provincial or county officials sometimes permitted farmers to sell grain and oilseeds to other buyers at market prices; however, the government only allowed such trade locally (within county borders) and on a small scale. Trade in farm products other than cotton and grain was also subject to restrictions, as government policies prohibited individuals and organizations other than the designated state agencies from specializing in commerce or engaging in long-distance transport.

After 1977 commercial policies changed as the government began to promote a policy of "multiple channels" for commerce. Beginning in 1981 individuals were permitted to establish small-scale businesses to conduct trade in animal products, vegetables, minor crops, and light manufactures such as textiles and clothing. In 1982 the government eased restrictions on the trade of grain by allowing individuals, non-commercial state agencies, enterprises and collectives to trade in grain both locally and long-distance once local grain quotas had been met. At this time the periodic market system, which historically had been an important channel for rural commerce, began to re-emerge.

Government planning of procurement and sales continued, but the scope of planning was gradually reduced. In the early 1980s many products were dropped from the list of items subject to delivery quotas and ration sales. While grain, oilseeds and cotton remained subject to plan, for grain and oilseeds the government reduced the level of mandatory quotas. Reductions in planning and the concurrent rapid growth in agricultural output greatly expanded the scope for market exchange.

At this time state commercial agencies became players in market trade. Under what was called "negotiated" procurement (*yijia shougou*), the state purchased farm output at prices which were set administratively to follow trends in supply and demand. In principle negotiated prices were to be slightly below market prices, and sales to the state at these prices were to be voluntary. Thus in the early 1980s farmers wishing to sell output beyond their quotas had several options. First, they could sell certain crops to the state at the above-quota bonus price (for grain and oilseeds this price was 50 per cent higher than the quota price; for cotton it was 30 per cent higher). Secondly, they could sell to the state at negotiated prices. Thirdly, they could sell to new market entrants at market prices.

Commercial reforms took a major step forward in 1984 when the central government announced a plan to eliminate planned procurement of farm products and expand the role of markets. This policy change was

---

4. Since the 1950s China's commercial administration has undergone several reorganizations. See Ministry of Commerce Institute of Economic Research, *Xin Zhongguo shangye shigao* (*A Commercial History of New China*) (Beijing: Zhongguo caizheng jingji chubanshe, 1984) and Contemporary China's Commerce Editorial Committee, *Dangdai Zhongguo shangye* (*Contemporary China's Commerce*) (Beijing: Zhongguo shehui kexue chubanshe, 1988), Vol. 1.

prompted by several factors. Rapid growth in agricultural production in the early 1980s had eliminated perceived shortages of farm products. In the case of grain, for which the government had a policy of purchasing as much as farmers wished to sell at the above-quota price, state commercial agencies had surplus supplies and overflowing warehouses. Grain procured at above-quota and negotiated prices was sold at considerably lower planned sales prices, causing substantial financial losses. By 1984 government spending on price subsidies was 22 billion *yuan*, equivalent to 14 per cent of total government budgetary revenues. Of this, 93 per cent was price subsidies on grain, oilcrops and cotton.[5]

In response, the government announced that starting in 1985 mandatory quotas for grain and cotton were to be replaced by procurement using voluntary advance contracts (*hetong dinggou*). For grain, the state would procure only wheat and rice under contract. Farmers would now sell all other varieties of grain either to the state at negotiated prices or on the market. Farmers would also sell any wheat and rice beyond the contracted quantities at negotiated or market prices. Free market exchange of grain was permitted even during the procurement season. For the first time in decades the government allowed cotton to be traded on the market. More generally, it planned to phase out state commerce for all but a handful of key farm products. Markets were expected to grow gradually to encompass most transactions.

As has been discussed elsewhere, the government retreated from the 1985 reforms after grain and cotton production fell in 1985. In 1986–87 it announced that grain and cotton procurement contracts were no longer voluntary. In ensuing years it reinstated its monopsony on rice and cotton, and prohibited grain trade on free markets unless local (county) quotas had been met.[6] Mandatory production targets, which had been abolished in 1985, were revived so as to ensure contract fulfilment.

Despite these reversals, the 1985 reforms fundamentally altered the commercial environment in rural areas. Evidence presented below shows an immediate and persistent increase in the importance of trade on the market and in commercial activity by new entrants (see Table 7, below). Furthermore, efforts to reform rural commerce did not entirely stop. In the late 1980s, for example, the government raised contract procurement prices for grain, oilcrops and cotton and announced that obligatory quotas for grain deliveries at negotiated prices were to be eliminated.[7] At this time it also began to reduce the scope of ration sales. Cuts in rationing were prompted by renewed growth in price subsidies. These had declined after the 1985 reforms, but rebounded to 37 billion

5. To cover the losses of money-losing commercial enterprises, the government made additional outlays totalling 9 billion *yuan* in 1984. *Zhongguo tongji nianjian, 1993* (*Statistical Yearbook of China, 1993*) (Beijing: Zhongguo tongji chubanshe, 1993), pp. 215, 231, 626.

6. *Zhongguo shangye nianjian, 1990* (*Almanac of China's Commerce, 1990*) (Beijing: Zhongguo shangye nianjianshe, 1990), p. 16.

7. This announcement suggests that negotiated grain procurement had not been entirely voluntary. See *Zhongguo shangye nianjian, 1990*, pp. 15–16, 47, and Terry Sicular, "Establishing markets: The process of commercialization in agriculture," unpublished manuscript, 1994.

yuan, equivalent to 12 per cent of government budgetary expenditures, by 1989.[8]

The pace of commercial reform once again accelerated in the early 1990s. A key component of the new wave of commercial reforms was the liberalization of grain markets. In 1991 the central government allowed regional experiments in grain market reform. The content of these reforms varied among localities, but generally followed one of two forms: elimination of rationing while maintaining mandatory contract deliveries (although sometimes at reduced levels), or elimination of both rationing and mandatory contract deliveries. Experimental areas also eased restrictions on grain trade in free markets.[9]

In 1991 153 counties nation-wide, including 107 in Guangdong province, had adopted such experimental reforms. By the end of 1992 more than 400, or nearly 20 per cent of the counties in China, had adopted them. The scope of grain market liberalization continued to widen in 1993.[10] By the autumn of that year more than 90 per cent of the provinces, 280 prefectures and cities, and more than 1,900 counties had dropped grain rationing.[11] Although many areas maintained mandatory grain contracts, in 1993 the central government increased contract prices to the level of market prices. This was intended to pave the way for the removal of mandatory procurement.

Parallel reforms occurred for cotton circulation. In 1992 the State Council approved an experimental policy deregulating cotton markets in selected provinces, including the major cotton-producing provinces of Shandong, Hebei and Jiangsu. These provinces were to eliminate mandatory production plans, abolish the state cotton monopoly and permit beyond-quota cotton to be sold on the market at market prices.[12] Farmers

8. Some 70% of these price subsidies was for grain, oilcrops and cotton. *Zhongguo tongji nianjian, 1993*, pp. 215, 231.

9. Andrew Watson, "Market reform and agricultural development in China," University of Adelaide Chinese Economy Research Unit Working Paper No. 94/3 (January 1994), pp. 12–14, Frederick W. Crook, "Reform of China's grain and oilseed markets," in U.S. Department of Agriculture, *China: Situation and Outlook Series*, RS-93-4, July 1993, pp. 12–15, and *Zhongguo shangye nianjian, 1992*, p. I-3.

10. *Zhongguo shangye nianjian, 1992*, p. I-3, and *Zhongguo shangye nianjian, 1993*, pp. I-3, IV-1 to IV-3. The expansion of the grain market reforms to other provinces in 1993 is reported by Ji Xirong, Dong Yiman and Sun Meijun, "Survey of grain circulatory restructuring in Hunan and Hubei," *Zhongguo nongcun jingji (China's Rural Economy)*, No. 2 (1993), pp. 45–48, translated in JPRS-CAR 93-036, 3 June 1993, pp. 24–27, and Cheng Jiyun, "Anhui province implements new policy on grain production and sales," *Nongmin ribao (Farmer's Daily)* (23 April 1993), p. 1, translated in JPRS-CAR 93-054, 30 July 1993, p. 35. Shandong adopted grain market reforms in 1993 (author interviews, Zouping county, Shandong, 1993–94).

11. "Moving ahead while tackling difficulties – correspondent summarizes new situation of all-out pursuit of economic system reform," *Zhongguo jingji tizhi gaige (China's Economic Structure Reform)*, No. 10 (1993), pp. 16–18, translated in JPRS-CAR 94-010, pp. 14–16.

12. Hunter W. Colby, "Discouraged by IOUs and pests, cotton farmers cut 1993 area," in U.S. Department of Agriculture Economic Research Service, *China: Situation and Outlook Series*, RS-93-4, July 1993, pp. 24–26, Dong Ying and Cheng Jianhua, "Historical retrospective on China's cotton system," *Zhongguo nongcun jingji*, No. 6 (1994), pp. 28–35, translated in JPRS-CAR 94-046, 15 September 1994, pp. 67–75, and Ren Fang, "China's cotton industry moves toward market system," *Jingji ribao (Economic Daily)* (22 December 1992), p. 2, translated in JPRS-CAR 93-009, 9 February 1993, p. 44.

delivering cotton to the state were no longer required to go to the designated state cotton procurement station in their township, but could choose to go to any procurement station they wished.[13] These measures were intended to generate competition among agencies buying cotton from farmers.

Central policy-makers recognized that deregulation of grain and cotton markets would need to be accompanied by reforms altering the role and function of state commercial agencies and enterprises.[14] Earlier reforms in other areas such as fiscal decentralization and enterprise management contracting had to some extent already affected state commerce, but did not address its particular problems, especially those in commerce for grain and cotton. In 1992/93 the central government announced major initiatives aimed specifically at the state grain system. Grain ration shops were to be contracted or leased out and held responsible for their profits and losses. Local grain bureaus that had previously handled grain procurement in rural areas were to be converted into trading companies and contracted out using various forms of contractual management responsibility systems under which they would be financially self-supporting and managerially independent from government administration. These grain trading companies were to be given greater authority to set prices, make personnel decisions and diversify into other lines of business. Similar reforms were discussed for the cotton commercial system.[15]

In 1993 and 1994, following unanticipated drops in both cotton and grain production, rapid increases in market prices for farm products and the re-emergence of general inflation, aspects of the new commercial initiatives were held in check or reversed. Indeed, the need to reassert controls over prices and markets was a major theme of Li Peng's government work report at the opening of the National People's Congress in March 1995.[16] Emphasis on enforcement of mandatory procurement quotas was renewed, and 29 of China's 35 largest cities had reintroduced grain rationing by early 1995.[17] While the grain enterprise reforms have apparently continued to be implemented, their progress has been slowed by various obstacles. State grain enterprises have large accumulated losses and debts, their warehouses are stocked with old, inferior grain,

13. Interviews in Zouping county, Shandong, 1992–94.

14. Dong Ying and Cheng Jianhua, "Historical retrospective," Li Wenru, "Taking price reform as the breach and enlivening grain enterprises as the focus – reform of grain circulation will take a big step," *Jingji cankaobao* (*Economic Reference News*), 10 December 1992, p. 1, translated in JPRS-CAR 93-008, 5 February 1993, pp. 38–39, *Zhongguo shangye nianjian, 1992*, p. I-5, and *Zhongguo shangye nianjian, 1993*, pp. I-4, I-5.

15. Dong Ying and Cheng Jianhua, "Historical retrospective," Li Wenru, "Taking price reform as the breach," Scott Rozelle and Albert Park, "Gradual reform and institutional development: the keys to success of China's agricultural reforms," unpublished manuscript, Stanford University, January 1995, pp. 7–8, and author interviews in Zouping county, Shandong, 1991–94.

16. Patrick Tyler, "Chinese leader says 'mistakes' by government fueled inflation," *New York Times*, 6 March 1995, pp. A1, A9.

17. Reports of renewed rationing can be found in various news sources, for example, in *China News Digest*, 1 May 1995, 9 January 1995, 12 December 1994, and 17–18 October 1994.

and their managers and staff are unused to facing the rigours of the market.[18] The drop in cotton production brought an end to experiments in cotton marketing: the Supply and Marketing Co-op system is once again the sole buyer and seller of cotton, and it continues as of yore to carry out quota procurement at planned prices.[19] Despite these reversals, the agenda for the next phase of commercial reform has been clearly laid out, and ongoing commercial subsidies create pressure on both central and local governments to move ahead with reform. Once agricultural production recovers and inflation slows, then, these commercial reforms are likely to resume.

The Development of Agricultural Commerce

China's development since the late 1980s reflects the impact of the commercial reforms described above. Commerce has grown rapidly. Between 1980 and 1992 retail sales (deflated to correct for inflation) grew at an average annual rate of about 8 per cent. In comparison, during the same period GDP (deflated) grew 9 per cent a year.[20] Data on retail sales understate China's commercial development because they do not count trade within rural areas. Although direct data on intra-rural trade are unavailable, the volume of trade on rural free markets captures a portion of this exchange. From 1980 to 1992 trade on rural free markets (deflated) rose 12 per cent a year, outpacing growth in both retail sales and GDP. These trends suggest that the commercial reforms were especially beneficial to the development of trade in the countryside.[21]

Expansion in the number of commercial businesses accompanied growth in trade volume. In 1980 China had 1.7 million retail businesses, one for every 675 people; by 1992 the number of retail businesses exceeded 10 million, or one for every 116 people. During the same period the number of free market places more than doubled, and the average number of people per market place fell from 24,000 in 1990 to fewer than 15,000.[22]

Commercialization is sometimes defined as the extent to which economic agents rely on purchases and sales rather than self-sufficiently

---

18. Ji Xirong, Dong Yiman and Sun Meijun, "Survey of grain circulatory restructuring," Zhan Zhongliang and Leng Chongzong, "The pros and cons of the reform of the grain and oil purchasing and marketing system," *Jiage yuekan* (*Pricing Monthly*), No. 3 (1993), pp. 33–34, translated in JPRS-CAR-93-039, pp. 30–33, and Zhou Jiyun, "Problems and suggestions stemming from changes in the wake of deregulation of grain prices and dealings," *Jiage yuekan*, No. 9 (1993), pp. 42–43, translated in JPRS-CAR 94-002, pp. 25–28.

19. Dong Ying and Cheng Jianhua, "Historical retrospective," and author interviews in Zouping county, Shandong, 1993 and 1994.

20. Retail sales are deflated using the national retail price index. These numbers are calculated using data from *Zhongguo tongji nianjian, 1993*, pp. 31, 238, 611.

21. Rural free market transactions are deflated using the free market price index. These numbers are calculated using data from *Zhongguo shichang tongji nianjian, 1993* (*Yearbook of China's Market Statistics, 1993*) (Beijing: Zhongguo tongji chubanshe, 1993), pp. 415, 459, and *Zhongguo shangye waijing tongji ziliao, 1952–88* (*Statistical Materials on China's Commerce and Trade, 1952–88*) (Beijing: Zhongguo tongji chubanshe, 1990), p. 399.

22. *Zhongguo tongji nianjian, 1994*, pp. 59, 499, and *Zhongguo shichang tongji nianjian, 1993*, pp. 47, 415.

supplying goods and services for their own use. The rise in commercialization so defined is clearly visible in China's rural areas. The income of rural households includes both cash income and in-kind income from items produced for their own use; similarly, expenditures of rural households include both self-supplied and purchased items. Between 1980 and 1993 the share of cash income in the total income of Chinese rural households rose from 52 to 68 per cent. During the same period cash expenditures rose from 63 to 83 per cent of their total expenditures. In the early 1990s roughly two-thirds of total consumption by rural households was purchased.[23] Although these statistics are imperfect, they indicate that by the 1990s China's rural population relied heavily on commerce in both their production and consumption activities.[24]

Commercial development requires supporting infrastructure and institutions. Since the late 1970s governments at both central and local levels have invested in transportation and communications infrastructure, with the result that between 1978 and 1993 the total mileage of surfaced roads rose by 47 per cent, of railway lines by 11 per cent and of double-track railway lines by 88 per cent. During the same period the number of telephones increased sevenfold, and the number of long-distance telephone lines rose more than twentyfold.[25]

An important institution facilitating commercial development in rural areas has been the rural market fair or periodic market. Between 1980 and 1993 the number of periodic market places in rural China increased from 38,000 to 67,000.[26] Even these numbers understate the expansion of trade through periodic markers, as the average volume of trade at each market has grown. By 1992 trade on rural free markets was equivalent to 34 per cent of retail sales in rural areas.[27] China's periodic market system has, moreover, expanded beyond its traditional scope. New markets are emerging at locations that historically were not market places, and the number of specialized and wholesale markets has grown. For some products an interlinked, three-tiered system of local periodic markets, regional wholesale markets, and national wholesale markets and commodity exchanges is emerging.[28]

23. *Zhongguo tongji nianjian, 1994*, pp. 276, 280; *Zhongguo tongji nianjian, 1993*, pp. 311, 315; *Zhongguo tongji nianjian, 1990*, pp. 312, 316; *Zhongguo tongji nianjian, 1986*, p. 675.

24. Because self-supplied items have been valued at below-market accounting prices, these numbers overstate the shares of cash income and cash expenditures. In recent years the State Statistical Bureau has increased the prices at which it values retained output, so that the degree of this bias has been reduced. The change in accounting practices, however, creates a problem of comparability over time. If valuation of retained output had remained constant, then growth in commercialization would be larger than that shown by the official statistics.

25. *Zhongguo tongji nianjian, 1994*, pp. 459, 472–73, 484–85.

26. *Zhongguo shichang tongji nianjian, 1993*, p. 415, and *Zhongguo tongji nianjian, 1994*, p. 499.

27. *Zhongguo tongji nianjian, 1993*, pp. 611, 625, and *Zhongguo tongji nianjian, 1994*, p. 499.

28. Interviews, Zouping county, Shandong, 1992–94, Andrew Watson, "The reform of agricultural marketing," and Guo Guorong and Li Ji, "Regional grain circulation becoming more market oriented," *Zhongguo nongcun jingji*, No. 9 (1994), pp. 36–41, translated in JPRS-CAR-94-055, 30 November 1994, pp. 57–62.

The Structure of Commerce: State, Plan, and Market

Discussions of reform in China and other socialist countries often employ phrases like "plan and market" or "state and market." Evidence on China's commercial development during the reform period reveals that the relationships between plan, market and state have become increasingly complex. Indeed, as originally understood these terms are no longer applicable.

Farm households in China now sell their products through a variety of channels, to a variety of buyers and at a variety of prices. As mentioned, periodic markets have become an increasingly important channel for exchange. Farm households also sell their products to commercial intermediaries and take their products directly to users. Buyers now include not only state commercial agencies, but also consumers, private merchants, collective and state-owned enterprises, and organizations such as schools, hospitals and government administrative offices. State commercial agencies buy and sell some farm products under plan at administratively-set prices. These same agencies also buy and sell products outside the plan at negotiated prices. Other organizations and agencies, as well as consumers and private merchants, purchase farm products from farmers at mutually agreed-upon prices determined by the market.

This multiplicity of commercial channels, agents and prices in rural China raises questions about the usual "plan versus market" or "state versus market" classifications. For example, if a farmer sells corn to a state-owned enterprise at a market price, is the sale through state or market channels? Is grain procured by the state Grain Bureau at negotiated prices plan or market trade? Three features of the reform environment make such classification difficult. First, many government agencies and state-owned enterprises have become active market participants. They now buy and sell outside the plan at market or near-market prices. Furthermore, the planned trade of these agencies is no longer divorced from the market, because the existence of market opportunities creates incentives to evade quotas, especially if planned prices deviate too far from market prices. To a greater or lesser extent, then, state agencies operate through markets or in accord with markets.

Secondly, for key products the dominant buyer (or seller) is often a state commercial agency. As discussed below, for example, the Cotton and Hemp Company continues to buy almost all cotton sold by farmers, and the Grain Bureau continues to dominate procurement of grain. The position of these state agencies at the local level often resembles that of a monopsonistic firm. Economists define a monopsonist as a buyer that, by virtue of its size in the market, has the power to set prices to its advantage. Trade by a monopsonist is a type of market trade, albeit in an imperfectly competitive market. This raises a question: should procurement at administratively-set prices by a state commercial enterprise be considered "planned" trade or simply "market" trade by a monopsonist?

Thirdly, the "state" is not a single, undifferentiated entity.[29] Farmers sell grain to the grain procurement station under their county Grain Bureau, the designated state commercial agent for grain. They also sell to state-owned food-processing enterprises, state-run livestock farms, and state grain bureaus from other localities. These various state agents need not act in co-ordination; indeed, they are likely to be competitive.

In view of these considerations, the distinction between "state" and "non-state" is no longer conceptually useful.[30] A more relevant distinction is that between purchases and sales by those government agencies that are officially designated to conduct trade, and purchases and sales by other, non-designated agents. The former are charged with the task of carrying out the broader commercial policies and objectives of the government. These are the agencies that conduct quota procurement and ration sales, manage state storage facilities, engage in open market operations so as to stabilize markets, and provide supplies for poverty and disaster relief. They are usually backed by a large bureaucracy, own substantial fixed capital in storage, transport and related facilities, and have well-established marketing networks. They may be concerned with profits and losses, but to a large degree their behaviour in the trade of designated products has been policy-driven, and so has differed from that of a market-oriented, profit-seeking enterprise.

Non-designated state agencies and state-owned enterprises share some of these features, but in their commercial activities they are more likely to behave like profit-seeking agents. Historically, they were required to purchase from and sell to the designated state agencies. During the reform period non-commercial state enterprises and agencies have been able to conduct independent trade, and they have done so as a way of increasing their earnings. Thus their commercial activities are more profit-oriented than policy-driven.

In view of these differences, the term "designated agencies" is used here to mean those government agencies and enterprises that are officially charged with the task of carrying out commerce for the products in question. Trade in grain by designated agencies refers to purchases and sales of grain by the state Grain Bureau and its affiliated agencies and companies. Trade in cotton by designated agencies refers to purchases and sales of cotton by the Cotton and Hemp Company and its affiliated agencies within the National Federation of Supply and Marketing Co-ops. Trade through "non-designated" channels refers to purchase or sale of farm products by all other agents. It obviously includes trade among private individuals, and also by collective enterprises and by government agencies and state enterprises that are not the official agents handling state commerce for the product in question. Independent purchases of

29. See Jean Oi, "Economic growth and local governments in Zouping county," unpublished manuscript, Harvard University, 1993, for an interesting discussion of this issue.

30. This distinction is also problematic because of the complexity of ownership forms in China. For example, township enterprises are officially classified as "collective," but they are often set up and run by local governments and thus are effectively local state enterprises. See Andrew Walder, "The varieties of public enterprise in China: an institutional analysis," unpublished manuscript, Harvard University, January 1994.

farm products outside designated state commercial channels by a state-owned industrial enterprise, a school or hospital, the military, or even by an office in the government bureaucracy are all classified as non-designated trade.

The term "market" should not be used in juxtaposition with "state" or "designated" because "market" refers to the nature of the transaction, while "state" and "designated" refer to the type of agent conducting the transaction. Economists view "market" transactions as voluntary exchange of mutually agreed upon quantities at mutually agreed upon prices. "Market" prices are determined by supply and demand, where supply is the quantity producers are willing to produce at each price, and demand is the quantity buyers are willing to buy at each price.[31]

Market trade need not take place in a perfectly competitive environment. As mentioned above, even if government agencies have monopoly or monopsony power, exchange can be voluntary in nature and prices can reflect supply and demand. For example, a state agency may have no competitors, but farmers could still have the freedom to decide how much they sell to the state. The government agency must then consider the farmers' response when setting its price. If it sets a higher price, farmers will want to sell more; if it sets a lower price, farmers will want to sell less. In other words, the state agency faces a trade-off between price and quantity, and the price that ultimately prevails will reflect the preferences of both the buyer and the sellers. This price may not be competitive, but it is nevertheless a "market" price, and the transactions that take place are "market" trade.

In contrast, "planned" trade refers to transactions where participation is non-voluntary or obligatory. It occurs when the quantity sold or purchased is subject to some constraint or coercion, and includes obligatory delivery quotas for sales to the government and ration quotas on purchases from the government. In the former instance the government imposes a minimum quantity of goods that must be delivered at the planned price; in the latter case, it imposes a maximum quantity that can be purchased at the planned price. "Planned prices" are the administratively-set prices that apply to such trade.

While planned trade is characterized by an obligatory delivery or ration quota, what matters is not the presence of a quota *per se*, but that it is enforced and compulsory. The nominal presence of a planned quota or target does not necessarily mean that producers must comply, nor does the absence of a quota or target mean that producers are free of obligations. Thus planned trade should not include sales to the state in the presence of a quota if the quota is not enforced. The importance of this distinction will become clear in the cases discussed below.

---

31. Note that the term "market" as used here is not limited to trade at periodic or free markets. "Market" trade also includes voluntary exchange that takes place in other venues.

Designated State Commercial Agencies: How Dominant Are They?

The issues discussed above naturally raise questions about the relative importance of trade by designated state agencies and planned trade. Available data on trade by state commercial agencies show that their market share has declined. Between 1978 and 1992 the share of state commercial agencies under the Ministry of Commerce, Ministry of Grain, and Supply and Marketing Co-ops in total procurements of farm products and in retail sales of consumer goods fell from over 70 per cent to under 35 per cent (Table 1).[32] A survey of a nation-wide random sample of farm households similarly revealed that 31 per cent of farm products sold by households were sold to state commercial departments in 1992.[33]

While these figures indicate that designated state agencies no longer dominate, these agencies still maintain an aggregate market share of 30 per cent. More importantly, for particular goods the state's market share is considerably higher. As shown in Table 2, in 1992 domestic purchases by state commercial agencies exceeded two-thirds of the total quantities purchased for a range of important consumer goods. Domestic sales by state commercial agencies were also high for many of these items. Similarly, state commercial agencies remain the dominant buyer of key farm products (Table 3).[34] For cotton, procurements by the Supply and Marketing Co-op system exceeded 90 per cent of total procurements from farmers in almost every year since 1978. For grain, procurements by the Grain Bureau declined after the introduction of the contract system in 1985, but since then have remained fairly stable at 70 to 80 per cent of the total. A nation-wide random sample survey of marketing by farm households confirms the dominance of designated state agents in the trade of key farm products. This survey found that in 1992 some 71 per cent of cotton sales, 48 per cent of grain sales and 66 per cent of tobacco sales by farm households went to state commercial departments.[35]

Whether these market shares translate into monopoly or monopsony power will depend on several factors. State commercial agencies are composed of multiple branches with offices at both central and local levels. If these different branches and levels compete with each other, then a large market share does not imply the presence of a unified

32. Aggregate numbers on the share of state trade are problematic because such statistics value state and non-state trade at different prices. State trade includes planned commerce at below-market prices, and so its relative size is understated. Non-state trade is also undercounted, but for a different reason: the official Chinese statistics exclude intra-rural trade, which is entirely non-state. Unfortunately, the net bias of these two counterbalancing effects is unclear, and it may have changed over time.

33. Central Policy Research Office and the Office of Rural Fixed Observation Sites of the Ministry of Agriculture, "Excerpts from a special survey report: 'Rural households and the market'," *Jingji ribao*, 4 January 1994, p. 1, translated in JPRS-CAR 94-014, 2 March 1995, pp. 23–25.

34. The figures in Tables 2 and 3 are in quantity terms, and so they do not suffer from the bias caused by the fact that state purchases and sales are valued at below-market planned prices.

35. The household survey gives lower shares for state commerce than the aggregate data because the survey probably counts intra-rural trade. Central Policy Research Office and the Office of Rural Fixed Observation Sites of the Ministry of Agriculture, "Excerpts from a special survey report."

Table 1: **A. Procurement of Agricultural Products by Designated State Agencies** (% of total procurements in parentheses)

Year	Procurement of agricultural products by the state commercial system	of which:		
		Ministry of Commerce	Grain Bureau	Supply and Marketing Co-ops
1978	435.5 (70.0%)	103.5 (18.6%)	150.2 (26.9%)	181.7 (32.6%)
1986	1,014.7 (51.0%)	178.6 (9.0%)	507.5 (25.5%)	328.6 (16.5%)
1990	1,666.7 (44.9%)	279.1 (7.5%)	833.0 (22.5%)	554.6 (14.9%)
1991	1,716.1 (41.2%)	266.8 (6.4%)	837.4 (20.1%)	611.9 (14.7%)
1992	1,501.3 (34.0%)	246.4 (5.6%)	739.3 (16.8%)	515.6 (11.7%)

B. Retail Sales of Consumer Goods by Designated State Agencies (% of total retail sales of consumer goods in parentheses)

Year	Retail sales by the state commercial system	of which:		
		Ministry of Commerce	Grain Bureau	Supply and Marketing Co-ops
1978	1,014.3 (80.2%)	492.0 (38.9%)	129.6 (10.2%)	392.7 (31.0%)
1986	1,671.6 (38.2%)	766.4 (17.5%)	339.9 (7.8%)	565.3 (12.9%)
1990	2,426.6 (33.5%)	1,272.2 (17.5%)	416.3 (5.7%)	739.1 (10.2%)
1991	2,709.9 (32.9%)	1,392.9 (16.9%)	544.2 (6.6%)	769.8 (9.3%)
1992	3,064.3 (31.6%)	1,580.4 (16.3%)	676.0 (7.0%)	807.9 (8.3%)

Sources:
   Agricultural procurement: *Zhongguo shangye nianjian, 1988*, pp. 618–19; *Zhongguo shangye nianjian, 1990*, pp. 526, 527; *Zhongguo shangye nianjian, 1991*, pp. XI-90, XI-93, XI-94. Retail sales: *Zhongguo shangye nianjian, 1988*, p. 618; *Zhongguo shangye nianjian, 1990*, pp. 526, 527; *Zhongguo shangye nianjian, 1991*, pp. XI-90, XI-93, XI-94; *Zhongguo shichang tongji nianjian, 1993*, pp. 237, 339.

monopolist. In addition, the quantity of output marketed domestically may not reflect the full size of the market. For certain farm products a high proportion of output is retained for home use. Thus even if a state agency is the largest buyer, it must compete with on-farm demand. Similarly, reforms in China's foreign trade regime have increased the

Table 2: **Domestic Trade in Selected Consumer Goods by State Commercial Agencies, 1992**

	Purchases	% of total purchases	Sales	% of total sales
sugar (1,000 tons)	3,776	80.9	2,268	62.3
pork and hogs (million head)	59.9	47.0	42.5	38.1
laundry soap (1,000 tons)	782	81.6	227	36.4
cotton cloth (million metres)	1,110	24.3	1,230	55.9
wrist watches (1,000s)	15,577	68.9	20,817	65.7
bicycles (1,000s)	22,101	70.3	18,400	77.5
home refrigerators (1,000s)	3,064	81.6	2,632	76.3
televisions (1,000s)	10,774	64.5	9,660	74.4

Note:
   Purchases are "net domestic purchases" (*guonei chun goujin*), defined as domestic purchases by the state commercial sector from units and individuals outside the state commercial sector at all prices for resale or for processing and then resale. Sales are "net domestic sales" (*guonei chun xiaoshou*), defined as domestic sales by the state commercial sector at all prices to units and individuals outside the state commercial sector. Total purchases and sales, used as the divisor in the second and fourth columns, are defined similarly but count purchases and sales by all commercial agents, including designated state agents and other agents.
Source:
   Zhongguo shichang tongji nianjian, 1993, pp. 313–14, 342–43.

influence of international supply and demand on domestic markets, and so for some goods state agencies may face competition from abroad.

   The contrasting cases of cotton and grain illustrate the unpredictable relationship between market share and monopsony power. Throughout most of the 1980s and early 1990s the Supply and Marketing Co-op system procured more than 85 per cent of cotton output (Table 3). Although some sources report that private traders, rural enterprises and even state textile factories illegally bought cotton from farmers,[36] such activities do not appear to have become widespread. The state's high market share reflects the government's monopsony policy and the fact that farmers, for a variety of reasons including government prohibitions on handicraft production and the non-competitiveness of handicraft spinning, retained little cotton for their own use.

   Competitive pressure from international cotton markets is weak, as international trade in cotton has been closely controlled. Imports and exports of cotton were handled centrally by the China National Textile and Fibre Import and Export Corporation until 1992, when provincial-level companies were given the right to import and export cotton.[37] Net imports are small: in recent years they have been less than 5 per cent of

36. See, for example, *Zhongguo shangye nianjian, 1990*, p. 76, and *Zhongguo shangye nianjian, 1991*, p. IV-39.
37. *Zhongguo shangye nianjian, 1993*, p. IV-26.

Table 3: **Procurement of Cotton and Grain by Designated State Commercial Agencies**

	Cotton			Grain		
Year	Procurement (1,000 tons)	% of total procurements	% of output	Procurement (m. tons)	% of total procurements	% of output
1980	260.9	100.0	96.4	58.7	95.8	21.8
1981	287.1	100.0	96.7	62.6	91.4	21.9
1982	341.3	99.9	94.9	73.6	94.3	24.4
1983	458.4	100.0	98.9	98.7	96.3	29.6
1984	517.5	99.3	82.7	111.7	95.3	33.0
1985	422.4	97.8	101.9	79.3	73.7	22.5
1986	328.2	86.5	92.7	94.5	82.1	27.7
1987	389.8	95.8	91.8	99.2	82.0	28.3
1988	360.4	95.4	86.9	94.3	78.6	27.5
1989	324.2	98.1	85.6	100.4	82.7	28.3
1990	397.9	97.3	88.3	95.5	68.2	24.6
1991	493.4	93.3	86.9	99.0	72.6	26.4
1992	369.3	84.7	81.9	96.9	73.2	25.5

Notes:

1. Cotton procurement is in units of ginned cotton. Grain procurement is in units of trade (husked) grain. In calculating the share of state procurement in total grain output, procurement is converted to original grain equivalents. Conversion rates are calculated from data on total procurement in *Zhonguo tongji nianjian, 1993*, pp. 364, 607, 609.

2. Here and in other tables, where different sources give figures for the same years, I use figures from the primary source over a secondary source, and from the more recent source over the earlier source.

Sources:

Output and total procurement of grain and cotton: *Zhongguo tongji nianjian, 1993*, pp. 607–609; 363–365. Cotton procurement by the Supply and Marketing Co-op system: 1979–85: *Zhongguo shangye waijing tongji ziliao, 1952–1988*, p. 245. 1978, 1986–87: *Zhongguo shangye nianjian, 1988*, p. 658. 1988–89: *Zhongguo shangye nianjian, 1990*, p. 564. 1990: *Zhongguo shangye nianjian, 1991*, p. XI-129. 1991–92: *Zhongguo shangye nianjian, 1993*, p. XII-110. Grain procurement by the state grain system: 1978–89: Scott Rozelle, Albert Park and Jikun Huang, "Dilemmas in reforming state–market relations in rural China," unpublished manuscript, Stanford University, February 1995. 1987: *Zhongguo shangye nianjian, 1988*, pp. 659–660. 1989: *Zhongguo shangye nianjian, 1990*, pp. IX-566, IX-571. 1990: *Zhongguo shangye nianjian, 1991*, pp. XI-131, XI-136. 1991: *Zhongguo shangye nianjian, 1992*, pp. X-131, X-136. 1992: *Zhongguo shangye nianjian, 1993*, pp. XII-113, XII-118.

domestic output, and domestic cotton prices have remained about 30 per cent below international prices.[38]

The 1993 reforms in cotton marketing discussed above had the potential to open up cotton markets to new entrants and generate competition, but these reforms have yet to be implemented. In fact, cotton procurement agencies at local levels have little incentive to implement them. The cotton monopsony enables these agencies to procure cotton at low planned prices from farmers. They can then earn extra-normal profits by selling it at higher wholesale prices (beyond-plan sales of cotton at the wholesale level can now be sold at market prices), or by using it to produce yarn and textiles, products which are no longer subject to planned allocation.

The situation for grain is different. Although the Grain Bureau is the largest buyer, its market power is limited because a large share of grain production is retained by farmers for their own use. This is one reason why procurements by the Grain Bureau account for only 25 to 30 per cent of grain output.[39] Thus on the grain market more broadly defined, state commercial agencies do not dominate.

In recent years the state's ability to act monopsonistically in grain markets has also been eroded by institutional reforms promoting intra-state competition. As mentioned above, the central government has adopted measures giving local grain bureaus more financial independence and encouraging them to pursue profits. These reforms have provided local governments with an incentive to support the liberalization of grain commerce, as measures granting more financial independence at local levels have increased local responsibility for price subsidies.

Plan Versus Market

China's commercial reforms have substantially reduced the importance of planned trade. The shares of agricultural procurement and retail sales at planned prices have declined from more than 90 per cent of their respective totals in 1978 to less than 20 per cent in 1993 (Table 4). Over the same period, the number of agricultural products subject to planned allocation fell from 113 to 10, of light industrial products from 158 to 10, and of heavy industrial products from more than 1,000 to fewer than 100.[40]

To the extent that planned prices are below market prices, the figures in Table 4 will understate the importance of planned trade. Other factors, however, could cause these figures to overstate the importance of planned

---

38. Terry Sicular, "Why quibble about quotas? The effects of planning in rural China," Harvard Institute of Economic Research Discussion Paper No. 1714, February 1995, p. 20, and Li Zhiqiang, "An analysis of China's cotton output in 1994," *Zhongguo nongcun jingji*, No. 6 (1994), pp. 25–27, translated in JPRS-CAR 94-045, 19 August 1994, pp. 83–86.

39. *Zhongguo shichang tongji nianjian, 1993*, p. 207, and Table 3.

40. These numbers include products traded at both state fixed and state guidance prices (*guojia dingjia, guojia zhidao jia*). *Zhongguo gaige yu fazhan baogao (1992–1993): Xinde tupo yu xinde tiaozhan (China Reform and Development Report (1992–1993): New Breakthroughs and Challenges)* (Beijing: Zhongguo caizheng jingji chubanshe, 1994), p. 54.

Table 4: **Planned Versus Market Components of Agricultural Procurements and Retail Sales**

Year	% of agricultural procurements at:		% of retail sales at:	
	Planned prices	Market prices	Planned prices	Market prices
1978	94.4	5.6	97.0	3.0
1985	60.0	40.0	66.0	34.0
1990	31.0	42.0	55.0	45.0
1993	17.3	82.7	16.4	84.6

Notes:
1. 1993 figures are preliminary.
2. Planned prices include "state fixed prices" (*guojia dingjia*) and "state guidance prices" (*guojia zhidao jia*). According to *Zhongguo gaige yu fazhan baogao*, p. 54, these two types of prices apply to goods subject to mandatory planned allocation.
2. The shares of goods traded at different prices are calculated using the prices at which the trade occurred. Since planned prices are lower than market prices, these shares understate the relative size of planned trade. If goods in all categories were valued at the same prices, then the share of planned-price trade would be higher.
Sources:
   Zhongguo wujia nianjian, 1993 (*Price Yearbook of China, 1993*) (Beijing: Zhongguo wujia nianjian bianjibu, 1993), p. 93; *Zhongguo gaige yu fazhan baogao*, p. 54.

trade. As mentioned above, "planned trade" is defined not by the presence of planned prices and quotas *per se*, but by whether or not the quota is enforced and compulsory. Analysis of plan versus market trade for grain and cotton reveals that this distinction is important.

Available evidence suggests that grain quotas are mandatory and enforced. For China as a whole, the level of the delivery contract or quota has been stable at 50 million tons during the late 1980s and early 1990s. In the late 1980s deliveries at the contract price were close to or exceeded the contract quota in every year but 1985, which year was aberrant because of initial confusion over whether the new grain contracts were mandatory (Table 5). In early 1991 and 1992 deliveries at contract prices fell below the quota, but this probably reflects the expansion of local experiments with grain marketing reforms at this time. Indeed, in view of the fact that such experiments had been adopted in nearly one-fifth of China's counties by late 1992, the level of quota fulfilment in 1992 seems high.

This high degree of quota fulfilment implies that grain quotas have been enforced. Price data also support this conclusion. In the 1980s and early 1990s planned prices for grain were substantially lower than both market and negotiated prices (Table 6). Quota fufilment remained high despite this price gap. Even in 1989 when market prices were double the level of contract prices, deliveries at the contract price were close to the contract level. The fact that farmers have continued to fulfil contracts even though contract prices have been well below market prices strongly suggests that the contracts were mandatory.

The significance of this compliance of course depends on the magnitude of the quota burden relative to total output. Over time grain output has grown and the quota has been reduced, so that the proportion of total output procured under plan has declined. In the mid-1980s the grain quota was equal to roughly 20 per cent of grain output; by the early 1990s it was about 13 per cent.[41] Even for fine grains, which is perhaps a more appropriate yardstick, the share of output purchased under plan has fallen: in 1992, for example, contract procurement of wheat was 18 per cent and of rice only 13 per cent of output.[42] The quota makes up a larger percentage of marketed output: in the early 1990s the contract was equivalent to about 37 per cent of total grain procurements at the farm gate.

Negotiated procurement of grain has grown substantially since 1980, and it now constitutes over half of state procurements (Tables 3 and 7). As mentioned above, at times the state has set quotas for negotiated procurement. Unfortunately, the extent to which these have been obligatory at the farm level is unclear. One source reports that quotas for negotiated deliveries were not imposed directly on farmers, but rather applied to local state procurement agencies.[43] Other sources note that local governments have met their negotiated grain quotas by restricting entry by non-designated agents. In the late 1980s such actions were supported by central policies such as the reintroduction of the state monopsony on rice and the closing of grain markets during the procurement season.

Data on negotiated prices suggest the presence of either compulsion or market barriers, at least during certain years. In 1986–89 the gap between market and negotiated prices for rice widened noticeably (Table 6), yet negotiated procurement of rice nearly doubled, rising from 9.4 million tons in 1986 to 16.7 million tons in 1989. Similarly, the gap between market and negotiated prices for wheat widened in 1991–92, but negotiated procurements of wheat rose 55 per cent in 1991 and another 27 per cent in 1992.[44]

Regardless of whether negotiated procurement is counted as part of market trade, market trade has clearly grown in importance. Purchases by non-designated agents, presumably all of which are voluntary, now account for nearly 30 per cent of total grain procurements (Table 7). This share represents a lower bound on the importance of market versus plan trade. To the extent that negotiated procurement targets were met through

41. Calculated using data in Tables 3 and 5.
42. I use a rate of 0.70 to convert husked rice into paddy equivalents (procurement is measured in husked rice, output in paddy). The output data are from *Zhongguo tongji nianjian, 1993*, p. 364; the procurement data are from *Zhongguo shangye nianjian, 1993*, p. XII-114.
43. Interviews, Zouping county, Shandong.
44. Data for state procurement of rice and wheat are from Scott Rozelle, Albert Park and Jikun Huang, "Dilemmas in reforming state-market relations in rural China," unpublished manuscript, Stanford University, February 1995.

Table 5: **Planned Procurement of Cotton and Grain by Designated State Commercial Agents**

	Grain				Cotton	
Year	Planned quota (m. tons)	Procurement at quota prices (m. tons)	Procurement at quota prices as a % of the quota	Procurement at quota prices as % of Grain Bureau procurement	Planned quota (m. tons)	Procurement by the Supply and Marketing Co-ops as a % of the quota
1984	–	–	–	–	4.25	121.8
1985	70.0	59.3	85.1	74.8	(4.25)	99.4
1986	60.5	62.2	102.8	65.8	(4.25)	78.1
1987	50.0	56.9	113.8	57.4	(4.25)	91.7
1988	50.0	50.5	101.0	53.6	(4.25)	84.8
1989	50.0	48.9	97.7	48.7	4.25	76.3
1990	50.0	51.8	103.6	54.2	(4.25)	93.6
1991	50.0	47.5	95.2	48.1	(4.25)	116.1
1992	50.0	45.3	90.6	46.7	(4.25)	85.5

Notes:

1. Grain is in units of trade grain, and cotton is ginned cotton.

2. Grain deliveries at quota prices usually exceed slightly the amount of grain deliveries in fulfilment of quotas. For example, in 1989 and 1990 procurement at quota prices was 102% of the quantity of grain delivered to fulfil quotas.

3. Data for cotton and for total Grain Bureau procurement are for the calendar year; data for the grain quota and quota-priced grain deliveries are for the procurement year.

4. Parentheses indicate an estimate based on available information. Data on cotton quota levels are incomplete. *Zhongguo shangye nianjian, 1988*, p. 86, states that the quota level in 1984 was set at 4.25 million tons; it also states that expected cotton procurement in 1987 was 3.88 million tons, or 87.8% of the quota. This implies that the quota in 1987 was about 4.4 million tons. Similar information for 1989 implies a quota of 4.25 million tons (*Zhongguo shangye nianjian, 1990*, p. IV-38). For 1991, *Zhongguo shangye nianjian, 1992*, p. IV-44, states that the cotton quota was fulfilled in 1992 for the first time since 1985, but does not give a figure for the cotton quota.

In light of this information, which suggests that the cotton quota has remained between 4.25 and 4.4 million tons since 1984, I simply use a figure of 4.25 million tons for all years. While the quota may have been higher in certain years (for example, 4.4 million tons in 1987 and 1990), in most of the years shown cotton deliveries would have been insufficient to meet even a 4.25 million ton quota.

Sources:

Cotton quotas: See n. 4 above. Cotton and grain procurement by designated state agencies: Table 3. Grain quotas: 1985: Terry Sicular, "Agricultural planning and pricing in the post-Mao period," *The China Quarterly*, No. 116, p. 690. 1986–87: *Zhongguo shangye nianjian, 1988*, pp. 51, 55. 1989: *Zhongguo shangye nianjian, 1990*, p. 47. 1990–91: *Zhongguo shangye nianjian, 1991*, p. IV-1, IV-3. 1991–92: *Zhongguo shangye nianjian, 1992*, pp. II-1, IV-2. Grain deliveries at quota prices: 1985–86, 1988: Rozelle *et al.*, "Dilemmas in reforming state–market relations in rural China." 1987: *Zhongguo shangye nianjian, 1988*, p. 659. 1989: *Zhongguo shangye nianjian, 1990*, p. 566. 1990: *Zhongguo shangye nianjian, 1991*, p. XI-131. 1991: *Zhongguo shangye nianjian, 1992*, p. X-131. 1992: *Zhongguo shangye nianjian, 1993*, p. XII-121.

Table 6: **Grain Prices** (*yuan* per ton)

	Rice					Wheat				
Year	Quota price	Negotiated price	Market price	Market price ÷ quota price	Market price ÷ neg. price	Quota price	Negotiated price	Market price	Market price ÷ quota price	Market price ÷ neg. price
1980	341	595	726	2.13	1.22	328	528	557	1.70	1.06
1981	342	608	742	2.17	1.22	326	519	548	1.68	1.06
1982	342	633	758	2.22	1.20	324	516	544	1.68	1.05
1983	337	634	732	2.17	1.15	325	493	520	1.60	1.05
1984	339	613	642	1.89	1.05	326	457	482	1.48	1.06
1985	462	585	622	1.35	1.06	441	442	466	1.06	1.06
1986	464	635	715	1.54	1.13	442	490	517	1.17	1.05
1987	508	756	841	1.66	1.11	443	546	576	1.30	1.05
1988	523	937	1,084	2.07	1.16	477	668	705	1.48	1.06
1989	672	1,356	1,573	2.34	1.16	507	928	979	1.93	1.05
1990	672	1,271	1,338	1.99	1.05	507	880	902	1.78	1.03
1991	645	1,100	1,204	1.87	1.09	584	810	922	1.58	1.14
1992	718	1,041	1,140	1.59	1.10	600	764	870	1.45	1.14

Notes:
1. Quota prices from 1978–84 are the original quota prices; from 1985 onward they are contract delivery prices.
2. Quota prices are for standard-grade rice and wheat. The rice price is a weighted average of the indica and japonica prices. Negotiated and market prices are calculated as the value of transactions divided by the quantity traded and reflect the average quality of rice or wheat traded. Some of the difference between market/negotiated prices and quota prices is therefore due to quality differences.

Source:
Courtesy of Scott Rozelle; see also Rozelle *et al.*, "Dilemmas in reforming state–market relations in rural China."

Table 7: **Market Trade in Grain: Purchases at Negotiated Prices and by Non-Designated Agents** (million tons)

Year	State negotiated procurement	Purchases by non-designated agents	Market trade as a % of total procurements	
			Low estimate (non-designated only)	High estimate (non-designated and negotiated)
1978	2.9	0.02	0.0	5.8
1979	5.2	1.04	1.7	10.4
1980	8.6	2.59	4.2	18.3
1981	10.6	5.86	8.6	24.0
1982	17.4	4.46	5.7	28.0
1983	7.5	3.79	3.7	11.0
1984	9.4	5.55	4.7	12.7
1985	19.7	28.33	26.3	44.6
1986	32.3	20.66	17.9	46.0
1987	42.3	21.72	18.0	52.9
1988	43.8	25.65	21.4	57.9
1989	51.5	20.98	17.3	59.7
1990	43.7	44.45	31.8	63.0
1991	47.9	37.36	27.4	62.5
1992	51.5	35.56	26.8	65.7

Sources:
Negotiated procurement: 1978–89: Calculated from data in Rozelle *et al.*, "Dilemmas in reforming state–market relations in rural China." 1986–87: *Zhongguo shangye nianjian, 1988*, pp. 55, 660. 1988–89: *Zhongguo shangye nianjian, 1990*, pp. 49–50, 571. 1989–90: *Zhongguo shangye nianjian, 1991*, pp. IV-5, XI-136. 1990–91: *Zhongguo shangye nianjian, 1992*, p. IV-1, X-136. 1991–92: *Zhongguo shangye nianjian, 1993*, pp. IV-1, XII-118. Purchases by non-designated agents: Calculated as the difference between total procurement and procurement by designated state commercial agents. See Table 5 for sources.

monopsonistic practices rather than by mandatory quotas at the farm level, or that negotiated deliveries were voluntary, negotiated procurement should also be counted in the market share. If so, by the early 1990s as much as 60 per cent of grain sales by farmers may have been market sales, up from less than 10 per cent in the late 1970s (Table 7).

For cotton, the state has maintained its monopsony and almost all cotton continues to be procured by the National Federation of Supply and Marketing Co-ops at planned prices. The state does not procure cotton at negotiated prices, and trade by non-designated agents has been minimal. Yet, despite the predominance of official procurement at planned prices, the force of planning for cotton is weaker than for grain. State cotton procurements were well below the national procurement target in almost every year from 1986 to 1992 (Table 5). Studies in cotton-growing regions show a similar pattern of underfulfilment. In Zouping county, Shandong, cotton deliveries between 1985 and 1993 averaged only 75 per cent of the quota.[45]

The level of cotton deliveries appears to be a function less of the quota than of the level of output, which varies from year to year. For the past decade cotton output has generally fluctuated between 4 and 5 million tons, but in 1984 it reached 6.3 million tons, and in 1991 5.7 million tons. These two years of abnormally high production are the only ones in which cotton deliveries exceeded the plan. Conversely, in the two years when output was below normal, 1986 and 1989, plan fulfilment was low. In 1986 cotton output was only 3.5 million tons, and in 1989 3.8 million tons.[46]

The quantity produced in turn depends in part on the profitability of growing cotton relative to other crops. Farmers reportedly grow insufficient cotton to meet plan targets because the returns to growing cotton have been low. Cotton is a high-cost crop that requires substantial application of labour and cash inputs. When the price of cotton falls relative to the prices of competing crops or purchased inputs, or relative to the returns from off-farm employment, farmers move out of cotton production. Thus the decline in cotton output during the late 1980s is not surprising, as at that time market prices for most farm products increased markedly while the cotton procurement price was relatively constant. Similarly, the recovery in cotton production in 1990–92 is probably linked to the fact that after 1989 the state raised its cotton procurement price by 27 per cent while market prices for other farm products were falling. (See Table 8.)

More fundamentally, persistent problems with fulfilment of cotton procurement plans reflect the uneven nature of the commercial reforms. The state monopsony on cotton has persisted well into the 1990s. Meanwhile, the government has opened up markets for most other goods and encouraged the development of off-farm activities. Such measures have increased indirect competition, and the government now faces a

45. Sicular, "Establishing markets."
46. *Zhongguo tongji nianjian, 1993*, p. 354.

Table 8: **Planned Cotton Prices and Their Relationship to Market Prices**

Year	Cotton planned price (yuan/ton)	Cotton planned price index (1984 = 100)	Grain market price index (1984 = 100)	Vegetable oils market price index (1984 = 100)	Fresh vegetable market price index (1984 = 100)
1984	3,616.0 (3,266.0)	100.0 (100.0)	100.0	100.0	100.0
1985	3,528.4 (3,266.0)	97.6 (100.0)	101.8	108.0	121.6
1986	3,440.8 (3,266.0)	95.2 (100.0)	122.8	117.5	129.9
1987	3,528.4	97.6 (108.0)	145.0	129.8	155.1
1988	3,528.4	97.6 (108.0)	180.1	153.8	201.8
1989	4,728.4	130.8 (144.8)	246.0	208.2	201.4
1990	6,000.0	165.9 (183.7)	200.2	198.2	191.7
1991	6,000.0	165.9 (183.7)	173.0	188.7	196.7
1992	6,000.0	165.9 (183.7)	172.5	177.2	203.9
1993	6,600.0	182.5 (202.1)	—	—	—
1994	8,100.0	224.0 (248.0)	—	—	—

Note:
In 1984–86 the government set different prices for cotton in North and South China; thereafter the cotton price was uniform nationally. Cotton prices during these years in parentheses, and the cotton price index numbers in parentheses, are for South China. All cotton prices are for standard-grade ginned cotton.

Sources:
Cotton prices: Dong Ying and Cheng Jianhua, "Historical retrospective"; "Cotton procurement price to increase in September," *Zhonghua disan chanye bao (China Service Sector News)*, 16 May 1994, p. 7, translated in JPRS-CAR 94-37, 17 June 1994, p. 57; *Zhongguo shangye nianjian, 1990*, p. 76; *Zhongguo shangye nianjian, 1991*, p. IV-38; author interviews, Shandong province. Market price indexes: *Zhongguo shichang tongji nianjian, 1993*, p. 459; *Zhongguo guonei shichang tongji nianjian, 1991 (Statistical Yearbook of China's Domestic Markets, 1991)* (Beijing: Zhongguo tongji chubanshe, 1992), p. 436; *Zhongguo guonei shichang tongji nianjian, 1992*, p. 430.

trade-off between the price it pays and the quantity of cotton farmers are willing to sell. Efforts to enforce targets and quotas perhaps influence the extent of this trade-off, but the government is unable to dictate quantities.

Why is the government able to enforce plans for grain but not for cotton? It is partly because farmers have reasons to produce grain regardless of planned prices and quotas. They produce grain beyond the quota because they need additional grain for use as food and animal feed, and because beyond-quota grain can be sold on the market at higher prices. Both the government and the farmers know that even in years when the harvest is poor, the quantity of grain produced will exceed the quota by a large margin. Thus even if planned prices for grain are low, quotas are fulfilled. In contrast, the state monopsony and prohibitions on textile production by non-designated agents means that the main reason for growing cotton is for sale to the state. Consequently, farmers have little incentive to produce unless the planned procurement price is high enough to make cotton production relatively profitable. Ironically, then, the liberalization of commerce for grain appears to have helped promote plan fulfilment, while lack of liberalization for cotton has had the opposite effect.

Conclusion

China's reforms in agricultural commerce have opened the way for extensive change in the rural economy. Agricultural commerce has grown substantially, and rural households now participate actively in markets. The institutions and infrastructure necessary for continued commercial development are gradually being established. Qualitative changes have occurred in state commerce and planning. State commercial agencies now participate in markets and increasingly respond to market forces. In some markets state commercial agencies continue to dominate trade, yet their ability to exercise market power is often limited by intra-agency competition, new entrants and indirect competition from other markets. The government continues to set planned prices and quotas, but the liberalization of trade for beyond-plan quantities has altered the force of planning.

Such developments necessitate a re-evaluation of what is meant by terms like "state," "plan" and "market." In view of changes in the nature and role of state commercial actors, the distinction between "state" and "non-state" agents is no longer relevant. As discussed above, a more useful distinction is that between state agents who are officially charged with policy-related commercial activities, referred to as "designated" commercial agents, and other, non-designated commercial agents. Similarly, given that plans are not always enforceable and that the so-called planned trade of designated state agencies sometimes resembles monopoly or monopsony behaviour, the terms "plan" and "market" need to be redefined. "Planned" commerce here refers to commerce under planned prices and quotas where the quota is in fact compulsory. "Market" commerce refers to voluntary exchange at mutually acceptable prices, whether in a competitive or monopsonistic setting.

The evidence presented in this article documents two major changes in China's commercial environment. First, commercial activity by non-designated agents has expanded and now accounts for well over half of retail sales and farm procurements. Secondly, the importance of planned trade has declined substantially and now most commerce appears to be voluntary and at prices reflecting supply and demand. Of course, China's market system is still imperfect. The degree of competition varies considerably among goods and among regions. Underdeveloped transport, storage and communications contribute to price volatility and allow monopoly power to persist at the local level. While state commercial agencies now have incentives to engage in market-oriented activities, they are not yet fully independent, profit-seeking actors. In addition, the legal and financial institutions that support commerce remain weak. Commercial agents, especially those handling seasonal goods like agricultural products, need reliable sources of credit. China's banking system, which still consists almost entirely of state-owned banks, does not provide credit to private merchants. Indeed, it has not reliably supplied loans even to designated commercial agencies. When credit is tight, bank funds set aside for loans to state commerce have been diverted to other uses.[47]

Despite such obstacles, commercial activity has continued to grow and the reforms have succeeded in establishing the basis of a reasonably competitive market system. This success is partly because the government has had a financial incentive to push the reforms along. Since the mid-1980s large, ongoing budgetary outlays on commercial subsidies have helped create a consensus for commercial reform at the central level. At the local level, cadres have been receptive to central initiatives because the burden of these subsidies has been increasingly paid out of local budgets.

A second reason for the success of China's commercial reforms is that new policies have made use of pre-existing institutions and actors. The periodic market system has played a key role in this regard. Although trade on periodic markets had been suppressed under Maoist policies, they survived in latent form. With the reforms, they immediately provided a lattice of commercial venues throughout the countryside. They have also served as an important avenue for entrepreneurial development. Selling at periodic markets requires minimal start-up costs and can be done on a small scale. Individuals, households, and even village or township governments that wish to set up businesses can begin by selling their wares at one of the smaller township or village markets. Successful businesses can expand to several markets that meet on different days, can attend larger markets in the county seat or a nearby city, and can ultimately graduate to a permanent establishment. The periodic markets thus provide an entry point and a path for the development of private, and also collective, commercial enterprise.

The reforms have allowed pre-existing actors to participate in the transformation of China's commerce. Rather than abolish the state commercial bureaucracy, China adopted measures that encouraged its component agencies to become market players. Agencies and enterprises within the state commercial bureaucracy already had capital, labour, access to credit, and political and business networks, so that they were well positioned to fill the vacuum created by market liberalization. Fiscal and

47. Cheng Enjiang, "Financial issues and the forces for grain marketing reforms in China," The University of Adelaide Chinese Economy Research Unit Working Paper No. 94/13, November 1994.

enterprise reforms gave them an incentive to engage in market-oriented activity and limited their market power by promoting competition among agencies in different branches and levels of government.

In principle private commerce could also provide competition, but typically private traders must begin from a small, relatively weak market position. Thus their ability to challenge the state commercial system is limited. Competition from pre-existing non-commercial state agencies and enterprises, and among pre-existing agencies within the state commercial system, is more likely to prevent designated state agencies from becoming entrenched monopolies. One lesson from China's commercial reforms, then, is that the transition to a competitive market economy benefits not only from policies allowing private commerce to develop, but also from measures promoting competition among state agencies and enterprises.

The Role of Ownership and Property Rights in China's Economic Transition

Louis Putterman

The ever-greater roles played by markets and pecuniary incentives, and the increasing decision-making authority of localities, enterprises and individuals, have been central elements of China's economic reforms. Compared with these radical departures from the past, change in the area of property rights has been ambiguous. Depending on one's perspective, China might be seen as on its way to establishing a socialist market economy, in which public and collective ownership forms are predominant, or well along the path to a radical transformation of property rights, including a *de facto* private agriculture, massive private foreign investment, stock markets and the growth of private enterprise. What role property rights have played in the successes and problems of China's reforming economy is similarly debatable. The view that property rights have remained largely "social" leaves open interpretive possibilities ranging from the conclusion that China offers evidence of the viability of a market socialist option, to arguments that the transformation of property rights remains a major hurdle on the road to an economy that can support sustained growth. The quite different view that sectors experiencing substantial privatization have been the main contributors to the achievements of the reform economy, and that those maintaining public ownership have held back economic growth, is also taken by some.

The nature of the property rights that have characterized China's economy during the years of economic reform, and the influence of property rights and property rights reform on the performance of the economy during that era are the subjects of this article. In reviewing the evidence, an attempt is made to sort through the views mentioned above, and others, and to draw warranted conclusions. The extensiveness of property rights changes and what China's experience reveals about the role of property rights in economic performance are analysed. That analysis cuts through the simpler dichotomy between private and public ownership that appears in much of the literature to a fuller characterization of property rights as bundles. Real world variability in the assignment and exercise of each of a number of relevant rights allows for a variety of forms. Although it is most convenient to begin the discussion with such familiar categories as state-owned firms and collectives, it will ultimately move to viewing such categories as encompassing configurations of property rights that have varied over time and among enterprises.

Many mainstream analysts have begun to view China's experience as constituting a distinctive reform path or model of transition from the socialist command economy. Thus, debate over the merits of "gradualism/evolution" versus "shock therapy/big bang" approaches has been stimulated by comparisons of Eastern Europe and the former Soviet Union (EEFSU)'s early 1990s recessions with China's rapid economic growth during the same period. China's resistance to advice that rapid price liberalization and privatization of state enterprises were requirements of successful reform plays a central role in that debate. While those who look favourably upon Chinese gradualism see evidence that publicly owned firms have become increasingly efficient *without* privatization, opponents of this view argue that state-owned enterprises (SOEs) have performed poorly, and that it is the large initial and subsequently expanding size of the "non-state" sector that accounts for the economy's dynamism under reform. Arguments that China's SOEs have exhibited "progress without privatization" come not only from those who view privatization as the ultimate goal,[1] but also from some who see market socialism as a desirable end state.[2] The relative merits of such perspectives are analysed in what follows.

Ownership and Owners

The period from 1978 to the early 1990s was marked by a massive shift from team and brigade to household level economic activity in agriculture and other small-scale sectors, and by a change in the composition of the industrial sector toward substantially more urban and rural collective participation, with significant new participation by foreign and domestic private firms (see Table 1).[3] Construction, trade and transportation sectors also saw declining state roles and increasing participation by individuals and rural collectives. While the return of domestic and foreign private firms to the Chinese landscape was ideologically momentous on any scale, their contribution to total output and employment in most sectors remained small. With land still collectively owned and with the lion's share of non-agricultural activity conducted by entities controlled by governments of various levels, the economy could still be construed as being overwhelmingly publicly owned. On the other hand, with households the effective "firms" in an agriculture still accounting for 29 per cent of national income and for 59 per cent of employment, and with some township and village enterprises reported to be private enterprises simply enjoying local official protection, the economy could be said to have already gone some distance towards "privatization." Delegation of many rights to the enterprise level could be seen as part of a parallel trend, but also, rather differently, as an updating of public ownership. Clarifying such ambiguities requires moving from a simple dichotomy of private and public to a richer characterization of property rights. This

1. Thomas Rawski, "Progress without privatization: the reform of China's state industries," in Vedat Milor (ed.), *Changing Political Economies: Privatization in Post-Communist and Reforming Communist States* (Boulder: Lynne Rienner, 1994), pp. 27–52.

2. For example, Peter Nolan, *State and Market in the Chinese Economy* (London: MacMillan, 1993), especially pp. 267–296.

3. Further details of these trends and associated references are available from the author upon request.

Table 1: **Shares of Industrial Output Value by Ownership Type** (%)

Year	SOE	COE	Township and Village	Individual	Other
1978	78	13	9	—	—
1984	69	17.9	11.8	0.2	1
1988	56.8	18.4	17.7	4.3	2.7
1992	48.1	13.2	24.9	6.8	7.1

Source:
   China Statistical Yearbook 1993.

section gives a basic framework for the discussion of property rights, and then applies it to major, and changing, forms observed in China.

"Ownership" refers to a bundle of rights that an agent is empowered to exercise over an asset or piece of property. In industrialized market economies, the core bundle of rights that comprise "ownership" are the right to utilize the asset (utilization right), the right to possess the fruits (and responsibility for the negative outcomes, such as damages and debts) of that utilization (return right), and the right to transfer these rights to another agent through gift or sale (alienation right).[4] This bundled ownership concept applies not only to discrete assets such as machines and buildings, but also to business enterprises, which are simultaneously both the property of persons or other entities and entities empowered to act as legal agents in their own right. As with other kinds of property, the owners of firms hold standard rights of utilization, return and alienation; here, these rights translate into a right to dictate what contracts the firm will enter into and how it will utilize the assets it owns, the right to the returns from and responsibility for the costs of such utilization, and the right to transfer ownership to other agents.

Although rhetorically viewed as natural entitlements, historical rights are created by social actors, result from struggles among various interests and are subject to change over time. For example, the liability for debts imposed by ownership has varied from time to time and in specific instances, being more limited in the case of corporate shareholding than in that of individual proprietorship, and being adjusted by changes in bankruptcy law. To give another example, rights of utilization are some-times circumscribed by laws governing employment or environmental protection, by zoning restrictions, and so on. Decision-making rights and revenue rights are partially separated when employees are granted profit shares but not control rights. A large literature (see below) debates the

4. Louis Putterman, "Ownership and the nature of the firm," *Journal of Comparative Economics*, Vol. 17, No. 2 (1993), pp. 243–263; Alan Ryan, "Property," in John Eatwell, Murray Milgate and Peter Newman (eds.), *The New Palgrave: Dictionary of Economics* (New York: Stockton Press, 1987), pp. 1029–31.

extent to which decision control and revenue rights are effectively separated in the modern corporation.[5]

Western economists view hired managers of corporations not as *de facto* owners, but rather as agents of owners. While shareholders cede powers of day-to-day management to those agents, ultimate control continues to rest in the shareholders, who expect managers to serve their interests by taking whatever actions raise the value of their shares. Managers' compensation is set by, and their positions depend upon the approval of, boards of directors who are elected by shareholders. Although there is considerable controversy surrounding the degree to which managers are in fact made to serve shareholder interests, the view that managers are free to pursue their own goals because shareholders' stakes in the corporation are too small to cause them to monitor managers' actions intensively is by and large rejected. Instead, economists believe that such forces as the potential for incumbent management to be ousted in take-overs, the adjustment of managerial compensation according to share price performance and related indicators, and the influence of managerial reputation on the firm's cost of capital, cause managers to act largely in shareholders' interests. Profit-sharing, bonuses and other forms of compensation linked to financial performance are also methods of addressing the managerial agency problem. Of course, the rights that managers obtain because of delegation or imperfect control by *de jure* owners can be viewed as making them *de facto* owners, in a certain sense, but this usage is potentially confusing and is generally avoided. A more helpful approach is to treat the crucial dimension of ownership as the right to make such decisions over the use of an asset as have not already been determined contractually by concerned parties. Such residual rights of control, including the right to appoint and remove managers, remain with the shareholders in the case of corporations.[6]

This framework is now used to analyse the nature of property rights changes in China since 1978. Consider first agriculture under the household responsibility system. As operators of individual parcels under that system, families obtained the right to most revenue from farming, but their right to choose how land was farmed was often restricted by *de facto* production planning,[7] and a substantial part of their output usually had to be sold to state agencies at below-market prices. Control over the allocation of a critical input, land, was held by village government,

5. See Putterman, "Ownership and nature"; Louis Putterman and Randall Kroszner (eds.), *The Economic Nature of the Firm: A Reader (Second Edition)* (New York: Cambridge University Press, 1996).

6. See Oliver Hart, "An economist's perspective on the theory of the firm," *Columbia Law Review*, Vol. 89 (1989), pp. 1757–74, and other references cited in Putterman and Kroszner, *Economic Nature of the Firm*.

7. Terry Sicular, "China's agricultural policy during the reform period," in Joint Economic Committee, Congress of the United States, *China's Economic Dilemmas in the 1990s: The Problems of Reforms, Modernization, and Interdependence, Vol. I* (Washington, D.C.: U.S. Government Printing Office, 1991) pp. 34–64, provides survey results showing that 80% of villages in eastern and over 50% in central and western China set plans for crop rotation and layout in 1987.

circumscribing farmers' rights to transfer it and to capitalize its scarcity value. By contrast, nonfarm household enterprises were characterized by relatively unrestricted private property rights.

In industry, SOEs, nominally owned by "the whole people," had before 1978 come increasingly to be controlled by a range of jurisdictions from the central state to provinces, municipalities and counties. Taking control by such jurisdictions as a starting point, reform gave enterprise *managers* the right to retain within their enterprises portions of the profits, and to make many decisions regarding production and input use. Thus, some utilization and return rights can be seen as having been devolved from state bodies to enterprise managers. But this devolution was limited because supervising entities could still transfer the devolved rights among managers, whom they appointed and removed. Thus residual control rights remained with the relevant state jurisdiction.

A conclusion of the last paragraph is that the devolution of some rights to enterprise managers in China can be viewed as the adjustment of an agency relationship, rather than a shifting of the locus of ownership. It is legitimate to ask, however, whether the various governmental levels and bodies in which formal ownership resides have demonstrated an ability to play the role that shareholders and other financial sector agents are presumed to play in Western economies – that is, to discipline managers successfully so as to elicit from them performance consonant with their own goals. In this connection, it is frequently observed that considerable indiscipline flows from the still-observed tendency to subsidize enterprises that incur losses, giving rise to "soft budget constraints."[8] In such an environment, it could be rational for managers to seek to maximize their own stream of wages, bonuses and benefits in kind, sometimes to the detriment of enterprise profits.[9] The more one sees grants of autonomy allowing managers to pursue private goals, the less effective the agency relation between owner and manager, and the more one might justifiably speak of *de facto* privatization. Still, supervising unit control over the appointment and compensation of managers argues that residual control rights do remain with the legal owner. In this connection, it is significant that Groves, Hong, McMillan and Naughton find the reforms to have improved managerial performance in China's SOEs by strengthening incentives generated by pay and appointment mechanisms.[10]

In addition to a clarification of the concepts of ownership and agency, understanding the nature of ownership changes under China's reforms also calls for an inquiry into the identities and nature of the owners. As

8. For a classic statement of this argument, see Janos Kornai, "The soft budget constraint," *Kyklos*, Vol. 39, No. 1 (1986), pp. 3–30. For applications to China, see Christine Wong, "The economics of shortage and problems of reform in Chinese industry," *Journal of Comparative Economics*, Vol. 10, No. 4 (1986), pp. 363–387; Bruce Reynolds (ed.), *Reform in China: Challenges and Choices* (New York: M. E. Sharpe, 1987); Andrew Walder, "Manager and factory in an era of reform," *The China Quarterly*, No. 118 (1989), pp. 242–264.

9. Terry Sicular, "Going on the dole: why China's enterprises choose to lose," unpublished paper, University of Western Ontario, May 1994.

10. Theodore Groves, Yongmiao Hong, John McMillan and Barry Naughton, "China's evolving managerial labor market," *Journal of Political Economy* (in press).

already mentioned, for example, "state ownership" is frequently – indeed usually – associated with sub-national jurisdictions, not the central state. At no level, however, is the "state" as such the relevant actor; state control means control by specific persons and groups of persons whose actions are constrained by particular organizational structures and rules. State officials act in the interests of the whole people,[11] or of top Party or government leaders, to the extent that they internalize their objectives or expect penalties for not doing so. The increasing autonomy of localities, and thus the ever-greater localization of putative "state" ownership rights in the reform period, has been accompanied also by evidence of declining discipline, or increasing instances of corruption, in which the resources of state entities have been turned to the profit of bureaucrats – again suggesting *de facto* private property.

Collective ownership is also a tricky category. In principle, a collective is a group of individuals who hold joint and indivisible ownership over property, perhaps through the pooling of formerly private assets or by virtue of joint production. But Chinese collective ownership was fictitious, with state and Party exercising real control over the management of "collective" assets, and the distribution of proceeds from their sale generally proscribed. It is true that collectives shared with producers' co-operatives the attribute that their members were to some degree residual claimants. This characteristic was in turn associated with harder budget constraints, greater labour intensity and wages more closely linked with productivity than those of counterpart SOEs, conditions thought conducive to economic efficiency.[12] But even in the reform era the property of townships and villages has remained under the control of local officials, so it makes more sense to think of "rural collective property" as rural local government property. Most urban collective property is also quasi-state-owned property controlled by various supervising bodies, not enterprise personnel. In increasing the autonomy of both kinds of collective enterprise, reform has increased the power of managers, not that of the nominal owners.

In sum, ownership reform in China has indeed been much less radical than have been the changes in the role of markets, international trade and other aspects of the economic system, less radical than the *proposed* privatizations of most EEFSU nations. Although the invitation to private domestic and foreign firms to participate in China's economy is of enormous importance, the more quantitatively significant changes have occurred in the proportions of collective, and especially rural, versus state-owned enterprises. At the same time, significant changes have occurred in the content of ownership, with both state and collective sectors seeing major devolutions of rights, although residual control rights and rights of alienation remained in official hands. These changes

---

11. Assuming, that is, that such an interest can be defined.
12. Martin Lockett, "The urban collective economy," in Stephan Feuchtwang, Athar Hussain and Thierry Pairault (eds.), *Transforming China's Economy in the Eighties, Vol. 2.* (Boulder, CO: Westview Press, 1988), pp. 118–137.

can be seen as creating new mechanisms of agency rather than transferring ownership, but unsuccessful application has acted to transfer *de facto* ownership in some cases.

How Have Property Rights and Their Reform Influenced Economic Performance?

China's rate of growth of GDP per capita rose from around 4 per cent during 1952–78 to over 7 per cent during 1978–92, with estimated per capita consumption more than doubling during the latter period.[13] These changes are attributed by the Chinese government and observers in China and elsewhere to changes in economic policies. To what degree can the improvement in China's rate of economic growth be attributed to changes in property rights? Would growth have been faster still if property rights had been more rapidly transformed? Does growth and marketization without massive privatization imply that a socialist market economy is feasible or desirable?

Agriculture scored the first major successes in China's economic reforms. While the acceleration of the growth rate of crop output value from the 2.5 per cent rate of 1952–78 to 5.9 per cent in 1978–84 proved somewhat impermanent, rural reform freed residents to shift to higher value activities, thus helping to account for growth rates of 4.7, 11.1, 6.4 and 18.9 per cent respectively for forestry, animal husbandry, sidelines and fishery output during 1984–92 (2.7, 10.9, 11.0 and 17.9 per cent respectively for 1978–92 as a whole).[14] To what degree is agricultural and rural growth attributable to property rights reform, or retarded by its absence?

Most authors have judged the change in the locus of day-to-day management and of the claim on net output to be the single most important cause of China's improved agricultural performance after 1978. Judgments to this effect by authors such as Nolan are supported by much-cited econometric studies by McMillan, Whalley and Zhu and by Lin, which attribute 78 and 86.5 per cent respectively of growth in output per unit of agricultural inputs to the adoption of the household responsibility system.[15] While increased crop prices are assigned a share of the

---

13. Estimates of the comparative GDP growth rate are given by Dwight Perkins, "Completing China's move to the market," *Journal of Economic Perspectives*, Vol. 8, No. 2 (1994), pp. 23–46 at pp. 24–25. *China Statistical Yearbook 1993* gives indexes of consumption in comparable prices (1952 = 100) of 177 in 1978 and 444.7 in 1992, implying a 2.5-fold gain.

14. Based on data on gross output in current prices in *China Statistical Yearbook 1993*, p. 301, deflated by the overall farm and sideline products purchasing price index (p. 202). Based on the same series, crop output value fell by − 1.8% a year during 1984–89 but rose by 3.0% a year during 1984–92 as a whole.

15. See Peter Nolan, *The Political Economy of Collective Farms: An Analysis of China's Post-Mao Rural Reforms* (Boulder, CO: Westview, 1988); John McMillan, John Whalley and Lijing Zhu, "The impact of China's economic reforms on agricultural productivity and growth," *Journal of Political Economy*, Vol. 97, No. 4 (1989) pp. 781–807; and Justin Yifu Lin, "Rural reforms and agricultural growth in China," *American Economic Review*, Vol. 82, No. 1 (1992), pp. 34–51.

credit in Lin's study, no study quantifies the impact of market liberalization *per se*. Still, the consensus is that a change in the assignment of
decision-making and revenue rights deserves more credit than marketization or other aspects of China's reforms in explaining agriculture's faster
growth.[16] While local officials (collectives) retained residual control,
then, the devolution of other rights played a critical role in getting the
reforms off to a successful start.

Beyond this point, observers differ in their assessment of whether
lingering collective institutions have hindered or enhanced rural economic performance. One widely held view is that failure to bestow
land-ownership on tillers has held back agricultural growth, because as
non-owners farmers have limited incentive to invest in land improvements and because rather than moving into the hands of those who find
their comparative advantage to lie in farming, land remains divided along
egalitarian lines and is inefficiently fragmented, with farming becoming
part-time or the occupation of women and the elderly. Residents' abilities
to capture implicit land rents so long as they continue to farm, but not
through sale upon leaving farming, also discourages migration, supporting a possibly inefficient policy of geographically dispersed (and rural)
industrialization. Still-substantial collective ownership in rural industry is
also sub-optimal, to such observers, since local governments at best
occupy an intermediate position between higher state levels and private
owners in their degree of efficiency, pursuing political goals like job
creation rather than profit maximization alone.[17]

Opposing views on land include the argument that limited farm
investment is mostly due to biased prices and interventions in crop choice
and that a more efficient allocation of land and farm investment could
also be induced through charging farmers scarcity rents for collectively
owned land and paying full compensation for improved land returned to
collectives.[18] Collective units' contributions to irrigation and mechanized
farming, and the decline of these inputs where collectives have been
weak, are also cited. There is no consensus on industrial location, with
many scholars sympathizing with China's official desire for a more
dispersed industrialization pattern, and China's relative avoidance of

16. Authors such as Sicular, Putterman and Rozelle indeed emphasize the incompleteness
of marketization up to the early 1990s in Chinese agriculture, not only because of the
importance of involuntary procurements, but also because of the indications that informal
restrictions on planting decisions and a bias towards self-sufficiency were outgrowths of the
procurement system and related policies. See Sicular, "China's agricultural policy"; Louis
Putterman, *Continuity and Change in China's Rural Development: Collective and Reform
Eras in Perspective* (New York: Oxford University Press, 1993); Scott Rozelle, "The
economic behavior of village leaders in China's reform economy," unpublished Ph.D.
dissertation, Cornell University, 1991.
17. See William Byrd and Lin Qingsong (eds.), *China's Rural Industry: Structure,
Development and Reform* (New York: Oxford University Press, 1990); and Susan Whiting,
"Contract incentives and market discipline in China's rural industrial sector," unpublished
paper, University of Michigan, May 1994.
18. Putterman, *Continuity and Change*. See also Paul Bowles and Xiao-Yuan Dong,
"Current successes and future challenges in China's economic reforms: an alternative view,"
New Left Review, No. 208 (1994), pp. 49–76.

"shanty-towns" still viewed as to its credit. Equality in land distribution and the availability of farming as a fall-back for rural residents are also seen both as conditions for general acceptance of the reforms and as contributors to the social stability required for change to proceed. The success of rural collective industry is seen by some[19] as belying beliefs in the superiority of private property rights, and by others as indicators of the at least temporary expediency of this form.[20] Econometric studies have yet to find evidence of superior efficiency on the part of private as compared with township and village owned rural industrial enterprises.[21]

In industry more generally, most authors concur that the increasing importance of the so-called "non-state" sector, primarily collectives, has been a major contributor to growth, with TVE and COE total factor productivity (TFP) growing at two to three times the SOE rate.[22] Thus, Jefferson writes that "the rapid growth of China's TVE sector has been critical to the success of that country's transition to a market economy."[23] Singh, Radha and Xiao find that the share of the non-state sector in industrial output is a good predictor of the average TFP of SOEs across provinces.[24] Econometric evidence that industrial growth would be faster still were more enterprises private is as yet unavailable. While the greater labour intensity of private enterprises could be taken to indicate that they are more efficient in their choices of inputs, it is not clear whether this reflects differences inherent in the form of ownership rather than differences in the types of activities undertaken and biases in the banking system's allocation of capital.

Foreign investment is also sometimes suggested as a source of differential efficiency, and the level of foreign participation may well help to explain differences in rates of growth across localities (as well as China's better performance than much of EEFSU). Since foreign ownership is not

19. E.g. Martin Weitzman and Chenggang Xu, "Chinese township-village enterprises as vaguely defined cooperatives," *Journal of Comparative Economics*, Vol. 18, No. 2 (1994), pp. 121–145.

20. See Chun Chang and Yijiang Wang, "The nature of the township-village enterprise," *Journal of Comparative Economics*, Vol. 19 (1994), pp. 434–452; Jiahua Che and Yingyi Qian, "Boundaries of the firm and governance: understanding China's township-village enterprises," unpublished paper, Stanford University Department of Economics, August 1994; and David Li, "Ambiguous property rights in the gray market: an analysis of the Chinese non-state sector," paper presented at the Allied Social Science Associations meeting, Washington, D.C., 7 January 1995.

21. These studies include Jan Svejnar, "Productive efficiency and employment," in Byrd and Lin, *China's Rural Industry*, pp. 243–254; Mark Pitt and Louis Putterman, "Employment and wages in township, village, and other rural enterprises," in Gary Jefferson and I. J. Singh (eds.), *Reform, Ownership and Performance in Chinese Industry* (forthcoming), and Xiao-Yuan Dong and Louis Putterman, "Productivity and organization in China's rural industries: an efficiency frontier analysis," unpublished paper, Brown University, August 1994.

22. See Table 4 in Gary Jefferson and Thomas Rawski, "Enterprise reform in Chinese industry," *Journal of Economic Perspectives*, Vol. 8, No. 2 (1994), pp. 47–70.

23. Gary Jefferson, "Are China's rural enterprises outperforming state-owned enterprises?" Research Paper No. CH-RPS#24, The World Bank, 1993.

24. Inderjit Singh, Dilip Ratha and Geng Xiao, "Non-state enterprises as an engine of growth: an analysis of provincial industrial growth in post-reform China," Research Paper No. CH-RPS#20, The World Bank, 1993.

a real option for the economy as a whole, the most important question for the purposes of this article is what impact domestic property rights have had on the ability to absorb foreign funds and know-how and to interact fruitfully with foreign trading and investment partners. There is again a lack of econometric evidence on this issue. Casual observation suggests that the combination of reduced bureaucratic "red tape" and access to funds and inputs have given TVEs an advantage in dealing with foreign investment. While for large-scale projects, SOEs are the partners of choice, and while some SOE joint ventures have performed well in adopting new technology, SOE's advantages come clearly from the nature of the Chinese institutional environment, and there is little that can be concluded about the influence of their ownership structure as a factor in its own right and apart from that environment.

Great controversy surrounds the questions of how much, if any, improvement in SOE performance has resulted from reforms in their management and incentive structures, and to what degree the continuing presence of a large SOE sector and the non-privatization of most SOEs has held back China's growth. Chen et al. estimate that the rate of growth of total factor productivity in the SOE sector accelerated from 0.9 per cent during 1957–78 to 5.5 per cent per annum during 1979–85.[25] Jefferson and Rawski identify 13 studies of TFP growth in China's SOEs during the 1980s, most based on sample surveys.[26] Nine report annual growth of TFP within the range of 2 to 4 per cent.[27] Of those remaining, two show higher and two lower rates of productivity change. In two studies, Groves et al. find links between grants of enterprise autonomy, use of bonuses, more temporary employees (including "contract workers") and higher enterprise productivity, and evidence that competition for managerial positions had improved enterprise performance.[28] Jefferson, Zhao and Lu find that in both the SOE and TVE sectors, managers of less profitable enterprises were more likely to be put on more autonomous, incentive-based contracts, and that when the selection bias inherent in this relationship is controlled for, those contracts are found to lead to greater productivity. While COEs, including TVEs, registered faster TFP growth than SOEs, this might be looked upon as catching up by the less productive sector.[29] Evidence of increasing allocative efficiency in China's industrial economy as a whole comes from Jeffer-

25. Chen Kuan, Gary Jefferson, Thomas Rawski, Hongchang Wang and Yuxin Zheng, "Productivity change in Chinese industry, 1953–1985," *Journal of Comparative Economics*, Vol. 12, No. 4 (1988), pp. 570–591.

26. Jefferson and Rawski, "Enterprise reform."

27. This range includes a growth rate estimate of 2.4% per annum obtained by Jefferson, Rawski and Zheng after switching from the two factor (capital, labour) production function of the earlier Chen et al. study to a three factor (capital, labour, intermediate inputs) set-up. See Gary Jefferson, Thomas Rawski and Yuxin Zheng, "Growth, efficiency, and convergence in China's state and collective industry," *Economic Development and Cultural Change*, Vol. 40, No. 2 (1992), pp. 239–266.

28. Theodore Groves, Yongmiao Hong, John McMillan and Barry Naughton, "Autonomy and incentives in Chinese state enterprises," *Quarterly Journal of Economics*, Vol. 109, No. 1 (1994), pp. 183–209; and Groves et al., "China's evolving managerial labor market."

29. Jefferson, "Are rural enterprises outperforming SOEs?"

son, Rawski and Zheng's finding that the average marginal revenue products of labour and of capital in SOEs and COEs showed some convergence during 1980–88, while average marginal returns to material inputs were almost identical (and economically quite reasonable) throughout that period.[30] Naughton draws a similar conclusion from evidence of converging rates of profit across different lines of industry.[31]

But at the very time that Western econometric studies were finding signs of responsiveness to reform on the part of China's SOEs, Chinese officials were bemoaning their continued poor performance.[32] While this apparent contradiction could come from technical problems with the aforementioned studies, the relative unanimity among them, their growing number and the qualitative robustness of their results to alternative specifications suggests that an explanation should be sought elsewhere. One possible explanation derives from noting that while productivity measures deal with the relationship between output and inputs, among which those of labour are measured in physical units (number of personnel), profitability depends on the relationship between revenue and expenditures (a financial measure). Thus, even if output per bundle of (partly physical) inputs is rising, profits could be falling or turning negative if wages, bonuses and other forms of managerial and worker compensation are rising too rapidly. While Naughton interprets falling average SOE profitability as a welcome sign of eroded monopoly profits, Woo *et al.* argue that it reflects financial indiscipline that makes the SOEs a drain on the economy.[33] The finding by Groves *et al.* that reform-induced incentives raised SOE workers' productivity and compensation but not their enterprises' profits may be consistent with this interpretation. Although Jefferson, Rawski and Zheng refute Woo's contentions by noting that growth of labour compensation was in line with that of productivity,[34] losses by SOEs rose from 2.6 billion *yuan* in 1984 to 18.6 billion *yuan* in 1992,[35] and official Chinese rhetoric on the eve of a new round of enterprise reforms in 1994 suggested widespread agreement in China at least that the SOEs remained a bastion of economic privilege, and that previous reforms in the sector had accomplished far too little.[36]

30. Jefferson, Rawski and Zheng, "Growth and convergence." See also Gary Jefferson and Wenyi Xu, "Assessing gains in efficient production among China's industrial enterprises," *Economic Development and Cultural Change*, Vol. 42, No. 3 (1994), pp. 597–615, which shows that the degree of convergence of factor productivities was greater for enterprises that sold more of their output outside state plans.
31. Barry Naughton, "Implications of the state monopoly over industry and its relaxation," *Modern China*, Vol. 18, No. 1 (1992) pp. 14–41.
32. See, for example, the report on Premier Li Peng's remarks to delegates attending the Pacific Rim Forum in *China News Digest*, 28 October 1994.
33. See Wing Thye Woo, Gang Fan, Wen Hai and Yibiao Jin, "The efficiency and macroeconomic consequences of Chinese enterprise reform," *China Economic Review*, Vol. 4, No. 2 (1993), pp. 153–168.
34. Gary Jefferson, Thomas Rawski and Yuxin Zheng, "Productivity change in Chinese industry: a comment," *China Economic Review*, Vol. 5, No. 2 (1994), pp. 235–241.
35. Sicular, "Going on the dole."
36. See the discussion in Wanda Tseng, Hoe Ee Khor, Kalpana Kochhar, Dubravko Mihaljek and David Burton, "Economic reform in China: a new phase," IMF Occasional Paper No. 114, Washington, D.C., November 1994.

Change in agricultural production relations, which can be viewed both as a property rights adjustment and as an agency mechanism reform, appears to be responsible for much of the improvement in agricultural growth and for the release of resources to other rural activities that have played key roles in raising China's economic growth rate. Changes in property rights seem to have been somewhat less important in the industrial sector, where changes in the relative shares of different enterprise types, increasing competition between enterprises of differing ownership and jurisdiction, the expanded role of the price mechanism, and international trade and investment appear to have played the more important roles. But here, too, devolution of some control and revenue rights seem to have contributed to productivity growth. Finally, the robust evidence of productivity growth among state firms that has now accumulated is not enough to offset concerns that while enterprise reforms may have improved SOE responsiveness as an agent of society or state, in a climate in which the government moves cautiously when at all against the privileges of SOE employees, the reforms have also empowered the latter to act as *de facto* owners and, in some cases at least, to claim an economically unwarranted share of the benefits of growth.

Property Rights and the "Chinese Model"

As indicated at the beginning of this article, the extent of property rights change in China plays an important part in broader discussions of the so-called "Chinese model" of evolutionary system reform. Three broad points of view regarding property rights in the transition from a planned economy are discussed in this section. The first argues that privatization is central to economic reform and efficiency, that failure to embark on a thorough privatization programme retards economic progress, and that little additional progress is therefore possible for China without such a programme. The second contends that comprehensive privatization will ultimately bring gains but that it is not necessary in the early stages of reform, and that China can continue to dispense with full privatization for some time to come. The third sees marketization but not privatization as desirable for an economy, so that consolidating and further adjusting the institutions of China's emerging socialist market economy is desirable, but increasing private ownership of enterprises and resources is not. While other views are possible[37] and while it may be difficult to show that these exact views are widely held, they cover a considerable spectrum of possibilities and will be helpful to organizing the discussion.

The view that privatization is indispensible and should be undertaken as early as possible has been the standard fare of Western economic

---

37. For example: it could be held that privatization was unnecessary in the past, but is critical at the present juncture; that China has already gone too far in "restoring capitalism"; and so on.

advice to the transforming economies.[38] Proponents hold that free prices and exchange cannot deliver efficient outcomes without private ownership of resources and firms, for without these agents lack the motivation to respond to price signals in economically optimal fashion. Managers of SOEs facing "soft budget constraints" will seek to expand operations even under dubious circumstances, since they can win in good states but cannot really fail. Collective ownership robs agents of efficient investment incentives. Absence of a land market leads to inefficient use of farm and commercial land. Massive wastage of resources continues in China because the government allows state workers to squander social funds, reserves the lion's share of investment funds for public enterprises, fails adequately to control the growth of the country's money supply, and discourages a subsistence-oriented agricultural population from better exploiting local resources through specialization and from competing for urban jobs through migration.

A proponent of this first view may use a variety of arguments to explain why China's economy has achieved such striking aggregate performance despite the very limited privatization that has occurred thus far. Internal and external strife followed by decades of Communist rule and continuing internal struggles kept China's economy so far below the potential inherent in its heritage of administrative capacity and culture, its relatively educated and skilled human capital stock, its proximity to rapidly modernizing neighbours and ties to communities of entrepreneurial overseas Chinese, and the backlog of importable technology in use in other countries, that the simple rectification of Mao-era excesses coupled with very modest liberalization could generate tremendous gains. In the terminology of economic theory, output can grow despite allocative and technical inefficiency; improvements in factor productivity, for example, could simply denote movement from, say, 80 per cent below the world technological frontier to 70 per cent below it, a position still indicative of considerable inefficiency. A few changes such as bringing competent personnel back from political banishment and introducing more up-to-date technology from abroad could account for much of the gain. And the fact that significant if still very incomplete efficiency gains could be induced in an agricultural sector constituting a large part of the economy by moving only half-way to private farming worked to China's advantage. Gains were also obtained from the growth of private enterprise in the rural non-farm sector and urban trade and services,[39] and from foreign

38. See, for example, Stanley Fischer, "Privatization in East European transformation," in C. Clague and G. Rausser (eds.), *The Emergence of Market Economies in Eastern Europe* (Cambridge: Blackwell, 1992), pp. 227–243; for an application to China, see Jeffrey Sachs and Wing Thye Woo, "Structural factors in the economic reforms of China, Eastern Europe, and the former Soviet Union," *Economic Policy*, Vol. 18, No. 1 (1994), pp. 102–145.

39. Note, however, that references to the "non-state sector" as a whole to explain China's "progress without privatization" are problematic for such arguments, since most of the "non-state sector" is actually controlled by local governments. Treatment of TVEs as "disguised private enterprises" is unwarranted as a generalization, and there is much evidence of dynamism among TVEs controlled by local governments in places like southern Jiangsu and Shandong. The notion that TVEs and other collectives are "co-operatives" and thus

investment. Finally, believers in the necessity of privatization may argue that China's growth rate is exaggerated by official statistics; they may direct attention to the fact that growth varies enormously among localities (with those most exposed to foreign investment growing the fastest); and conclude that the easy gains from limited reform have already been exploited, so that delaying more comprehensive reform threatens the tentative progress that has occurred to date.

Proponents of the second view can point out that virtually no country, past or present, has rivalled China's rate of economic growth since 1978,[40] so claims that growth would have been faster still with more privatization lack empirical support. Post-1989 experience in EEFSU suggests that radically transforming all aspects of an economic system simultaneously or in close succession may be unwise because institutions require time to take root and evolve in a given society. Comparing China's "touching the stones to cross the river" reform philosophy with the shock therapists' assertion that "one must cross a chasm in a single bound," advocates of this view find merit in the first aphorism and ask whether the chasms into which some EEFSU countries fell were not of their own making.

While the second view differs from the first in holding that the use of markets and price signals can increase efficiency even without privately owned firms, it too accepts that private ownership offers the only truly satisfactory long-term solution to the problems of motivating energetic profit-seeking behaviour. However, the fact that outright privatization is not yet on the agenda of China's leaders does not worry the evolutionist. China's economy has been growing at historic rates, and such objectives as improving macroeconomic control and addressing bottlenecks in strategic sectors (energy, transportation) may deserve precedence over privatization on the official agenda. More work is also needed to build up social insurance mechanisms so that the impact of more radical enterprise reform on workers will be adequately cushioned. Finally, further separation of ownership and control, as envisaged in the current corporatization programme, may succeed in eliciting significant further gains in public enterprise efficiency.[41]

The third view differs from the first two views not only in positive beliefs about what does and does not promote economic vitality and growth, but also normatively, such as in placing a higher priority on equality and the amelioration of poverty, and in judging economic freedoms on instrumental grounds. To a supporter of this view, the goals of social justice for which traditional socialism stood are valid and

---

footnote continued

"quasi-private" is also largely refuted by this discussion. Finally, while public TVEs may indeed *resemble* private enterprises because local governments cannot provide soft budget subsidies, this scarcely permits the privatization proponent to redefine them as such.

40. See Shahid Yusuf, "China's macroeconomic performance and management during transition," *Journal of Economic Perspectives*, Vol. 8, No. 2 (1994), pp. 71–92.

41. See Adrian Wood, "Joint stock companies with rearranged public ownership," *China Economic Review*, Vol. 4, No. 2 (1993), pp. 181–194.

limiting private concentrations of wealth so as to achieve those goals is justified. The history of central planning, however, has shown that managing the details of production and resource allocation from one administrative centre produces results inferior to those of decentralization and reliance on markets. Whereas the privatization advocate goes further and asserts that private ownership of enterprises is the only viable route to prosperity, the market socialist rejects this view, appealing to China's recent experience as evidence that market socialism is workable.

To others, market socialism is a baseless dream. State ownership of firms and capital means state interference with management, distorted managerial incentives from the "soft budget constraint," and the absence of any agent with a strong incentive to maintain social property and to seek out its best uses. The market socialist might reject these conclusions, arguing that while the experiences of Communist Yugoslavia and Hungary may have seemed to lend support to such arguments, that of China since 1979 shows that they need not be correct. The phenomenon of soft budget constraints seems to be less of a problem when the responsible jurisdiction is a local one, and when numerous public entities compete against one another and with private competitors. Local officials have also exhibited great entrepreneurial talents and energies on behalf of publicly owned entities in China.[42] While soft budget constraints and government intervention continue to be problematic for larger SOEs, these problems may be overcome following the completion of more thorough-going price reform, creation of a social safety net for SOE employees, continued growth of non-state employment and earnings, and enterprise reforms further separating management from ownership. Shareholding public entities forbidden by a strong legal framework from attempting to dictate actions to enterprise managers will step back and concentrate on looking after their financial interests in maximizing the profit and tax returns on their enterprises. Any residual inefficiency on the part of public firms may be more than offset by the contribution of the institution of public ownership to the achievement of distributive and other social goals.

One irony of the market socialist position is that it appears to have as limited a constituency in China as in the West. Official Chinese enunciation of a socialist market programme seems to be one more in a series of compromises between socialist ideologues and reformers; there are no ideolgues of market socialism itself. Thus, even if China's recent experience is the most supportive evidence to date that some form of market socialism could be viable, failure of the Soviet model, the "no more experiments" attitude that has followed that failure throughout the ex-Communist world, collapse of Communism as a world movement, rapid

---

42. Thus, Bowles and Dong ("Successes and challenges") quote enthusiastically Thomas Rawski's reference to "entrepreneurial leaders in hundreds of counties and thousands of production brigades" and Shahid Yusuf's discussion of "the entrepreneurial zeal of local officials." (See Rawski, "Chinese industrial reform: accomplishments, prospects, and implications," *American Economic Review, Papers and Proceedings*, Vol. 84, No. 2 (1994), p. 273, and Yusuf, "China's macroeconomic performance.")

private economy growth in neighbouring countries, and burgeoning consumerism and the priority attached to economic goals in China, make long-term commitment to the socialist market concept appear doubtful. As the political old guard pass from the scene and as the most recent and radical wave of reforms become entrenched, continuing movement towards a more conventional market economy, including largely private ownership of resources and enterprises, appears the more likely outcome. Indeed, once the bulk of the SOEs have been converted to joint stock companies with upwards of 50 per cent of their shares in the hands of individuals and large chunks of the remainder held by local or functionally oriented public entities upon which the central government will find it hard to exert pressure, *de facto* privatization may well have reached a level from which it will be impossible to turn back. Conversion of many TVEs to an individual shareholding basis has also recently become popular in a number of localities. Even if a core of enterprises producing, say, 20 per cent of GDP were to remain in government hands, this would be no more than the corresponding share in non-socialist, post-War France. For this reason, the lessons of China's experience with respect to the viability of market socialism are arguably of more academic than practical interest.

The debate between evolutionists and privatization "fundamentalists" may also be of mostly academic interest. This is because the routes respectively followed by EEFSU and China since the end of the 1980s have been determined much more by political and international than by domestic economic factors. In EEFSU, popular rejection of Communist rule and the desire to emulate Western prosperity combined with massive external indebtedness and the profferment of aid and policy assistance packages by Western countries to pave the way for attempts at rapid privatization and economic liberalization. While some citizens may now doubt that the advice offered was truly in their best interest, the initial stages of these programmes have already been completed, and economic growth has resumed in most countries in already altered institutional landscapes. In China, by contrast, the Communist Party has remained in power with enough continuity of personnel and doctrine that its initiation of more rapid and radical reforms was at the very least improbable. This is especially the case since, to quote a recent IMF report, "the Chinese economy, unlike those of other former centrally planned economies in transition, was not in a deep crisis of macroeconomic instability just before reforms were implemented."[43] No reform Communist, including Yugoslavia's Tito, Hungary's Kadar and the Soviet Union's Gorbachev, had initiated massive privatization of a state sector while in power.

It is plausible to suppose that if the Communists had fallen from power in China in the late 1970s or 1980s, the shift to a more conventional market economy would have proceeded more rapidly. It is an open question, however, whether such a shift would have generated a more

---

43. Michael Bell, Hoe Ee Khor and Kalpana Kochhar, "China at the threshold of a market economy," IMF Occasional Paper No. 107, Washington D.C., September 1993, p. 6.

rapid rate of economic growth or achieved as acceptable a distribution of growth's benefits as did the policies of the CCP under Deng Xiaoping. The question mark attached to the growth rate follows from the fact, already alluded to, that the rate that was in the event achieved is more or less historically unsurpassed, so that there is no empirical basis on which to demonstrate that it was surpassable. One can suggest specific policies that might have generated more efficiency and more investment, such as more complete and immediate decontrol of agricultural prices or a less bureaucratically controlled environment for foreign investors. But some free market style policies might well have reduced growth, at least for a time. A greater opening of China's markets to imports causing some de-industrialization, along East European lines, comes to mind.[44] And full liberalization would have led to social tensions to which any government would have been forced to respond in one manner or another. It is not clear that the expedients adopted by the CCP, influenced by its ideology and internal struggles though they were, were any less satisfactory from the standpoints of growth, equity and stability than those that a non-Communist government would have been led to adopt.

Conclusion

Compared to changes in the roles of market forces, incentives and international trade in its own economy, and compared with intended and sometimes achieved rates of change in ownership in some transitional economies of EEFSU, property rights reform has been gradual and limited in China. Agricultural land remains collective property, only some smaller state enterprises have been privatized and the most quantitatively significant change in industrial ownership is the rise of TVEs, among which local public ownership has remained predominant from the standpoints of output and investment. For further signs of change, one must look to the smaller private and foreign-invested sectors or look more closely at the content of property rights, which have been unbundled and significantly devolved from public owners to managers in both agriculture and industry.

The effects of these changes in property rights are clearest in agriculture, where the shift from teams to households as production units appears to have significantly enhanced production incentives and speeded the release of resources to other sectors. The contribution of reforms in industry is less clear, because evidence of increasing technical efficiency in many enterprises is clouded by problems of financial performance,

44. Of course, even a non-Communist Chinese government may have been unlikely to follow a *laissez faire* approach. Policies modelled after the export-oriented economies of Japan, South Korea and Taiwan, where a strong state role was combined with private ownership and markets, would perhaps have been more likely, as well as more effective, making the *laissez faire* benchmark a somewhat unfair standard of comparison. See Alice Amsden, *Asia's New Giant: South Korea and Late Industrialization* (New York: Oxford University Press, 1989) and Robert Wade, *Governing the Market: Economic Theory and the Role of Government in East Asian Industrialization* (Princeton: Princeton University Press, 1990).

signs of rent-capture by employees, and unwanted impacts on government revenue and inflation. However, increased competition between industrial units, including the rapid expansion of the role of TVEs, has clearly contributed to growth, as has the transfer of methods associated with foreign investment and trade.

Limited reform in the ownership of enterprises is a key element of the "evolutionary" reform model that is associated with China. Whether deferring privatization has retarded China's economic growth is a much debated question. Its experience also reopens debate about the potential of market socialism. Gradualism has to date been a reflection of China's political evolution, and it seems likely to continue changing into a conventional market economy, if the absence of market socialists is any indication. Although the record might have been improved in some specific respects, I am nevertheless drawn to the conclusion that in view of the existence of social conditions calling for caution in some aspects of liberalization, and in the absence of more successful growth stories than that of post-1978 China, it is doubtful that a more economically liberal regime could have produced a significantly better overall record of growth, especially if social equity and stability are accorded any weight.

The Role of Foreign Trade and Investment in China's Economic Transformation

Nicholas R. Lardy

In the almost two decades since economic reform began in China the role of the foreign sector has burgeoned in ways that no one anticipated. The volume of foreign trade and the role of foreign capital are both far greater than could have been foreseen based on the modest Chinese economic reforms initiated in the late 1970s. By the mid-1990s China had become one of the world's largest trading nations, the recipient of more foreign direct investment than any other country in the world, the largest borrower from the World Bank, the largest recipient of official development assistance in the form of low-interest, long-term concessionary loans from industrialized countries, and, except for the Czech Republic, the only transition economy with ready access to international capital and equity markets.

This article attempts to analyse how important foreign trade and foreign capital have been to China's growth acceleration in the reform period and to identify those institutions and policies that have been most effective in this process. It then seeks to analyse the extent to which China's experience is relevant to other transition economies.

Foreign Capital

China has become a major participant in international capital markets. It has borrowed money from multilateral lending institutions such as the World Bank and the Asian Development Bank; from national development banks such as the Japanese Overseas Economic Co-operation Fund; from national export-import banks such as the United States Export Import Bank; and from commercial banks. In addition China has floated both debt and equity issues on international capital markets. Finally, as noted above, China has become a major recipient of foreign direct investment. Indeed, in 1993 China was the site of more foreign direct investment than any other country.[1] In 1994 gross foreign direct investment inflows into China were exceeded only by those into the United States.

Foreign direct investment. Chinese data on foreign direct investment are given in Table 1. The data show it grew from modest amounts of a few hundred million dollars annually in the late 1970s and early 1980s to almost four billion dollars annually in the late 1980s. Because many foreign invested projects were delayed in the aftermath of Tiananmen, actual investment showed no growth in 1990. However, beginning in 1991, China attracted greatly increased amounts of foreign direct

1. World Bank, *World Debt Tables: External Finance for Developing Countries, 1994–95* (Washington, D.C.: The World Bank, 1994), Vol. 1, p. 16.

Table 1: **Foreign Direct Investment in China, 1979–94** (millions of US$)

Year	Contracted	Actual
1979–82 (cumulative)	6,999	1,767
1983	1,917	916
1984	2,875	1,419
1985	6,333	1,959
1986	3,330	2,244
1987	4,319	2,647
1988	6,191	3,739
1989	6,294	3,773
1990	6,987	3,755
1991	12,422	4,666
1992	58,736	11,292
1993	111,435	27,514
1994	81,406	33,787

Note:
   The data reported above are inclusive of foreign direct investment in equity joint ventures, contractual joint ventures, wholly foreign-owned enterprises and joint exploration as well as foreign investment in leasing, compensation trade, and processing and assembly.
Sources:
   Ministry of Foreign Trade and Economic Relations, *Zhonghua renmin gongheguo duiwai jingjimaoyibu xinwen gongbao* (*The Bulletin of the Ministry of Foreign Trade and Economic Relations of the People's Republic of China*), No. 2 (25 April 1994), p. 10. Xinhua News Service, "Zhongguo qunian liyong waizi 337 yi duo meiyuan" ("Last year China's utilized foreign direct investment exceeded US$33.7 billion"), *Jinrong shibao* (*Banking Times*), 26 January 1995, p. 1.

investment. It more than doubled in both 1993 and 1994 and rose a further one-fifth in 1994 to reach almost $34 billion actual investment.

   The dramatic increases in foreign direct investment in the first half of the 1990s appear to be caused by four factors. First, the magnitude of aggregate foreign direct investment flowing to developing countries increased significantly in the 1990s. Average annual flows in 1990–93 were double those of 1987–89.[2]

   Secondly, China's seeming political stability in the wake of Tiananmen, combined with the explosive growth of the domestic economy after 1992, led to a fundamental reassessment by foreign firms of China's economic and investment potential. China was deemed a less risky political and economic environment by risk assessment organizations such as the Economist Intelligence Unit.[3] Many multinationals decided that they could not afford not to invest in the world's fastest growing emerging market.

   2. *Ibid.* p. 159.
   3. On a scale in which 100 is the riskiest rating, China rated 15 in 1988, one of the EIU's lowest risk ratings. This jumped to 35 in 1989 but by 1992 had fallen back to 25. *The Economist*, 21 May 1994, p. 120.

Thirdly, China systematically liberalized its foreign investment regime. Some of the special provisions to attract foreign direct investment, which in the late 1970s and early 1980s had only been available in the four special economic zones in South China, were made much more widely available. For example, special tax concessions, liberalized land leasing and other inducements were made available in a growing number of open coastal cities, economic development areas and high technology development zones, increasing the attractiveness of China as a site for foreign investment. China also opened up sectors such as retailing, power generation and port development that previously had been off limits for foreign investors.[4] Liberalization of foreign participation in property development in the early 1990s led to particularly significant foreign capital inflows directed toward the development of residential housing, retail complexes and other projects.

Fourthly, foreign direct investment flows increased in part because of the phenomena of recycled capital of Chinese origin. In order to take advantage of the special tax and other incentives provided to foreign invested enterprises, Chinese firms moved money off-shore and then recycled it back into China disguised as "foreign investment." The World Bank guessed that these might comprise as much as 25 per cent of gross investment inflows in 1992.[5]

Foreign borrowing. China's second largest source of foreign capital, after foreign direct investment, has been borrowing. The cumulative amount of foreign borrowing from all sources is reflected in Table 2. The data show China's total external debt rising from well under $1 billion in 1978, as reform was just getting under way, to $93 billion by the end of 1994. To put these numbers in perspective, only Indonesia among low and lower-middle income economies has a larger outstanding debt. China's external debt is only modestly smaller than the two most heavily indebted upper-middle income economies, Mexico and Brazil.

However, China's debt burden remains modest. In part this is because its exports are so much larger, relative to its outstanding debt, than those of Brazil and Mexico, which the World Bank classifies as moderately and severely indebted, respectively.[6] For example, on average in 1991–93 China's total external debt relative to earnings from the export of goods and services was less than half that of Mexico and less than a third that of Brazil.[7]

In addition, a relatively large share of China's external debt is concessionary with grace periods of up to ten years before repayments of principal must begin and/or carrying below market interest rates. Even its

4. Nicholas R. Lardy, *China in the World Economy* (Washington, D.C.: Institute for International Economics, 1994), pp. 63–71.

5. Peter Harrold and Rajiv Lall, *China. Reform and Development in 1992–93*, World Bank Discussion Paper No. 215 (Washington, D.C.: The World Bank, August 1993), p. 24.

6. Severely indebted countries are those for which either the ratio of the present value of debt service to GNP exceeds 80% or the ratio of the present value of debt service to exports of goods and services exceeds 220%. For moderately indebted countries the ranges of the values of these variables is from 48 to 80% and from 132 to 220% respectively.

7. World Bank, *World Debt Tables 1994–95*, Vol. 1, pp. 55–56.

Table 2: **China's External Debt, 1978–94**

Year	Millions of US$
1978	623
1979	2,183
1980	4,504
1981	5,797
1982	8,358
1983	9,609
1984	12,082
1985	16,722
1986	23,746
1987	35,296
1988	42,362
1989	44,812
1990	52,554
1991	60,851
1992	69,321
1993	83,573
1994	92,806

Sources:
World Bank, *China: Macroeconomic Stability in a Decentralized Economy* (Washington, D.C.: The World Bank, 1994), p. 184. The People's Bank of China, *China Financial Outlook 1994* (Beijing: China Financial Publishing House, 1994), p.58. Xinhua News Agency, "Woguó waizhai changzhailu he zhaiwulu diyu guoji gongren jingjie xian shuiping" ("China's external debt, debt service ratio, and debt-to-export ratio are lower than the international warning levels"), *Renmin ribao (People's Daily)*, 21 July 1995, p. 1.

non-concessionary debt carries favourable interest rates since China is the only transition economy, except for the Czech Republic, that enjoys an investment grade rating on its sovereign debt, allowing it to sell its bonds internationally with a lower interest rate than the market would otherwise demand.[8]

These factors reduce China's debt service, including both amortization and interest payments, below what it would otherwise be. For example, at year-end 1993, of China's total external debt of $83.6 billion, a little over $10 billion was owed to the World Bank and other multilateral

8. Moody's rates China's long-term sovereign debt at A3 while Standard and Poor's gives a rating of BBB. Both are investment grade ratings. Other transition economies that have rated sovereign debt, but which have been assigned below investment grade ratings, are Hungary and Slovakia. *Transition*, Vol. 5, No. 9 (November–December) 1994, p. 13. Both agencies initially assigned ratings to the Bank of China, the Industrial and Commercial Bank, the People's Construction Bank of China, the Bank of Communications, China International Trust and Investment Company (CITIC), and the Guangdong International Trust and Investment Company (GITIC) that were identical to those they gave to China's sovereign debt. However, in April 1995 Moody's downgraded the first four of these to Baa. Prior to that it had watchlisted CITIC for a potential downgrade. Although Baa is still an investment grade rating, the downgrade led the Bank of China to cancel a HK$5 billion floating rate certificate of deposit issue.

lending agencies. A large share of this debt is to the World Bank's soft loan window, the International Development Association (IDA). Loans from IDA bear no interest at all and since 1989 even the initial commitment fee borrowers were once charged has been eliminated.[9] Debt from official bilateral creditors stood at almost $23 billion. Thus borrowing from private creditors on commercial terms comprised only about three-fifths of China's total external debt.

Foreign equity investment. In addition to foreign direct investment and borrowing abroad, China has sold equities for hard currency on both domestic and international markets. The market for B shares in Chinese companies, which are priced in domestic currency but paid for in hard currencies, began in 1992. In that year the B shares of nine companies were listed on the Shanghai stock exchange. Thirteen companies were listed in 1993, with ten more in 1994. By the end of 1994 the B shares of 34 Chinese companies were traded on the Shanghai and Shenzhen stock markets.

Sales of Chinese companies on international markets began in the autumn of 1992 when China Brilliance Automotive was listed on the New York Stock Exchange.[10] At about the same time the Chinese Securities Regulatory Commission approved a plan to list nine Chinese state-owned companies on the Hong Kong Stock Exchange beginning in 1993. More issues were sold in New York in 1993 and 1994. Table 3 shows that the proceeds from the international sale of equities and debt instruments roughly doubled in 1993 compared to the previous year. Based on sales of bonds and equity on international markets to September 1994, proceeds in 1994 probably increased by about 25 per cent over 1993.

The data summarized above suggest that China was awash in foreign capital in the mid-1990s. In 1994 gross capital inflows exceeded $53 billion, including about $17 billion in borrowing from commercial banks, international organizations, bilateral development banks and international bond markets; $34 billion in foreign direct investment; and about $2.5 billion in equity investments. These numbers might suggest that China is heavily dependent on foreign capital to finance investment and thus to generate the rapid economic growth of the 1990s. However, this conclusion would not be warranted. After taking into account outflows of Chinese capital and changes in holdings of foreign exchange, at least to

9. Technically the fee is still set annually by the Executive Directors of the World Bank. But it has been set at zero from fiscal year 1989 to fiscal year 1995.

10. Technically China Brilliance Automotive Holdings Limited is a Bermuda-based holding company, not a Chinese company. However, since the holding company's only asset is a 51% ownership in the Shenyang Jinbei Passenger Vehicle Manufacturing Company, Ltd., for practical purposes it may be regarded as a Chinese company. The holding company was established in 1992, only a few months before the initial public offering of the stock on the New York Stock Exchange. According to some sources the Bermuda holding company was created simply to escape the approvals required by China's Securities Regulatory Commission for overseas listings of Chinese firms.

Table 3: **China's International Equity and Debt Issues, 1991–94** (millions of US$)

	Equity	Debt
1991	11	115
1992	1,049	1,289
1993	1,908	3,184
1994*	1,939	3,134

Notes:
    *To the end of September 1994.
    The value of international equity issues is inclusive of listings of Chinese companies in New York and Hong Kong, the value of B share offerings in Shenzhen and Shanghai, and the value of so-called "back door listings" in which China-backed companies obtain a listing on the Hong Kong Stock Exchange by purchasing a relatively dormant existing listed company. The company then injects assets financed by rights issues and placements. The best examples are Citic Pacific, controlled by Beijing-based CITIC, and Guangdong Investment, controlled by the Guangdong provincial government.
Sources:
    International Monetary Fund, *International Capital Markets: Developments, Prospects, and Policy Issues* (Washington, D.C.: International Monetary Fund, 1994), p. 127. World Bank, *World Debt Tables: External Finance for Developing Countries, 1994– 95* (Washington, D.C.: The World Bank, 1994), Vol. 1, pp. 103, 116–17.

the end of 1994 foreign capital appears to have been an insignificant source of investment in China.

A quick accounting explains the paradox. First, capital inflows may be used to finance a current account deficit (when imports of goods and services exceed exports of goods and services) or may added to the foreign exchange holdings of the government, enterprises or individuals. Secondly, capital inflows must be measured on a net basis, that is, outflows of capital must be taken into account.

The first adjustment is somewhat easier than the adjustment from gross to net. Official holdings of foreign exchange by the People's Bank of China more than doubled in 1994, from $21.2 billion at year-end 1993 to $51.6 billion at year-end 1994.[11] In addition, individual holdings of foreign exchange in the Bank of China and other banks authorized to accept foreign exchange deposits, which since August 1992 have not been included in China's official foreign exchange holdings, grew by about $6 billion in 1994.[12] Retained foreign exchange earnings of the Bank of China and other financial institutions presumably also rose. Thus, holdings of foreign exchange appear to have increased by at least $36 billion in 1994.

11. Zhu Baihua and Ou Yangwei, "Zhongguo waihui chubei yu wubai yi meiyuan" ("China's foreign exchange reserves exceed $US50 billion"), *Renmin ribao* (*People's Daily*), 28 January 1995, p. 1.

12. Personal savings in foreign exchange denominated accounts amounted to some $20 billion at the end of 1994. "BOC says $20b saved in foreign currency," *China Daily*, 11 January 1995, p. 7.

The adjustment from gross to net capital flows is more difficult because of incomplete information. Outflows on the capital account include amortization of previously contracted foreign debt, officially recorded foreign direct investment abroad by Chinese companies and unrecorded capital outflows. Amortization of existing debt was around $7.5 billion in 1994. Official Chinese balance of payments data, which are published with a considerable time lag, show that China's annual foreign direct investment abroad grew steadily from $20 million in 1982 to $913 million by 1991.[13] Most international observers put the actual amount considerably higher. China's foreign direct investment outflows in 1994 may have been about $5–10 billion. This would be roughly consistent with reports of the increases in the stock of Chinese foreign direct investment abroad. Chinese authorities placed cumulative Chinese investment in Hong Kong alone at $19.2 billion by the end of 1994, an amount that is far larger than could be accounted for by China's officially reported capital outflows.[14] Finally, the errors and omissions entry in the balance of payments, presumably largely reflecting unrecorded capital outflows, was $24.9 billion in 1992 and $20.9 billion in 1993.[15] Based on China's current account surplus of $7.7 billion in 1994, the estimated $36 billion increase in foreign exchange holdings, and other known or estimated components of the capital account, unrecorded capital outflows and the net capital inflow can be estimated at $7 to $12 billion and $28.7 billion, respectively.[16] Increases in holdings of foreign reserves more than absorbed net capital inflows. Thus, unless foreign direct investment outflows or unrecorded capital outflows have been overestimated there appears to have been no foreign contribution to capital formation in China in 1994.

Because of the many uncertainties surrounding entries in the capital account in China's balance of payments data, it is instructive to examine China's current account, that is, the balance on trade in goods and services. Ignoring for the moment changes in reserve holdings, any current account deficit (surplus) must be financed with a capital inflow (outflow). In short, net capital inflows must be used either to finance a current account deficit or be added to foreign exchange holdings. Thus, after adjusting for changes in holding of foreign reserves, China's net capital inflows over time can be measured by its cumulative current account deficit.

13. State Statistical Bureau, *1979–1991 Zhongguo duiwai jingji tongji daquan (1979–1991 China Foreign Economic Statistics)* (Beijing: Chinese Statistical Publishing House, 1993), pp. 9–11.

14. New China News Agency, Hong Kong Branch quoted in Hong Kong Economic and Trade Office, *Hong Kong Digest Issue No. 1/95*, pp. 5–6.

15. World Bank, *China: Macroeconomic Stability in a Decentralized Economy* (Washington, D.C.: The World Bank, 1994), p. 14.

16. Net capital inflow equals changes in reserves ($36.4 billion) minus current account surplus ($7.7 billion). Unrecorded capital outflows estimated from: gross capital inflow ($53.2 billion) minus gross capital outflow equals net capital inflow ($28.7 billion) where gross capital outflow is the sum of amortization ($7.5 billion), Chinese foreign direct investment abroad ($5–10 billion) and unrecorded capital outflows.)

Table 4: **China's Current Account, 1978–94** (millions of US$)

1978	− 932
1979	− 2,489
1980	− 3,281
1981	1,319
1982	5,748
1983	4,487
1984	2,509
1985	− 11,810
1986	− 7,334
1987	300
1988	− 3,802
1989	− 4,316
1990	11,997
1991	13,273
1992	6,401
1993	− 11,609
1994	7,660

Sources:
World Bank, *China: Macroeconomic Stability in a Decentralized Economy* (Washington, D.C.: The World Bank, 1994), p. 177. International Monetary Fund, *International Financial Statistics*, June 1995, p. 166. Xinhua News Agency, "Woguo qunian guoji shouzhi zhuangkuang haozhuan" ("China's balance of payments situation improved last year"), *Renmin ribao*, 18 July 1995, p. 1.

Two points emerge from an analysis of the data on China's current account deficit in Table 4. First, on a year-by-year basis China's current account position, whether deficit or surplus, has been relatively small. For example, even China's record current account surplus of about $13 billion in 1991 was only 3.7 per cent of GNP.[17] Moreover, the average current account deficit or surplus over the 12-year period was less than half that of 1991. Thus, China's average annual current account position has been quite modest.

More importantly, over time China's cumulative current account position is insignificant. From the beginning of 1982 to the end of 1993 it was actually a positive $5.846 billion. This does not mean that China experienced a net outflow of capital, for changes in China's foreign exchange reserves have been ignored.

17. World Bank, *China: Macroeconomic Stability in a Decentralized Economy*, p. 14. Even this calculation, since it utilizes the official exchange rate to convert China's GNP in *yuan* into U.S. dollars, overstates the magnitude of the surplus. Taking into account the real purchasing power of the Chinese currency, China's estimated GNP would be at least three times higher and the current account surplus as a percentage of GNP only one-third, or even less, than the 3.7% estimate.

Table 5: **Investment and Savings, selected years** (% Gross Domestic Product)

	1980	1990	1991	1992	1993
Gross domestic investment	30	35	35	38	43
Gross national savings	28	38	39	39	40
Net foreign savings	2	− 3	− 4	− 2	2

Source:
  World Bank, *China: Macroeconomic Stability in a Decentralized Economy*, p. 8.

Over the same period China's total foreign exchange reserves rose by $44.2 billion.[18] Thus China's cumulative capital inflow over the period is the difference between the increase in reserves and the current account surplus or about $38.4 billion. This is a very modest amount, regardless of one's view of the degree to which using the official exchange rate to convert *yuan* to dollars understates the size of China's real GNP. Even using the official exchange rate, which results in the lowest estimate of aggregate output, China's cumulative gross domestic product from 1982 to the end of 1993 was $4,100 billion. Thus cumulative net foreign capital inflows would amount to less than one per cent of cumulative output. Purchasing power parity estimates of Chinese output in 1990 place GDP at from 3.5 to 8 times the level calculated on the exchange rate.[19] If the same relationship holds over the entire period, China's cumulative net capital inflow over 12 years could have been as low as one-tenth of one per cent of Chinese GDP. In short, cumulative net foreign capital inflow relative to cumulative output of the Chinese economy over the 12 years was less than one per cent and may have been vanishingly small.

The same point is borne out by examining data on the relative importance of net foreign savings and gross national saving in financing gross domestic investment. Data for selective years are shown in Table 5. They show that the contribution of net foreign savings to gross domestic investment varies; in some years it is positive and in others negative. Thus, contrary to what one might believe from observing the flood of foreign capital flowing into China, on a net basis such inflows have not contributed to domestic capital formation in China.

Although foreign capital has not made a major impact on China's savings-investment balance, it has contributed significantly to the transfer to China of advanced technology and managerial practices in many industries; to the expansion of China's trade; and indirectly to the supply of foreign exchange.

18. Based on estimated total reserves of $49 billion at year-end 1993 and the official figure of $4.773 billion for year-end 1981. Chinese Finance and Banking Society, *1993 Zhongguo jinrong nianjian (Almanac of China's Finance and Banking 1993)* (Beijing: Zhongguo jinrong nianjian bianjibu (Chinese Finance and Banking Compilation Department), 1993), p. 368.
  19. Lardy, *China in the World Economy*, p. 15.

Table 6: **Exports of Foreign Invested Enterprises, 1985-94**

Year	Millions of US$	Percentage of total exports
1985	320	1.1
1986	480	1.6
1987	1,200	3.0
1988	2,460	5.2
1989	4,920	8.3
1990	7,800	12.5
1991	12,100	16.8
1992	17,400	20.4
1993	25,240	27.5
1994	34,710	28.7

Note:
Exports are inclusive of those produced by equity joint ventures, contractual joint ventures, and wholly foreign-owned firms.
Sources:
Nicholas R. Lardy, "Chinese foreign trade," *The China Quarterly*, No. 131 (September 1992), p. 711. New China News Agency, "Zhongguo duiwai maoyi zongjine qunian zengzhi 1957 yi meiyuan" ("China's foreign trade increases to reach $195.7 billion"), *Renmin ribao*, 10 January 1994. Li Xiaolei, "Sanzi qiye waimao jinchukou zengjia" ("Foreign trade imports and exports of foreign invested enterprises increase"), *Renmin ribao*, 18 January 1995, p. 1.

Effect on foreign trade. The transforming effect of foreign investment on China's economy is revealed in Table 6, which shows exports generated by foreign invested enterprises. The small amounts of foreign direct investment in the late 1970s and early 1980s initially made a negligible contribution to China's total exports. As late as 1985, six years after the passage of China's foreign investment law and five years after the establishment of special economic zones, the exports of foreign invested enterprises were only $320 million, barely over one per cent of China's total exports. From that modest base they expanded dramatically, reaching about $35 billion by 1994, almost 30 per cent of China's total exports.

Exports produced by foreign invested firms are predominantly products assembled from imported parts and components. In addition, many Chinese firms also produce processed exports using parts and components supplied by or purchased from foreign firms. Total processed exports grew to $57 billion in 1994, almost half of China's exports.[20] They comprised about 60 per cent of $100 billion in manufactured goods exports that year. In recent years about half of these exports have been produced by foreign-funded firms.

20. "Wo jiagong maoyi jinchukou qunian tupo qianyi meiyuan" ("China's import and export processing trade broke through the level of US$100 billion last year"), *Renmin ribao*, 23 January 1995, p. 1.

Effect on the supply of foreign exchange. Under the provisions of China's foreign exchange control system, foreign-funded enterprises have had full control of their foreign exchange earnings from exports throughout the reform period. Most importantly, a very large share of the exports of foreign-funded enterprises are processed products such as machinery, electronics and garments. Export earnings are largely used to pay for imported components and assemblies used in the production of these goods. For example, in 1994 foreign-funded firms exported $30.58 billion in processed products but imports of parts, components and the equipment needed to carry out the processing amounted to $28.09 billion.[21]

Despite their heavy expenditures on imported parts and components, foreign-funded firms generally have been net sellers of foreign exchange, first through informal markets and, since 1985, in the swap markets for foreign exchange. Their net sales of foreign exchange rose from $442 million in 1988 to more than $3 billion in 1994.[22]

Foreign Trade

More outwardly oriented economies usually achieve higher rates of savings and investment, and greater efficiency in the use of investment resources, both of which contribute to higher rates of growth. Efficiency gains may accrue not only from economies of scale but, more importantly, from the stimulus that international competition provides for technical change and managerial efficiencies.[23] The World Bank in particular believes that success in the promotion of manufactured exports provides a powerful mechanism for technological upgrading and thus a source of rapid productivity growth in the high performing economies of East Asia.[24]

The pace of growth of Chinese exports shown in Table 7, particularly manufactured exports, compares quite favourably with the countries the World Bank has identified as the high performing economies of East Asia. Not only have China's exports grown more rapidly than those of any other country, the commodity composition has shifted decisively toward manufactured goods. By 1994 China exported manufactured goods worth more than $100 billion and was probably the eighth largest such exporter in the world. At growth rates observed in recent years, by the year 2000 China's exports of manufactured goods will surpass those of the United Kingdom.

What is less clear is whether this growth has stimulated the postulated improvement in productivity in manufacturing that was characteristic of

21. "Processed goods lead exports to new high," *China Daily*, 24 January 1995, p. 5.
22. Nicholas R. Lardy, *Foreign Trade and Economic Reform in China, 1978–1990* (New York: Cambridge University Press, 1992), p. 61. Zhu Baihua, "Wo waihui tizhi gaige qujian chengxiao" ("A preliminary view of the results of China's foreign exchange system reform"), *Renmin ribao*, 20 January 1995, p. 1.
23. Gershon Feder, "On exports and economic growth," *Journal of Development Economics*, No. 1–2 (1983), pp. 60–61.
24. World Bank, *The East Asian Miracle: Economic Growth and Public Policy* (Oxford: Oxford University Press, 1993), pp. 22–23.

Table 7: **Chinese Exports, 1978–94**

Year	Exports Billions of $	Of which manufactured exports Billions of $	% of total exports
1978	9.8	—	—
1979	13.7	—	—
1980	18.2	9,005	49.7
1981	22.0	11,756	53.4
1982	22.3	12,271	55.0
1983	22.2	12,606	56.7
1984	26.1	14,205	54.3
1985	27.4	13,522	49.4
1986	30.9	19,670	63.6
1987	39.4	26,206	66.5
1988	47.5	33,110	69.7
1989	52.5	37,460	71.3
1990	62.1	46,205	74.4
1991	71.8	55,698	77.5
1992	85.0	67,948	79.9
1993	91.8	75,090	81.8
1994	121.0	101,330	83.7

Note:
Data for 1978 and 1979 were compiled by the Ministry of Foreign Economic Relations and Trade. A breakdown of manufactured goods for these years is not available since the Ministry combined data on exports of manufactures and mineral products in a single category.
Sources:
State Statistical Bureau, *Zhongguo tongji nianjian 1993* (*Chinese Statistical Yearbook 1993*) (Beijing: State Statistical Publishing House, 1993), p. 634. "Wo waimao jinchukou zaichuang jiaji" ("China's foreign trade again achieves fine results"), *Renmin ribao*, 14 January 1995, p. 1.

the other high performing economies in East Asia. If enhanced productivity had spread to the state-owned industrial sector, this presumably would be reflected in evidence of increasing ability to compete with foreign firms either in international or domestic markets.

As already suggested, the most impressive export performance in China has been by foreign-funded enterprises and Chinese firms engaged in export processing. For the most part the latter appear to be township and village enterprises rather than state-owned enterprises. Although exports of state-owned manufacturing firms have grown significantly, their contribution to export growth looks quite modest when measured against the share of manufactured goods that they produce. State-owned firms, which produced two-thirds of all manufactured goods in 1985, have contributed a rapidly declining share of annual incremental exports. In 1986 and 1987 they accounted for more than four-fifths of the growth of exports; in 1991–92, when they still accounted for fully half of all manufactured goods production, their contribution was only a fifth.[25]

Foreign invested enterprises contribute such a small share of total manufactured goods output that they are not even listed as a separate category in the industrial output data published by the State Statistical Bureau in its annual *Statistical Yearbook of China*. The output of foreign-funded enterprises, along with that produced by firms with a variety of less important forms of ownership, is included in the category "other," which expanded from about one per cent of output in 1985 to 7 per cent by 1992.[26] Yet the contribution of foreign-funded enterprises to annual incremental exports rose from 4 per cent in 1986 to an average of three-fifths in 1992–94. By 1994 foreign-funded enterprises accounted for 15 times more exports than would have been expected on the basis of their contribution to output.[27] In short, it is not easy to make the case that state-owned firms have become increasingly successful competitors in the international market.

What about in domestic markets? To what extent are state-owned manufacturing firms successfully competing with foreign firms in the Chinese market? A fully satisfactory answer to this question lies well beyond the scope of this article. However, some important evidence, such as the structure of tariff and non-tariff protection that insulates Chinese industry from international competition, does exist.

A World Bank study of China's trade regime showed that Chinese import tariffs in 1992 were relatively high by international standards, particularly for manufactured consumer goods.[28] In addition, China imposes a variety of non-tariff barriers including a mandatory import plan, canalization of imports and import licensing. The sectors with the highest concentration of these non-tariff barriers are iron and steel products, textile yarns and machinery.[29]

An evaluation that takes into account the high degree of dispersion of China's nominal import tariff levels is even more revealing. Economists have long noted that if tariffs are below average on primary and intermediate goods then the effective rate of protection afforded to the final good will be substantially above the nominal tariff rate applied to that good. The World Bank's analysis of effective rates of protection showed that valued added at international prices was negative in 10 of 19 sectors examined, including petroleum refining, machinery, building materials, wood and pulp, food processing, textiles, apparel, paper, and miscellaneous manufactures. This means that under the assumptions of the model "none of these activities would appear to be able to survive under

25. Thomas G. Rawski, "Export performance of China's state industries," unpublished manuscript, March 1994, Table 3.

26. State Statistical Bureau, *Zhongguo tongji nianjian 1993* (*Statistical Yearbook of China 1993*) (Beijing: Chinese Statistical Publishing House, 1993), p. 409. The note defining the scope of the category "other" is at p. 471.

27. Based on the estimate that they account for 2% of manufactured goods output.

28. World Bank, *China: Foreign Trade Reform* (Washington, D.C.: The World Bank, 1994), pp. 55–56.

29. *Ibid.* p. 67.

full trade liberalization."[30] The study quickly adds that, because the analysis is based on quite aggregate categories, it would be incorrect to assume that the production of every good in each of these sectors would wither if subject to the full force of international competition. But the results are "indicative of the highly distorted nature of the Chinese trade regime."[31]

Moreover, even some major industries that have positive value added at international prices are heavily insulated from international competition. For example the chemical industry, China's fourth largest, receives an effective rate of protection from imports of more than 110 per cent.[32] It is difficult to envisage that this industry has begun to feel the effects of international competition.

Chinese assessments of the challenge that would be presented by the reduction of tariff and non-tariff protection that presumably would accompany its participation in the General Agreement on Tariffs and Trade (GATT) generally confirms the analysis of the World Bank. An authoritative analysis of the State Planning Commission's Economic Research Institute reported that if China were to accede to the GATT, "the branches of industry that would take the greatest pounding, in order, are the electronics industry (computers, video cameras, xerographic copiers, colour television tubes, cameras, and broadcast and communications equipment), motor vehicles and trucks, petroleum refining, numerically controlled machine tools, and instruments."[33]

In short, the partial evidence that is available suggests that state-owned industries have not participated proportionately in the growth of China's exports. Since they are heavily insulated from international competition, they also appear ill-prepared to compete with foreign firms in China's domestic market. Thus if productivity has been rising in the state-owned sector in China, it would appear to be stimulated by processes that are quite different from those that were important in other high performing economies in East Asia.

China's Trade Reform Strategy in Comparative Perspective

Any comparative assessment of China's foreign trade and investment reform strategy needs to take into account two respects in which China differed fundamentally from many other transition economies. First, China was never a formal member of the Council of Mutual Economic Assistance (CMEA) and at the time economic reform began in China it had been trading predominantly with Western market economies for almost two decades. Thus it avoided the major disruption of trade

30. *Ibid*. p. 75.
31. *Ibid*. p. 75.
32. *Ibid*. p. 74.
33. State Planning Commission Economics Research Institute Task Force, "Dui huifu guanmao zongxieding diwei hou de xiaoyi fenxi he duice" ("An effective analysis and countermeasures after China resumes its place in the General Agreement on Tariffs and Trade"), *Guoji maoyi* (*International Trade*), No. 2 (1993), p. 10.

associated with the collapse of intra-CMEA trade in the early 1990s, which followed the formal introduction of convertible currency settlements in world prices on 1 January 1991 and the decision to dissolve CMEA in June 1991.[34] In the case of Russia, exports to former CMEA countries fell by more than three-quarters between 1990 and 1992 and imports fell by five-sixths.[35] The collapse of intra-CMEA trade, in turn, was one of the most important factors leading to declining real output in Russia and Eastern Europe.

Secondly, China began its economic reform with virtually no external debt. It had imposed a policy of extreme financial self-reliance, right up until the time economic reform began. Its trade with the rest of the world was small and imports were all financed by export earnings. Thus China had not borrowed significant amounts on international markets.[36]

By contrast the former Soviet Union under Gorbachev between 1987 and 1991 had borrowed heavily from the West to finance its budget deficit. External debt shot up from $14.2 billion at the end of 1984 to $56.5 billion by the end of 1991.[37] However, this borrowing was utilized largely to finance current consumption rather than investment that would contribute to Soviet export earnings. As a result, as early as 1989 the USSR began to delay repayment of some external obligations. By the end of 1991, when Russia had become an independent sovereign entity, its unpaid international obligations were around $6 billion.[38] Although it was already in default on its debt, Russia assumed responsibility for almost all the debts of the former Soviet Union which, it was revealed in late 1994, meant year-end 1991 total external indebtedness was $103.9 billion. As a result of IMF and World Bank lending and modest amounts of official commodity credits from Western governments, by mid-1995 Russian external debt amounted to $130 billion.[39] Since this was more than twice the value of its exports outside the FSU, Russia sought to reach an agreement on rescheduling payments on outstanding debts from the Soviet era, which would presumably facilitate its return to international debt markets. In short, Russia was handicapped in its transition since its huge existing prior debt plus falling exports meant that debt rescheduling, if not default, was almost inevitable. That in turn deprived Russia of access to commercial credit in the early years of its economic transition.

China's strategy of external reform was quite gradual. Key institutional reforms, such as ending the monopoly powers of state-owned trading companies, were phased in over more than a decade.[40] Even as

34. Harriet Matejka, "Post-CMEA trade and payments arrangements in the East," in Jozef M. van Brabant (ed.), *The New Eastern Europe and the World Economy* (Boulder, CO: Westview, 1993), p. 63.

35. Anders Aslund, *How Russia Became a Market Economy* (Washington, D.C.: The Brookings Institution, 1995), p. 46.

36. China's borrowing in the pre-reform period was limited to short-term trade financing.

37. Aslund, *How Russia Became a Market Economy*, p. 49.

38. *Ibid.* p. 50.

39. John Thornhill and Andrew Fisher, "Russia pleads for easier payment of Soviet debts," *The Financial Times*, 6 July 1995, p. 2.

40. Lardy, *Foreign Trade and Economic Reform*, pp. 39–41.

late as 1993 only 839 Chinese manufacturing companies had been granted the right to trade directly in the international market.[41] By contrast in Russia all firms were given the right of direct international trade almost from the outset of reform in January 1992.[42] Similarly the process of convergence of Chinese domestic with international prices for traded goods lasted well into the 1990s whereas, with a few exceptions, prices were liberalized in Russia within a year or so of the break-up of the Soviet Union. The story is similar on import subsidies. As a percentage of gross domestic product they were initially much larger in Russia, but they were abolished in 1994. In China they persisted well beyond the first decade of reform.

China's comparatively gradualistic approach in the external sector was appropriate, given its initial economic conditions and the slow pace of reform in the domestic economy, particularly in the state-owned manufacturing sector. The immediate freeing of all prices in an environment in which state-owned enterprises were still not subject to hard budget constraints would have led, as it did in Russia, to skyrocketing prices for industrial goods. For the same reason moving rapidly to current account convertibility would have caused massive excessive devaluation of the *renminbi*. In short, application of the Russian model in China probably would have created severe macroeconomic imbalances.[43]

The challenge China faces now is to co-ordinate the further liberalization of its trade regime, particularly reducing various barriers to imports, with the reform of the state-owned sector, especially in manufacturing. Subsidies to state-owned enterprises, increasingly in the form of bank loans that are not repaid, absorbed about 10 per cent of gross domestic product in 1993, "an unsustainable structural situation" according to the World Bank.[44] Reform in the state-owned sector will require a substantial degree of industrial restructuring, a process that has been largely postponed.[45] Liberalization of China's import regime, which would subject Chinese firms to increasing international competition, should be an important tool to facilitate industrial restructuring.

Conclusion

Despite the impressive expansion of exports, large inflows of foreign direct investment and access to international capital markets that is

41. "The Ministry of Foreign Economic Relations and Trade quickens the approval of foreign trading rights of production enterprises," *Guoji shangbao* (*International Business*), 9 February 1993, p. 1. At the end of 1992 China had 8.61 million industrial enterprises of which 1.03 million were state-owned.

42. Aslund, *How Russia Became a Market Economy*, p. 147.

43. Ronald I. McKinnon, *The Order of Economic Liberalization: Financial Control in the Transition to a Market Economy* (Baltimore: The Johns Hopkins University Press, 1993), pp. 217–225.

44. Harry Broadman, *Meeting the Challenge of Chinese Enterprise Reform*, World Bank Discussion Paper No. 283 (Washington, D.C.: The World Bank, 1995), pp. 15–16.

45. Nicholas R. Lardy, "Trade expansion and domestic structural adjustment in China, Japan, and the United States," paper presented at the Trilateral Workshop, Beijing, October 1995.

unparalleled among transition economies, it is still premature to judge that China's external sector reforms have been a stunning success in comparison with others. China has had rapid export growth, but this has depended to an unprecedented degree on foreign invested firms. There is nothing wrong with reliance on foreign-funded enterprises, *per se*. But, combined with the protection provided to state-owned industries, it has inhibited productivity growth, especially in intermediate input industries where prices are still above international levels.[46] Thus rapid export growth from foreign invested firms, a large share of which is export processing, has limited backward linkages and the domestic content of exports is very low. To some extent export industries appear to be enclaves and China's state-owned industries have underparticipated in export growth by a wide margin. Over the longer term it will be difficult for China to sustain the growth of exports at a rate anywhere near that of the past decade unless there is widespread industrial restructuring.

China in recent years has attracted far more foreign direct investment than all the other transition economies combined. But, as already noted above, such investment in China is substantially overstated because of the recycling phenomenon. Moreover, the real difference that remains after correcting for this factor may reflect primarily the relatively early stage of the economic transitions of the former Soviet Union and Eastern Europe. As the data in Table 1 reflect, foreign direct investment in China in the first decade of reform was quite modest compared to the inflows recorded in the early 1990s. Foreign direct investment in the six countries of Eastern Europe was $2.4 billion, $3.3 billion and $5.0 billion in 1991–93, amounts that compare quite favourably with direct foreign investment in China at a comparable stage of its transition a decade earlier.[47]

Finally, China's better access to international capital markets was at least partially due to its lack of pre-reform borrowing. At the outset of their reforms Russia, Bulgaria and Poland struggled to generate trade surpluses in order to service debts accrued under old regimes. Ultimately they defaulted and so access to international capital markets was limited to debt restructurings, lending by international organizations and credits extended by Western governments to promote their own exports. By contrast China, with ready access to international borrowing, enjoyed the luxury of running relatively large trade deficits in the first three years of economic reform.[48]

Moreover, China's access to international capital has improved over time. The sale of equities on international markets, for example, did not start until 1992 and bond sales were relatively modest until the same

---

46. World Bank, *China: Foreign Trade Reform*, p. 77. Vinod Thomas, "China: assuming its role in global trading," unpublished manuscript, 1994, p. 8. World Bank, *China Updating Economic Memorandum: Managing Rapid Growth and Transition* (Washington, D.C.: The World Bank, 1993), p. 55.

47. Barry P. Bosworth and Gur Ofer, *Reforming Planned Economies in an Integrating World Economy* (Washington, D.C.: The Brookings Institution, 1995), p. 140.

48. Lardy, *China in the World Economy*, p. 30.

year.[49] Again that suggests, as in the case of foreign direct investment, that the access to international capital markets of other transition economies may compare more favourably to China after their reforms are a decade and a half old.

49. *Ibid.* pp. 60–62.

China's Macroeconomy in Transition

Barry Naughton

Is macroeconomic stability the Achilles heel of the Chinese economy? Recurrent bouts of inflationary disorder lead some observers to worry that the Chinese government is unable to control the economy. Macroeconomic difficulties show up in a pattern of repeated boom and bust cycles, in which each boom is accompanied by an acute inflationary phase and significant disruption. Moreover, since the reform era began, the peak annual inflation rate of each successive cycle has been higher than that of the preceding one.[1] The most recent attempts to cool off the economy have only led to additional questions. An austerity policy was decreed at the end of June 1993, yet inflation actually accelerated in 1994, and it was not until mid-1995 that it dropped to the levels of mid-1993. The Chinese government was engaged in a quest for an economic "soft landing" for two years without a net reduction in the inflation rate!

Macroeconomic issues also attract attention because of their link to broader questions about the future of Chinese society. For centuries, China has been plagued by the two extremes of dictatorship and chaos. Today, it has thrown off the main institutions of economic dictatorship – the system of central planning – and has created the rudiments of a market economy. But it is possible that the improved economic conditions produced by reform will be threatened by a descent into economic chaos? More broadly, it is obvious that the Chinese political system has not achieved real legitimacy or widespread support among the population. The current government is woefully inadequate to cope with the growing diversity and emergent political demands of Chinese society. In this context, macroeconomic instability often seems to stand in for the spectre of broader social unrest. During the period when the government is temporarily able to maintain direct political control over a changing society, macroeconomic weakness is brought in to demonstrate the paradoxical weakness that shadows this apparently strong government.[2]

Even on more narrowly economic grounds, it is common to view China as lacking the macroeconomic institutions required to manage a market economy, thus having little protection from economic disorder. Economics-based approaches may stress the relative strength of local governments and their client enterprises[3]; or they may deduce problems from the

1. Inflation, as measured by the retail price index, peaked at 6.0% in 1980, 8.8% in 1985, 18.5% in 1988 and 21.7% in 1994.

2. Kathleen Hartford, "The political economy behind Beijing Spring," in Tony Saich (ed.), *The Chinese People's Movement: Perspectives on Spring 1989* (Armonk, NY: M. E. Sharpe, 1990), pp. 50–82. Hartford's reasoned arguments become grotesques in Richard Hornik, "Bursting China's bubble: the Muddle Kingdom," *Foreign Affairs*, Vol. 73, No. 3 (1994), pp. 28–42.

3. For example Christine Wong argues, "In the 1990s, the tenuous hold of the central government over macroeconomic control is under assault, with traditional administrative

evolution of macroeconomic magnitudes such as central government budgetary revenues (which are declining) or central bank lending (which fluctuates but is sometimes large).[4] These views are useful in directing attention to a crucial unresolved area in China's economic reform process. It is indeed true that reform of the institutions of macroeconomic control is currently the most urgent need in the reform process, as well as one of the most difficult. However, this article argues that it is simply not the case that the Chinese central government is a feeble state, bereft of effective instruments of macroeconomic control and doomed to a process of economic disintegration. Indeed, anyone who sees the Chinese central government *solely* as a weak government is seriously misperceiving the situation. Instead, the Chinese central government combines paradoxical elements of strength and weakness, and attempts to achieve multiple and sometimes conflicting objectives, including some that require ambitious intervention in the economy.

This combination of conflicting and paradoxical elements often results in inconsistent or destabilizing policies. But there is nothing in the fundamental characteristics of China's macroeconomy that dooms the effort of reformers to establish a stable and consistent policy package. The macroeconomy is *not* the Achilles heel of the reform process. Instead, it is argued that the quest for macroeconomy stability should be seen as an inherently extremely difficult process in a transitional economy. On balance, China has done reasonably well: probably better than anyone had any right to expect. But there are still serious challenges facing policy-makers, and these challenges will become much more formidable if the political process breaks down after the death of Deng Xiaoping.

This article addresses a few of the many issues relating to Chinese macroeconomic policy. The first section details the basic conditions that structure China's macroeconomic problems. Most important is the remarkable shrinkage in the size of the state budget, caused by the rapid entry of new firms that has led to increased competition and the erosion of the previously protected monopoly profits of state-owned enterprises (SOEs) in industry and trade. This process has also led to a distinct division of labour between state and non-state firms across industrial sectors. The second section shows that the retreat of the state from most spheres of the economy has not been accompanied by a similar reduction in state fixed investment. On the contrary, the state has maintained a

---

footnote continued

restraints … rapidly losing potency, while effective indirect mechanisms are slow in developing. Local governments have led this assault." "China's economy: the limits of gradualist reform," in William A. Joseph (ed.), *China Briefing 1994* (Boulder: Westview Press, 1994), p. 50.

4. A recent World Bank report, *China: Country Economic Memorandum: Macroeconomic Stability in a Decentralized Economy* (26 October 1994), argues that People's Bank of China (PBC) lending represents a hidden budget deficit and attempts to quantify it. PBC lending to state banks has been large since 1988, but soared to 8.5% of GDP in 1993. The World Bank authors guess that 60–80% of this is for "policy loans" (i.e. government ordered spending) and reclassify it as additional deficit spending (see n. 20, below).

vigorous and intrusive role in investment, actually growing in the past few years (1992–94). In the third section, the enormous pressures on the banking system created by shrinking state revenues and large state investment are described. The fourth section discusses two other problems that disrupt macroeconomic stability: deficit SOEs and new problems related to the maintenance of external balance. The final section includes a few predictions about future policy and stability.

The article's conclusions can be summarized as follows. First, the overall process of macroeconomic policy-making does not reveal a government bereft of effective instruments. Rather, it shows a government whose policies are clumsy and often delayed, but which eventually responds and achieves results. Secondly, because current problems are difficult and are not about to disappear, continued recurrent inflationary bouts and instability can be expected. This is not because the government is without instruments, but because it is subject to intense, often contradictory, pressures in complex situations, and will inevitably make mistakes. Thirdly, financial reform is a focus of current contradictions and the main area where radical economic reforms are needed. Many of the required measures and institutions have been proclaimed – such as central bank independence – but the point is to make them actually work. When it is considered that the key economic fundamentals are in place – with high domestic saving, rapid growth and the institutional outlines in place – there are some grounds for optimism despite the formidable problems.

The Context of Evolutionary Reform

Even in a developed market economy, macroeconomic policy-making is difficult and often surrounded by controversy. In the United States, the Federal Reserve Board possesses abundant sources of information and controls powerful instruments to intervene in sophisticated capital markets. Moreover, the Federal Reserve Board possesses a relatively straightforward and unitary objective: maintaining price stability. Despite these advantages, hundreds of millions of dollars are spent annually anticipating and placing wagers on policy moves by "the Fed." In a formerly socialist transitional economy, little of the sophisticated institutional apparatus of macroeconomic policy implementation is available. The absence of well-functioning institutions not only makes it more difficult to achieve price stability, it also complicates the overall process by requiring policy-makers to pay attention to multiple objectives. While policy-makers in China or other transitional economies strive for price stability, they must also foster new financial institutions. Fundamentally, financial institutions exist to channel saving into investment, which is necessary for economic growth. Yet in the course of reform, these institutions must undergo massive change. Macroeconomic policy-makers must thus strive for price stability, insure investment finance through existing institutions and reform those institutions. Inevitably, these complex objectives generate conflicts.

The basic context within which the changing role of planners and macroeconomic institutions in China must be placed is the process of marketization and the overall evolutionary reform strategy of "growing out of the plan."[5] In the unreformed economy, planners had direct control over saving and investment. Virtually all national saving was carried out in the state sector, more particularly in state manufacturing enterprises. Those enterprises operated in a protected environment, with prices set at generous levels by the government, and they earned very large profits. They remitted almost all their surpluses to the government budget. Household savings were small, so the allocation of government investment funds by the central planners basically determined the economy-wide balance between saving and investment. What is traditionally thought of as monetary policy (supply of money and credit and establishment of interest rates) was not very important in the planned economy. Prudent fiscal policy was all that was required, and in practice this meant setting the growth of state investment at sustainable levels.

The most crucial step in economic reform was the ending of the government monopoly over the economy, and especially over industrial production and investment. The industrial system was changed by entry of new producers, including township and village enterprises, private firms and new locally-run state firms. Not surprisingly, entry was most rapid in those sectors where profits were high, as was true generally in manufacturing. Competition eroded the huge surpluses that state firms had been accustomed to earning, thus upsetting government budgets and the entire balance of saving and investment in the economy. Many of the government institutional and policy changes that marked the reform era can be seen as responses to this changing environment.

With this came massive change in the role of the government budget. In 1978, government budgetary revenues at all levels came to 35.5 per cent of gross national product (GNP); according to preliminary figures, in 1994 the comparable figure was only 12.7 per cent.[6] Scaled to GNP, budgetary revenues have fallen steadily to about one-third of their 1978 level. Under the pressure of this erosion in revenues, budgetary expenditures have been cut back as well. Overt deficits have been kept to moderate levels: between 2 and 3 per cent of GNP in most years, including 1994. Deficits of this size are not in themselves enough to destabilize an economy, but they are enough largely to eliminate the ability of policy-makers to use "fiscal policy" to affect the macroeconomy. Policy-makers don't have the revenue available to reduce the deficit, and they don't dare run a larger deficit for fear that this would signal economic difficulties. Budgetary authorities have therefore been forced to resign themselves to simply managing the decline in revenues

5. Barry Naughton, *Growing Out of the Plan: Chinese Economic Reform, 1978–1993* (New York: Cambridge University Press, 1995).

6. Liu Zhongli, "Report on the implementation of the state budget for 1994 and on the draft central and local budgets for 1995," *Beijing Review*, 3–16 April, 1995, pp. VI–VIII. *Zhongguo tongji nianjian 1994 (China Statistical Yearbook 1994)* (Beijing: Zhongguo tongji chubanshe, 1994), pp. 213–221; Naughton, *Growing Out of the Plan*, pp. 337–39.

and expenditures in an orderly fashion.[7] Previously, only fiscal policy was important; since reform, fiscal policy has been rendered impotent. By contrast, whereas monetary policy used to be fairly trivial, today only monetary policy can really matter for macroeconomic stability.

Since revenues and expenditures are closely related, Figure 1 displays only budgetary expenditures. Two facts emerge clearly. First, the reduction in overall budgetary outlays has been massive and sustained: from 35 per cent to just below 15 per cent of GNP. Secondly, perhaps even more surprisingly, the changes have had very little overall quantitative impact on what might be thought of as "ordinary government," that is, the category of government expenditures labelled "current expenditures" in Figure 1. Reductions in expenditures have been concentrated in investment, defence outlays and subsidies. Budgetary outlays for investment were at their highest in 1978 at 16.2 per cent of GNP and have declined steadily since to only 2.7 per cent of GNP in 1994. Military expenditures peaked in 1979 at 5.6 per cent of GNP and generally declined – notwithstanding a blip in 1989–90 – to 1.3 per cent of GNP in 1994. And subsidies – lumping together price subsidies and subventions to loss-making SOEs – peaked in 1981 at 8.2 per cent of GNP and declined to 1.5 per cent of GNP by 1994.[8] By contrast, government current expenditures have been maintained at almost exactly 10 per cent of GNP throughout the entire reform era.[9] Thus, despite the dramatic decline in revenues, the share of GNP going to administration, education and other ordinary government has been sustained.[10]

The majority of the decline in budgetary revenues is clearly as a result of remittances from industrial SOEs plummeting. Until the end of 1993 this decline was understandable given the absence of tax reform and the continuing reliance on the old budgetary system, under which SOE profit remittances funded the bulk of government activities. Since 1 January 1994, however, a new tax system has been established that nominally has many of the desirable characteristics of a modern system. It creates a nearly uniform value-added tax and a profit tax that applies equally to all

7. In this sense, Chinese policy-makers are in the same position as American policy-makers or those of most other countries. Very few countries are currently able to use fiscal policy as a flexible element of overall macroeconomic policy.

8. There are numerous issues relating to budgetary data that cannot be discussed here. Real military outlays are substantially greater than budgetary data reveal, both because the military controls revenue off the books, and because some military expenses are "buried" under other headings. In addition, Chinese budgetary data do not cover social security expenditures by SOEs which are significant. There are many types of "extra-budgetary" funds: the majority are best described as enterprise funds, but some are more like fiscal revenues and ought to be included in budgetary accounts.

9. The different evolution of different functional components of expenditures explains some of the changing relation between central and local government. The central government is responsible for most investment and defence, while local governments are responsible for most current expenditures. Thus a decline in investment and defence relative to current outlays implies a decreasing central government share of expenditures, all else constant.

10. It is true that the share of GNP channelled through the budget to education, health and other expenditures should be increased, and that maintenance of the pre-reform share of GNP is inadequate. The point here is simply to argue that, on balance, these outlays have been shielded from the worst effects of eroding budgetary resources.

Figure 1: **Evolution of Budgetary Expenditures (% of GNP)**

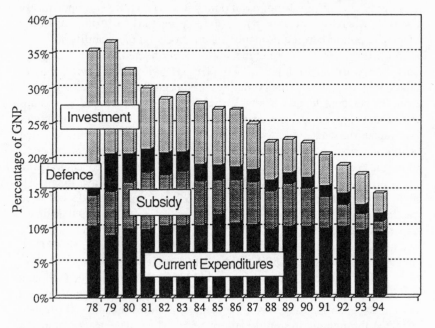

Sources:

   Zhongguo tongji nianjian 1994 (Statistical Yearbook of China 1994) (Beijing: Zhongguo tongji chubanshe, 1994), p. 217; Liu Zhongli, "Report on the implementation of the state budget for 1994 and on the draft central and local budgets for 1995," *Beijing Review*, 3–16 April, 1995, pp. VI–VIII.

ownership forms.[11] However, it has thus far been unable to slow the fall in government revenues. Not only did 1994 continue the pattern of declining revenues established in previous years, there are also ominous signs that revenue collection in the first half of 1995 was even slower than in 1994.[12]

As described above, it might appear that the decline in budgetary revenues was a purely negative phenomenon: government saving declined, and fewer resources were available for public investment and services. There was, though, another side to the story. By permitting entry into lucrative manufacturing and trade sectors, the government created new opportunities for private and local interests, and investment by households and non-state enterprises increased. In order to finance those investments, these entities increased their saving as well, and this compensated for much of the reduction in government saving.[13] Non-state firms stepped up their internal saving as SOEs were forced to reduce

11. Tsang Shu-ki and Cheng Yuk-shing, "China's tax reform of 1994: breakthrough or compromise?" *Asian Survey*, Vol. 34, No. 9 (September 1994), pp. 769–788.
   12. "China shows early signs of missing deficit goal," *Reuter*, 13 July 1995, electronically transmitted.
   13. Naughton, *Growing Out of the Plan*, pp. 142–44.

theirs. As these decentralized entities invested more in the economy, they took over many activities that had previously been dominated by the government. Thus although the government had fewer resources to invest, the need for it to finance all types of investment was eliminated. Moreover, the economy benefited from de-monopolization. It became more diverse and resilient, and developed stronger self-regulating mechanisms, as some decisions were taken out of the hands of central planners.

New division of labour. The result has been the emergence of a *de facto* division of labour between competitive sectors with investment from non-state enterprises, and non-competitive (or not fully competitive) sectors that continue to be dominated by state investment and especially by central government activity. This division of labour began to emerge in the early 1980s, and developed steadily in the 1990s. Figure 2 displays one way to look at it. Industrial sectors are arranged in three groups, roughly according to the share of SOEs in gross output.[14] At the top are the non-competitive sectors, in which state output is dominant. Most prominent are the natural resource sectors and utilities, where the government has simply decreed that SOEs will retain a monopoly or near-monopoly position. The remaining sectors are the heavy materials industries that exhibit substantial economies of scale (such as steel and chemicals). In these sectors, the entry of new producers has not fundamentally altered the ownership structure, because of both administrative regulation and economic factors.

A second group comprises three sectors – tobacco, food processing and beverages – in which SOEs are still extremely important. The government continues to control a large part of the agricultural procurements required as inputs, and it reserves these inputs for SOEs. In some cases, such as cigarettes, the national government intentionally maintains control in order to protect revenues. In other cases control is decentralized, but local agencies cling to it to generate revenues for client enterprises. As a result of these lingering distortions, these sectors are not fully competitive either.

The third group is the competitive sector which makes up the largest part of Chinese industry. The sectors classified as competitive make up 53 per cent of industrial output in the data shown in Figure 2, and an even larger proportion of total industrial output including very small-scale firms. The share of competitive sector output produced by SOEs is quite modest: only 27 per cent of the covered output. Yet these competitive sectors account for fully 71 per cent of the output of non-state firms

14. Chinese authorities do not publish a breakdown of all industrial output. The data in Figure 2 are calculated by summing the data on independent accounting enterprises and village-run collectives, for which sectoral and ownership breakdowns are available. *Zhongguo tongji nianjian 1994*, pp. 373, 378, 388, 395. The data shown account for 88% of all industrial output. SOEs account for 48% of this output, compared with the 43% of total output they are known to account for. Of the output excluded from Figure 2, SOEs account for only 10% and non-state firms, mostly small-scale private firms, account for 90%. Compare Richard F. Garbaccio, *Reform and Structural Change in the Chinese Economy: A CGE Analysis*, Ph.D. dissertation, University of California, Berkeley, May 1994, pp. 102, 106–107.

Figure 2: **Ownership Structure of Industrial Sectors (% of Gross Output Produced by SOEs)**

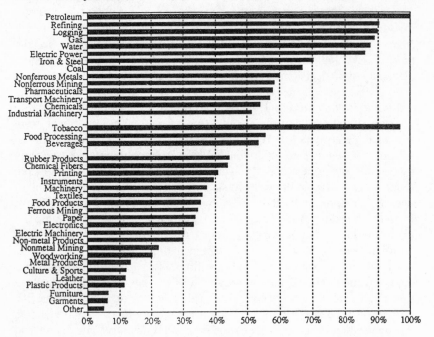

Source:
Zhongguo tongji nianjian 1994, pp. 373, 378, 388, 395. See discussion in nn. 14 and 15.

covered. Put another way, a large majority of non-state industrial output is in the competitive sector, which is most of Chinese industry. Conversely, a large majority of state industrial output is in non-competitive sectors: these account for more than two-thirds of SOE output and SOEs produce about two-thirds of the output of these sectors. The non-competitive sectors represent a minority of Chinese industry, but account for the bulk of resource extraction, utilities and capital intensive materials industry. In this respect, the Chinese state sector is beginning to resemble the state sector in other mixed market economies, with a strong tendency to concentrate on infrastructure and a few heavy industrial sectors.

This division of labour occurred as the result of a complex process. On one hand, new entrants were able successfully to out-compete state firms in some competitive sectors. Output of competitive sectors grew and the need for government investment there was reduced. On the other hand, with robust economic growth, the need for government investment in public goods and infrastructure *increased*. The result was pressure on government to concentrate investment on infrastructure provision and strategic industrial sectors. The initial government response stressed primary energy production (given China's severe energy crisis in the early 1980s), but gradually the emphasis shifted to infrastructure. Central government planning did not cease, but it was focused on a narrower range of activities, the scope of which was determined by the growth of market forces.

Intervention in Investment

Does the rapid decline in government (and SOE) saving and state investment financed through the budget, as documented above, mean that overall investment in state-owned units declined as well? In fact, contrary to what might be supposed, overall state investment has remained large and even increased in the 1990s. The contrast between high and rising state investment and low and declining state financing for investment represents the fundamental conflict underlying macroeconomic policy decisions. This section examines overall quantitative trends in government investment, their sectoral impacts and the implication for understanding central and local government roles in the economy.

Quantitative investment trends. From a starting point in 1978 where nearly all fixed investment was in the state sector, the state share of fixed investment first dropped quickly and then declined more slowly until the end of 1988. However, this reduction was not sustained. In 1985, the state accounted for two-thirds of both total fixed investment and total industrial output. After 1989, the state share of industrial output continued to decline, reaching 40 per cent in 1994, but its share of investment remained stubbornly high, and even increased to 69 per cent in 1994.[15] A significant part of this investment, particularly during the 1990s, went to support infrastructure construction. China has experienced extremely rapid rates of overall economic growth, which would have been inconceivable without generally adequate provision of infrastructure. Although bottlenecks have repeatedly re-emerged under the pressure of rapid growth, government investment has generally been sufficient to overcome them and prevent growth from faltering. Adequate provision of infrastructure must be considered the second key element of successful Chinese growth policy, along with vigorous entry and investment in competitive sectors. These have enabled a self-sustaining growth process to become established during the course of transition from a planned to a market economy.

Figure 3 provides a general view of government investment in physical infrastructure and social sector fixed capital.[16] Infrastructure investment

15. *Zhongguo tongji nianjian, 1994*, pp. 140–41; *China's Latest Economic Statistics* (Hong Kong: China Statistics Information Consultancy Service Centre, January 1995). The shares are not directly comparable, since the investment figures include non-industrial investment and also lump joint-venture investment in with the state sector if an SOE is a joint venture partner. A correction to make the data comparable is possible for 1993 and would reduce the state investment share to 61.5%. The trends are quite robust, however.

16. The following discussion defines infrastructure as consisting of (1) electric power; (2) transportation; (3) telecommunications; (4) urban water supply; and (5) rural water conservation. Social sector investment comprises (6) education construction and (7) health and welfare construction.

Figure 3: **Infrastructure Investment**

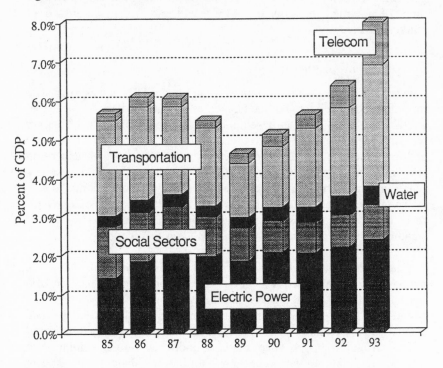

Sources:
    Zhongguo tongji nianjian 1994, pp. 148–49; 16–61. *Zhongguo guding zichan touzi tongji ziliao* (*China Fixed Capital Investment Statistical Materials*) (Beijing: Zhongguo tongji chubanshe, various years).

(physical and social) surpassed 5 per cent of GDP in 1984, and has been maintained at that level since, except in 1989. Since 1992, spending of this type has grown extremely rapidly, and it reached 8 per cent of GDP in 1993. Excluding the social sectors, physical infrastructure expenditure reached 6.5 per cent of GDP in 1993, well above the average of developing countries (4 per cent) and close to the 7 per cent "recommended" by the World Bank.[17] Only in the social sectors has performance seriously lagged: investment eroded from 1.3 per cent of GDP in 1985 to only 0.9 per cent in 1993. Weak social sector investment is attributable to the state's continuing fiscal difficulties and the absence of alternative financing arrangements.

Central and local government investment. The pattern of a continued high level of state investment requires a closer look at the role of central and local governments, since both are included in the general category of state investment. The categories of "central" and "local" are not sym-

17. World Bank, *World Development Report 1994* (Washington, D.C.: International Bank for Reconstruction and Development, 1994).

metrical. Central government investment is co-ordinated through the State Planning Commission, generally reflects central government policy and is roughly equivalent to government investment in other developing countries. By contrast, local investment in state-owned units is the aggregate of investment by local governments as such (for example, urban infrastructure investment), and of state-owned enterprises nominally under the authority of local governments.[18] In practice, many of those state-owned enterprises have gained substantial autonomy in recent years, and their activities correspond to that of parastatals in other developing countries. Moreover, local state-owned unit investment includes investment under the supervision of governments ranging from provinces – which have populations of up to 110 million people – down to counties and even occasionally townships with total populations of only 100,000. It is thus exceptionally difficult to generalize about local state investment in China.

A majority of state investment is local: about 60 per cent in recent years, but slightly higher in 1993–94. Despite ongoing decentralization, central government investment has remained substantial. In 1978, before reform began, investment in central government projects amounted to 8.7 per cent of GDP, and in 1993 it was 8.6 per cent; 1994 preliminary figures indicate a similar 8.3 per cent (see Figure 4). Local government investment increased significantly early in the reform era, and it also fluctuates more than that in central government. Before reform, in 1978, investment in local government projects was 9.9 per cent of GDP, and after considerable fluctuation equalled 17.0 per cent of GDP in 1994. Together, central and local governments invested a whopping 25.3 per cent of GDP in state-owned units under their control in 1994 (down slightly from the total in 1993). These state investment rates are higher than any other period of the PRC outside the Great Leap Forward.[19]

The sectoral composition of central and local state investment differ substantially. The Centre devotes 37 per cent of its investment to infrastructure, including the bulk of that in power and telecom; in addition, it provides nearly all of that in primary energy (coal, gas and oil), which accounts for 23 per cent of its investment. Some 12 per cent of its investment is spent on scientific research and "other," both of which presumably involve national security. As a result, in the central government's investment outlays, infrastructure, primary energy and "science and other" together account for 72 per cent. Only 28 per cent is available for all other uses, and in practice much of this is taken up by investments in industrial sectors characterized by substantial economies of scale: metallurgy, chemicals and transportation equipment. The central government invests almost nothing in the competitive sectors shown in Figure 2. By contrast, local governments commit almost nothing to primary

18. All "state" investment in China is classified according to the level of subordination of the enterprise with the primary responsibility for the investment project, regardless of actual financial participation, which can be more complicated.
19. Central investment is slightly understated since all housing has been deemed local.

Figure 4: **Fixed Investment: Total and State Investment**

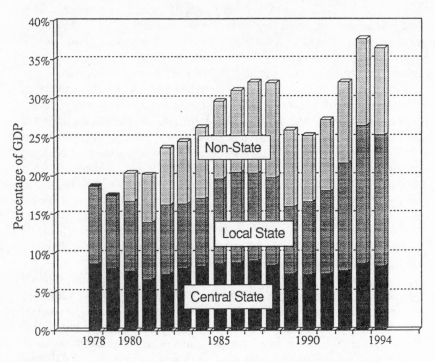

Sources:

   Zhongguo guding zichan touzi tongji ziliao, various years. *China's Latest Economic Statistics* (Hong Kong: China Statistics Information Consultancy Service Centre), January 1995; February 1995.

energy and "science and other," and about 25 per cent to infrastructure (especially transport, water and social infrastructures). In total, only 30 per cent of state investment under local control goes to infrastructure, energy, and "science and other." Locals have 70 per cent available for other uses, and while they also invest in metallurgy, chemicals and machinery, they have substantial funds available for competitive sectors.

   Strengthening of traditional planning organs. One consequence of the increased level of government investment in the 1990s has been a strengthening of the traditional planning organs, especially the State Planning Commission (SPC), where until 1989 the tendency had been for these to lose influence. The traditional plan was frozen and then shrank, greatly limiting the discretionary power of the State Planning Commission. At the same time, alternative centres of economic expertise and forecasting advice developed in the semi-autonomous "think tanks" set up under Zhao Ziyang's auspices. Since 1989, though, planners have become more confident and more interventionist. They have sought to reinvent themselves as guardians of the public interest and agents of a national industrial policy, based on their interpretation of Japanese and

Korean experience. Industrial policy has been popular – at least within government – and the SPC has been able to ride a "hot" agenda item back into political influence. In addition, the SPC's renewed influence reflects the weakening, and in some cases elimination, of alternative centres of economic policy-making advice in the wake of June 1989.

Increasing infrastructure investment in the 1990s is thus part of a broader process of increasing central government intervention in the investment process. While traditional allocation of materials is no longer a significant part of SPC power, substantial instruments are used primarily to shape the flows of investment. These include:

- In consultation with the Ministry of Finance, setting the aggregate quantities of budgetary investment; and in consultation with the People's Bank of China, setting the quotas for bank lending for fixed investment.
- Allocation of budgetary grants for capital construction (technical transformation grants are allocated either by the Economics and Trade Commission or by individual ministries).
- Allocation of a large proportion of bank credits for fixed investment projects, the amount of which fluctuates, but has probably been above half of state bank fixed investment lending in the past two years.
- Allocation of that portion of foreign exchange earnings that are under central government control.

Yet the technical capabilities of the SPC are far more limited than their Japanese or Korean counterparts. In practice, the SPC is more like a broker than a steerer. It does not have detailed project planning capabilities, nor does it have great skills in project evaluation or economic analysis. There is a mis-match between capability and ambition at the SPC level.

Pressures on the Banking System

The preceding sections have shown that there is a fundamental tension between the disappearance of government saving and continued high levels of investment in SOEs. Where does the money come from to fund state investment? Fixed investment is now predominantly funded by a combination of bank loans and various types of retained and earmarked funds. The banking system, in particular, channels financial surpluses (savings) from the household sector to the enterprise sector, a process known as "intermediation." Thus, the Chinese financial system increasingly resembles that in a developing market economy. It is entirely normal that investment be funded through a combination of retained earnings and bank credit derived from household saving balances. However, the financial system is highly distorted by the continuing pressure from the government to provide funds for its priority projects (at both central and local government levels). This is evident both in the banking system and in the disposition of retained funds. Large sums of money are retained within the government sector, either within SOEs or as various types of earmarked funds, and these are intermediated by government bodies outside the formal banking system. Thus both the banking system and the system for using retained funds are influenced to a high degree by government officials at the central and local levels.

An overview of investment financing is provided in Table 1. In the investment statistics, various types of retained funds and informal loans are lumped into the category of "own funds" (*zichou zijin*), for which further detailed breakdowns are not available. However, judging from sample surveys and partial statistics, it is possible to estimate roughly the magnitude of some of these flows. Table 1 shows that almost a quarter of total investment is financed by bank loans, and half from "own funds." Within the "own funds" category, an estimated 13 per cent of total investment is raised by private firms, households and joint stock companies, that is through formal or informal capital markets. Another 18 per cent is the retained funds of SOEs. An estimated 9 per cent is "fund raising" – various forms of informal borrowing, not approved by the central government, that transfer funds from households and other businesses to SOEs. Finally, another 10 per cent comes in the form of government earmarked funds (*zhuanxiang jijin*). These are really quasi-tax revenues, quite formalized in some cases (such as electricity funds that are levied nation-wide at the rate of 2 *fen* per kilowatt-hour), but in other cases simply extraordinary levies imposed arbitrarily by local governments. (The three biggest formalized levies are those on electricity, railroad freight and vehicles: together they amount to over 1 per cent of GDP in extra-budgetary funds.) Thus, despite the large size of the funds deposited in China's banking system, this is only one part of the huge flow of funds into investment. Roughly the same amount flows into fixed investment outside the banking system – not counting enterprise funds used in the enterprise in which they are retained – as flows into fixed investment through the banking system. However, very little is known about this complex and diverse set of financial institutions.

The formal banking system is subject to multiple forms of government intervention. Earmarked bank loans have long been an important part of bank fixed investment lending, but there may have been a tendency for the proportion of bank lending subject to earmarking to increase in the 1990s, following the reassertion of industrial policy after 1989. The central government thus compels the banking system to provide credit for its priority projects. In this respect, the central government is no different from local governments: both put the banking system under constant pressure to provide funds for their projects. Indeed, the proportion of central and local government projects funded by bank loans is nearly identical, notwithstanding the different sectoral composition of central and local investment.

In addition, the government generally maintains fairly high levels of central bank (PBC) lending to the specialized (commercial) banks. To a substantial degree, PBC lending is offset by excess deposits maintained at the PBC by the specialized banks. Thus, PBC lending is a way to exercise control over commercial bank deposits, moving funds from one location

Table 1: **Financing of Total Fixed Investment, 1993 (estimated)**

Source of Finance	Percentage
Budgetary	3.7
Bank loans	23.5
Foreign investment	7.3
Own-funds (retained and raised)	50.0
of which: private firms and households	10
joint stock and co-ops	3
state and collective	37
of which: enterprise retained	18
"fund-raising"	9
government earmarked	10
Other	15.6

Sources:
   Zhongguo tongji nianjian, pp. 140–41. Breakdown of own-funds based on sample surveys, see *Zhongguo jinrong nianjian 1993*. (*Almanac of China's Finance and Banking 1993*), pp. 268, 277–78. See also *Zhongguo touzi nianjian 1993* (*China Investment Yearbook 1993*), pp. 16–17.

to another in accord with central government priorities. Finally, and perhaps most important, interest rates are regulated at well below market clearing rates. In effect, the banking system is forced to subsidize government enterprises and investment projects. On balance, these add up to a very substantial reliance on the banking system by the government to substitute for its declining direct budgetary revenues.

The *de facto* tax rate on the banking system is thus extremely high. Depositors get less than they could earn for their funds elsewhere, and borrowers (other than favoured state clients) find their access to funds obstructed. Although the bank system provides a service in intermediating funds from savers to borrowers, the transaction is highly taxed by the government. Indeed, it is remarkable that China's household saving rate has remained as high as it is, given the low return to much of this saving. As a result of this high "tax rate," there is a strong temptation for both savers and borrowers to opt out of the formal state-run banking system and try to make deals through other kinds of institutional arrangements. When this occurs, it is called "disintermediation."

Under the current system, the disintermediation crisis is the most typical kind of financial crisis. When inflation occurs, savers are more highly taxed (because interest rates rise more slowly than does the inflation rate), and they may wish to shift into durable goods that won't depreciate with the currency. When liberalization occurs, both savers and borrowers may find new institutional forms (stocks, bonds, non-bank financial institutions, credit clubs) that allow them to circumvent the banking system with its high tax rates. When both inflation and liberaliza-

Figure 5: **Growth of Cash and Savings Deposits**

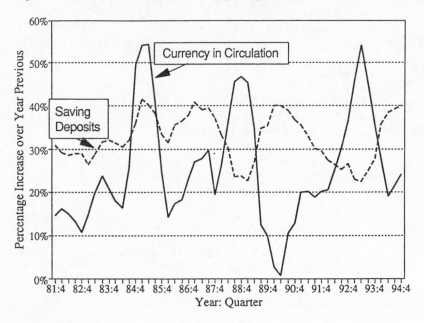

Source:

Zhongguo jinrong (*China Banking and Finance*), Beijing periodical, various issues.

tion occur at the same time (as is usual in China), the effects are particularly severe.

China has experienced two very severe, very obvious disintermediation crises over the past ten years, and probably several smaller ones. The most severe ones occurred in 1988 and 1992–93. They can be clearly seen in Figure 5 as the episodes when household saving deposit growth slows or stops while currency in circulation grows rapidly. Households removed funds from the banking system and either hoarded them or put them into other types of investment. Disintermediation can also begin as funds "escape" from the banking system as individuals and organizations seize the opportunity to loan funds into high-return activities. The 1992–93 crisis was particularly interesting in this respect. At the end of 1992, the bank statistics were at their most misleading, since 120 billion *yuan* had been channelled through the inter-bank market and outside the banking system. They were thus "missing," and are listed on the bank balance sheet as a large negative "other" entry.

Disintermediation crises have interesting effects. They put the banking system into a severe credit squeeze, because suddenly the deposit base drops, despite the rapid growth of the price level and credit. They cannot simply be ignored. The dilemma at that point is whether the central bank should inject additional liquidity into the system. To do so is to threaten higher inflation but not to do so is to put the banking system into an impossible squeeze. In fact, in both 1988 and 1993, the PBC did so, and there was thus a substantial jump in PBC lending precisely in those years.[20] The effect is particularly strong when policy-makers demand a special effort to provide funds for agricultural procurements, which requires additional central bank lending.

The disintermediation crisis is the characteristic form of Chinese macroeconomic imbalance, because it is the stage at which economic accountability finally emerges. Without sensitive signals from interest rates or asset markets, Chinese policy-makers do not get clear messages about the macroeconomic problems they are creating until the disintermediation crisis emerges. Even when economic problems mount, the temptation is enormous to continue to push for additional investment and more growth until the last possible moment. In practice, that moment is generally when a disintermediation crisis emerges. Then and only then are policy-makers forced to adjust their policies.[21]

Macroeconomic Dynamics and Other Pressures

The preceding sections have sketched out a view of China's macroeconomic problems that differs from the popular wisdom both in substance and in emphasis. Instead of seeing macroeconomic difficulties as deriving from a weak central government with inadequate control instruments, it instead portrays difficulties as coming from an activist, interventionist central government with substantial power but immature financial institutions and inadequate capabilities for monitoring the economy. The popular wisdom interprets each episode of loss of macroeconomic control as a symptom of overall weakness, and suggests that it is a harbinger of a coming breakdown of control. The view presented here suggests that the short-term loss of control is due to a competition among government agencies with contradictory objectives (or possibly among competing objectives held by individual leaders). As a result, it suggests that control is likely to be re-established once macroeconomic problems compel temporary agreement that macroeconomic stability is the most important short-term objective. Indeed, that has been precisely the outcome after each inflationary episode in China, including the most recent.

The primary locus of stabilization policy has shifted to monetary policy with the onset of the reform era. However, monetary policy is subject to unrelenting pressure from government officials at both central and local levels. In essence, government officials want the banking system to

20. The disintermediation crisis explanation is superior to the World Bank analysis reported above in n. 4. They interpreted the high level of PBC lending in 1993 as evidence of a chronic, increasing disguised budget deficit. I interpret it as largely a short-term response to a disintermediation crisis. In the following year, 1994, PBC lending dropped almost to zero. This is compatible with the disintermediation crisis explanation, but is either incompatible with the "disguised deficit" interpretation, or else means that the deficit was miraculously closed within a single year.

21. In 1992–93 official recognition of overheating was further delayed by Deng Xiaoping's "bundling" economic reform and rapid growth into a single package. Opposition to expansionary macroeconomic policy was construed as opposition to reform.

extend more credit to their priority projects, and they thus create constant pressure for a more rapid growth of credit, and thus of money supply as well. In order to complete the picture, it is necessary briefly to discuss two other sources of macroeconomic instability. The first is deficit SOEs and the second is the problem of instability imported through the foreign trade account.

According to conventional wisdom, China's inflationary tendency results from the government propping up obsolete state-run factories. This amounts to a substantial hidden budget deficit and feeds inflation. While this story is not completely wrong, it is doubtful that it provides much explanatory power. The basic fact is that current subsidies going to state-run enterprises are moderate in size, whereas overall investment flows are very large. It is much more likely that the sources of macroeconomic imbalance lie with investment policy. Macroeconomic imbalances are the flip side of the aggressive infrastructure and industrial policy described above. Total direct government subsidies for prices and to loss-making enterprises have declined steadily during the 1990s, because of the success of price reform. In 1994 they amounted to only 1.5 per cent of GDP, by far the lowest since the beginning of reform. There are without doubt significant hidden subsidies going to state industry, in the form of guaranteed access to relatively cheap credits. But even here caution must be observed. The total increment in credit to industrial enterprises from the state banking system in 1993 was 3.5 per cent of GDP. In addition, there are substantial subsidies in the form of low interest rates – which are very large when inflation is high and real interest rates significantly negative, but moderate when inflation is low and real interest rates poke into the positive range. All together, if current subsidies to the state sector amount to 3 or 4 per cent of GDP (a generous estimate), this is certainly wasteful, but is simply not enough continuously to tip the economy into an inflationary spiral, not when it is generating saving at the rate of over 35 per cent of GDP, as China is.

Nevertheless, SOEs represent a burden on the banking system, and thus are a factor tending to destabilize macroeconomic policy. According to a recent statement by Chen Yuan, vice-head of the PBC, about a fifth of the state banking system's loans are overdue (but still paying interest), and about 3 per cent of loans have been classified non-performing. Most of both categories are loans to SOEs.[22] These numbers represent real challenges to the banking system. Great care must be taken to clean up the bank balance sheets properly, write off non-performing loans and put the banks in a healthy position so they can compete in the new market economy.

Why is the assessment of the SOE problem in this article so different from the popular wisdom? First, the popular wisdom does not adequately distinguish between support for SOEs as a waste or as an obstacle to improving efficiency on the one hand, and support for SOEs as a source

22. Associated Press, "China banks to go commercial?" 20 June 1995, over China News Digest.

of macroeconomic instability on the other. In examining the macroeconomic impact of a government action, the crucial question is not whether the activity is wasteful, but rather whether the action is adequately funded. If a real use of resources is not adequately funded, it will be inflationary to the extent that the government ends up "printing money" to support the activity. Some support for SOEs undoubtedly does come in this form, but although the amount is not really known, it is probably not large. The bigger expenditure is in the form of loss-making enterprises, and most of those losses are fully funded by deductions from profits which would otherwise be remitted to the government. Secondly, the popular wisdom is overly influenced by imprecise statements from Chinese sources. Complaints about SOE losses have been expressed in China for over 15 years, but the nature of the phenomena complained about has changed dramatically. Throughout the 1980s, the overwhelming majority of SOE losses were incurred by commercial units supplying food to urban dwellers. What were then labelled "SOE losses" were in fact policy-determined payments to urbanites. In the 1990s, those losses have been nearly eliminated by price reforms. Meanwhile, industrial SOE losses, which were insignificant in the 1980s, have become substantially more important, though they are only a fraction of the magnitude of the earlier food subsidies. Government officials are naturally concerned because they are used to treating industrial SOEs as their "cash cows." Moreover, as state employees themselves, government officials are understandably somewhat obsessed with the tough problem of how to restructure SOEs without creating mass unemployment. But these very real issues do not necessarily imply that SOEs are a destabilizing factor in the economy.

Finally, the popular wisdom lumps all SOEs into a single category. In fact, as shown in Figure 2, SOEs are evolving in different directions in different sectors. In certain sectors in which SOEs are dominant – including electricity generation, steel making and cigarette production – SOEs continue to be highly profitable. In others, including coal and petroleum extraction, losses are substantial partly because of continued government distortions of the price structure. On balance, SOEs are a significant obstacle to further economic reform and improved efficiency. Privatization could begin immediately and be carried out quickly in the competitive sectors. Progress in non-competitive sectors would be slightly slower, since a regulatory framework needs to be created in those areas. But there is no reason not to proceed with privatization and rapid restructuring of SOEs. Conversely, though, there is no reason to believe that the continued presence of SOEs prevents urgently required financial reforms, or makes macroeconomic stability impossible.

A second factor that can destabilize the macroeconomy in today's China is exchange rate policy, which was particularly important in 1994. On 1 January 1994, China devalued and unified the currency at a rate around 8.7 RMB to the dollar. For most purposes this was a substantial devaluation. China's exports responded to the stimulus, and the trade balance swung from a deficit of $12.2 billion to a surplus of $5.35 billion. The magnitude of the change can be better appreciated if only "ordinary" trade is looked at. This is carried out primarily by Chinese foreign trade corporations (FTCs), setting to one side the roughly 30 per cent of China's exports carried out by foreign invested enterprises (FIEs). FIE exports are important, but are not highly sensitive to the exchange rate in the short term because they import a large share of their inputs. By contrast, ordinary exports are highly sensitive to exchange rate fluctuations. During the first eleven months of 1994, ordinary exports increased 42 per cent, while ordinary imports actually declined 5.4 per cent, so the surplus on ordinary trade jumped to $26 billion from a little over $6 billion.[23] This dramatic shift resulted in a huge inflow of income from foreign trade.

In the face of this inflow, the Chinese government had a number of alternatives. It could have allowed the RMB to appreciate (that is, allow its value to increase relative to the dollar, since dollars were less scarce and less valuable), undoing some of the devaluation at the beginning of the year and eventually shrinking the trade surplus. Secondly, it could have encouraged imports, which would have had some benefits: increased import of grain would have moderated inflationary pressures created by the year's poor harvest, and increased imports from the United States would have reduced trade tensions. The government actually pursued a third option, which was to buy with RMB the dollars earned by exporters, thus increasing foreign exchange reserves and maintaining a stable exchange rate. China's foreign exchange reserves increased 140 per cent during 1994, to reach $51.6 billion, and jumped to $58 billion by the end of March 1995. Thus foreign exchange reserves increased by a total of about $30 billion in 1994, roughly equivalent to the surplus on ordinary trade. At 8.5 RMB to the dollar, this means that the government injected about 250 billion *yuan* RMB into the domestic economy.

With the central bank pumping a substantial amount of money into the economy to purchase foreign exchange reserves, it had little or no leeway to create money by extending new central bank loans. Indeed, on the central bank balance sheets, the increase in new foreign assets (foreign exchange reserves) accounted for 87 per cent of base money creation during the first eleven months of 1994.[24] The central bank made very little money available in new domestic central bank lending. In that sense, monetary policy was quite tight. Total credit (state banks plus rural credit co-operatives) increased at the moderate rate of 20 per cent in 1994. This explains the phenomena of 1994 and 1995. Money supply growth has been fairly rapid – M2 grew 34.4 per cent in 1994 and currency in circulation grew 24 per cent – yet the banks proclaim that they are following a tight monetary policy and enterprises complain about the difficulty in getting bank loans.[25] In fact, the domestic economy faces relatively tight money, while the export sector is awash with liquidity.

23. Yao Keping, "An analysis of 1994 balance of payments and a projection for 1995," *Zhongguo jinrong*, No. 4 (1995), pp. 39–40.

24. *Ibid.* p. 40.

25. Monetary data from *Zhongguo jinrong*, No. 3 (1995), pp. 44–45.

This helps to resolve the paradox raised in the first paragraph of this article: China's "soft landing" after the July 1993 initiation of austerity policies took so long because it conflicted with the inflationary forces emanating from the export sector.

Some Implications and Conclusion

There are some clear implications to the preceding analysis. First, the attempt by the government to steer the economy and commandeer resources from the banking system is the ultimate source of macroeconomic imbalance. The imbalances occur not so much because of the continuing cost of propping up a state sector, but rather because the government is committed to maintaining very high rates of new investment in priority sectors, but doesn't have the direct command over resources to pay for it. Moreover, it is currently locked into a difficult set of interactions. It has been "successful" in pumping up large investments in key infrastructure sectors. That has allowed growth to accelerate and insured the profitability of non-infrastructural investments, typically made by decentralized agents. But as inflationary problems increase, the government's investment effort may prove to be unsustainable. With direct control concentrated on infrastructure investment, any cutbacks in central government control will first affect infrastructure investment, and may therefore aggravate bottlenecks and imbalances. There may be a rapid fall from the high-growth path which China has followed for the past few years.

Secondly, given the lack of accountability in the system, the result is likely to be a continued series of macroeconomic crises, as the government continually runs up against the limits of what it can exact from the economy as a whole, and from the financial system in particular. Difficulty in controlling the economy is not caused by an absence of control instruments. Indeed, the Chinese government has repeatedly shown the ability to impose austerity programmes, reduce the growth of bank credit and ultimately bring inflation down, but its resources to those instruments is delayed until after the crisis is full-blown. The real problem is the absence of day-to-day restraint that prevents crises from emerging.

Thirdly, policy-makers in China have already recognized that financial reform is one of the most crucial and most urgent needs of current reform. Indeed, the basic outline of a direction for financial sector reform was passed with the Banking Law of 1995. This set out a vision of independent commercial banks not subject to government intervention. In order to help implement this vision, the State Development Bank and two other government "policy lending" banks were created during 1994 to assume the burden of government-directed loans. Yet it is clear that it will take far more than a simple declaration of principles to implement banking reform effectively. In the first place, the banking system continues to be under pressure from the government's conflicting objectives (indeed, sometimes from the conflicting objectives of different parts of the government). Even if the State Development Bank succeeds in taking over a large portion of the government-directed lending of the commercial banks, it will require a major commitment to prevent central and local government agencies from imposing new lending requirements on the commercial banks. Moreover, banks will inevitably need some facility for restructuring their existing loans, giving them a mechanism to write off bad loans or transfer them to a new facility. Finally, some commitment to liberalize interest rates significantly will be required to make the vision a reality.

Development of capital markets had lagged behind because it is difficult; because there are still ideological obstacles; and because government officials want to retain the power to influence investment and are thus ambivalent about future reform. A foreshadowing of the difficulties of financial sector reform is apparent in the failure of government efforts to shift the investment system to repayable grants. The government has received very little in the form of repayment for past investment in this form.[26] In the financial arena, perhaps more than in other areas, successful reform appears to require a substantial, sustained exertion of political will by a committed central government. In both the banking system and the taxation system, nominal reforms have already been adopted that outline the basic steps required. The question is whether the political system can generate sufficient unity of purpose to make implementation of those reforms a reality.

26. *Zhongguo jinrong nianjian 1992* (*Almanac of China's Finance and Banking 1992*) (Beijing: Zhongguo jinrong chubanshe, 1993), p. 296.

China in Transition: The Political Foundations of Incremental Reform*

Steven M. Goldstein

As the People's Republic of China approaches a half century of existence, it seems to be an anomaly. Not only has it survived "the mass extinction of Leninist regimes,"[1] it also continues along the path of reform. And this is despite the widely accepted assumption that Soviet-style systems are, by their very nature, incompatible with the assumptions of systemic reform – namely, the gradual and incremental transformation of economic and political systems by leaders who "use and build upon the existing structures of society."[2]

Several of the contributions to this volume discuss aspects of this gradualist strategy of moving from plan to market from an economic perspective. This one explores its political dimensions. However, because China's economic reform is a bundle of many different policies, what follows cannot pretend to be a comprehensive analysis.[3] Rather, it focuses on a single policy outcome – the emergence and development of the "non-state" sector – which is considered to be an essential element in the gradualist strategy in industry and uses it to draw some broader conclusions about the political foundations of reform.

The discussion begins on a comparative note by outlining the assumptions that have guided analyses of reform in Soviet-type systems. This is followed by a description of the manner in which these assumptions have been reflected in reform proposals and outcomes in Eastern Europe and the former Soviet Union (EEFSU). This provides the basis for consideration of what it might be about China's political institutions and processes that has conditioned an apparently quite different outcome. Finally, I assess the impact which this aspect of the reform strategy has had on the nation's political economy, concluding with a discussion of the challenges its results pose for the Chinese polity.

Reform in Soviet Systems

Gradualism or piecemeal reform is not the only distinctive aspect of the Chinese reform. The post-Mao economic reforms have proceeded at

* My thanks to Zimu Zheng for research assistance, to Zvi Gitelman, Jean Oi and Andrew Walder for their comments, and to the Fairbank Center, Harvard University – and especially Nancy Hearst – for providing an hospitable research environment.

1. Ken Jowitt, "The Leninist extinction," in Daniel Chirot, (ed.), *The Crisis of Leninism and the Decline of the Left* (Seattle & London: University of Washington Press, 1991), p. 79. For stylistic purposes, I have omitted the italics found in the original.

2. Michel Oksenberg and Bruce J. Dickson, "The origins, processes, and outcomes of great political reform: a framework of analysis," in Dankwart A. Rustow and Kenneth Paul Erikson (eds.), *Comparative Political Dynamics: Global Research Perspectives* (New York: Harper Collins, 1991), pp. 235–262.

3. Thus, in at least in one area, agriculture, one might question just how gradualist the strategy was.

a pace, and with a scope, that has exceeded political reform. This runs counter to the conventional wisdom that reform of Leninist-Stalinist systems requires comprehensive economic reform (big bang or shock therapy) preceded by, or at least closely linked to, an equally comprehensive dismantling of the institutions of Communist Party rule.[4] This highlights an obvious problem with the juxtaposition of gradualist reform in China to the theories of shock therapy, which have been applied to the reform of socialist countries *no longer* under the authoritarian rule of a dominant Communist Party. This, of course, is not the case in China. However, as shown below, this does not necessarily render comparisons with China invalid. Much of the intellectual foundation of shock therapy is based on a view of the logic of the socialist political economy deduced from the unsuccessful reforms of the 1960s and 1970s as well as from the fate of the Gorbachev reforms. Thus, a discussion of shock therapy embedded in the intellectual framework of these deductions (which are, themselves, more directly applicable to the situation in China) is a necessary introduction to the political bases of the post-Mao reforms.

"You can't cross an abyss in two leaps" is the response of advocates of the big bang to "crossing the river by feeling for the stones underfoot" – the central metaphor of Chinese gradualism.[5] This approach to economic reform was proposed as Communist Party rule eroded in Eastern Europe and the Soviet Union. It assumes that change must be carried out rapidly and on a broad front.[6] This derives from a belief in the centrality of market liberalization and privatization as well as the presumption of their incompatibility with a planned economy. Moreover, it is believed that the logic of this planned economy makes the introduction of any one aspect of marketization (that is, profit) dependent on other changes (such as market prices, freedom from plan quotas) if it is to be effective since "altering one or a few [characteristics] is merely disruptive of the stable functioning of the system and of its effectiveness."[7]

This approach is tied to political considerations as well. In the 1930s Joseph Stalin presided over the creation of a political system whose aim was industrialization and which was structured so that administration and

4. As Peter Nolan writes, "It has become a part of the conventional wisdom among policy advisors on the reform of the former Stalinist economies that sweeping economic and political reform are inseparable." Peter Nolan, *State and Market in the Chinese Economy: Essays on Controversial Issues* (London: MacMillan, 1992), p. 218.

5. Juliet Johnson, "Should Russia adopt the Chinese model of economic reform?" *Communist and Post-Communist Studies*, Vol. 27, No. 1 (1994), p. 61.

6. Jan Prybyla, "The road from socialism: why, where, what and how," *Problems of Communism* Vol. XL, Nos. 1–2 (January–April, 1991), p. 9. For another vigorous defence of the concept, see Josef C. Brada, "The transformation from Communism to capitalism: how far? how fast?" *Post-Soviet Affairs*, Vol. 9, No. 2 (1993), pp. 87–110.

7. Richard E. Ericson, "The classical Soviet-type economy: nature of the system and implications for reform," *Journal of Economic Perspectives*, Vol. 5, No. 4 (Fall 1991), p. 24. See also, Peter T. Knight, *Economic Reform in Socialist Countries* (Washington, D.C.: The World Bank, 1983), pp. 25–26.

planning would take the place of the market. The logic of the system was the "fusion of politics and economics."[8] To many observers, this fusion provided the key to understanding the fate of reforms in socialist systems during the 1960s and 1970s when efforts gradually to introduce elements of the market into the planned economy were overwhelmed by the command sector. Such efforts, János Kornai contended, created a situation of "dual dependence" whereby firms looked to both the market and the state authorities. The latter, because of their greater power, took precedence and weakened the effectiveness of market mechanisms. Kornai thus identified the "stubborn inner contradiction in the whole reform process": gaining the participation of the very people who will lose a part of their power if the process is successful.[9]

It was a contradiction not easily resolved. Greater marketization would confront obstacles as bureaucracies undermined or distorted reforms that would erode their power. Precedent changes in those political structures which drew their authority from the command economy were thus necessary. Yet, where would the political power to make these changes be found? In the years before the Gorbachev reforms, this interdependence between political and economic reform was seen as the principal bar to a fundamental economic reform of Soviet-style systems. The central dilemma of reformers was that while the inter-related nature of the economic system required broad and rapid change (what came to be called shock therapy), the fusion of that system with political institutions made such change unlikely.

For many, Mikhail Gorbachev's policies confirmed both the fruitlessness of partial economic reform and the need for precedent political change to achieve systemic economic reform.[10] In the early years of his reform, concrete examples of Kornai's contradiction were evident as ministries frustrated attempts to lessen controls over enterprises; local Party cadres constrained private enterprise; and collective farm bureaucrats resisted greater initiatives for work groups. In time, an increasingly radicalized Gorbachev realized that existing institutions could not be the basis for economic reform. Yet, to carry out institutional reform required autonomous power outside the existing political structures. It was not only economic change that required political reform, it was the politics of reform itself. Gorbachev's democratization of public life, his move to a government-based presidency and the empowering of Republic Soviets

8. Seweryn Bialer, *Stalin's Successors: Leadership, Stability, and Change in the Soviet Union* (Cambridge: Cambridge University Press, 1980), ch. 1. Wlodzimierz Brus has argued that it is "the amalgamation of strictly political with economic power which makes the Communist mono-archy so special." Wlodzimierz Brus, "Political pluralism and markets in Communist systems," in Susan Gross Solomon (ed.), *Pluralism in the Soviet Union* (New York: St Martin's Press, 1982), p. 113.

9. János Kornai, "The Hungarian reform process: visions, hopes, and reality," *Journal of Economic Literature*, Vol. XXIV (December 1986), p. 1729.

10. See for example, Graeme Gill, "Sources of political reform in the Soviet Union," *Studies in Comparative Communism*, Vol. 24, No. 3 (September 1991), pp. 240–41.

may be seen as attempts to escape the policy gridlock by creating new institutions capable of implementing economic reform from outside the old system of fused power.[11]

In the end, Gorbachev was defeated by existing institutions as well as the vulnerability of new institutions. Wlodzimierz Brus and others have suggested that Gorbachev was trapped in a Catch-22 of reform in Soviet-style systems: unable to restructure political institutions inhibiting economic reform, he embarked first on a path of political reform to create new, autonomous bases of power which so weakened political power that not only was economic restructuring impossible but political and economic disintegration resulted. In other words, Gorbachev's approach of political reform precedent to economic reform, while in accord with the logic of the fused system, could not be implemented because of that very same systemic logic.[12]

Reform in China in Comparison

This logic did not escape Deng Xiaoping whose infrequent discussions of political reform were linked to economic reform.[13] However, rhetoric aside, political reforms in China were modest, seeking to create a more rationalized and liberalized authoritarian system while resisting any political pluralism or democratization.[14] Deng, many would say, had learned from Gorbachev's fate, resisting any reforms that would weaken China's Leninist political system.

The discrepancy between the nature of the political system and extent of economic reform prompted a widely accepted view that China has defied both the systemic logic and historical experience of other socialist states by being transformed "from a command economy to one in which

11. *Ibid.* Christopher Young, "The strategy of political liberalization: a comparative view of Gorbachev's reforms," *World Politics*, Vol. 45, No. 1 (October 1992), pp. 47–65 and Philip G. Roeder, *Red Sunset: The Failure of Soviet Politics* (Princeton: Princeton University Press, 1993), ch. 9.

12. Wlodzimierz Brus, "Marketization and democratization: the Sino-Soviet divergence," *Cambridge Journal of Economics*, No. 17 (1993), pp. 433–444. This is also Roeder's point in *Red Sunset*. See also George W. Breslauer, "Evaluating Gorbachev as a leader," reprinted in Alexander Dallin and Gail Lapidus (eds.), *The Soviet System in Crisis* (Boulder: Westview Press, 1991), pp. 178–209, Tsuyoshi Hasegawa, "Connection between political and economic reform," in Gilbert Rozman with Seizaburo Sato and Gerald Segal (eds.), *Dismantling Communism: Common Causes and Regional Variations* (Baltimore: The Johns Hopkins University Press, 1991), pp. 94–99, David Lane and Cameron Ross, "Limitations of party control: the government bureaucracy in the USSR," *Communist and Post-Communist Studies*, Vol. 27, No. 1 (1994), pp. 19–38, and Michael McFaul, "State power, institutional change, and the politics of privatization in Russia," *World Politics*, Vol. 47, No. 2 (January 1995), pp. 224–25.

13. For example, in 1986, he told a Japanese visitor that "… unless we modify our political structure, we shall be unable to advance the economic reform or even to preserve the gains that we have made so far." Deng Xiaoping, *Fundamental Issues in Present-Day China* (Beijing: Foreign Languages Press, 1987), p. 149.

14. For an elaboration of these terms see Nina Halpern "Economic reform and democratization in Communist systems: the case of China," *Studies in Comparative Communism*, Vol. 22, No. 2/3 (Spring/Autumn, 1989), pp. 139–152.

the market and non-state-owned enterprises dominate economic life"[15] without political reform. For most who accept the logic of the big bang, economic reform in the absence of political reform can yield only partial change. Yet those economists such as John McMillan and Barry Naughton who ascribe China's success to gradualism argue that such partial reform can fundamentally transform a Soviet-style system. They present the "key features of China's economic reforms" as:

First, massive entry of non-state firms; second, a dramatic increase in competition, both among state firms and between state firms and non-state firms; and, third, improvements in the performance of state-owned firms resulting from state-imposed market-like incentives.[16]

In this view, while certain of the post-Mao reforms (such as dual pricing, greater autonomy in production and marketing, increased managerial authority) have been aimed *directly* at the planning system, more significant change has been affected *indirectly* through the creation of a more marketized, "non-state" sector outside the state planning system. In Brus' opinion "allowing and promoting the growth of a new type of economy alongside the old one has probably been as important for the comparative success of the Chinese reform" as agricultural or foreign trade policy.[17]

The idea that planned economies might be reformed through the creation of a virtual parallel economy is not new. It was discussed in Hungary before the fall of Communism and continues to be offered as an evolutionary alternative to the big bang in EEFSU. In the pre-1989 period Ivan Szelenyi advocated a "socialist mixed economy" which he believed would offer a "third road" that was neither Western capitalism nor Soviet Communism.[18] "Socialism may still be reformable," he maintained, "… if it allows the emergence of firms with hard budget constraints, that is private enterprises." Similarly, János Kornai argued that "the appearance of a vital nonstate sector represents something brand new and important in the history of socialist countries."[19] This "socialist mixed economy" appeared to skirt the problems that necessitated a big bang. Rather than unravel the Soviet-style economy, a new, private sector would be created alongside the old. Yet Kornai and Szelenyi suggested that the socialist mixed economy avoided this problem only to confront another pitfall –

15. The quotations are from Susan Shirk's, *The Political Logic of Economic Reform in China* (Berkeley: University of California Press, 1993), p. 346.

16. John McMillan and Barry Naughton, "How to reform a planned economy: lessons from China," *Oxford Review of Economic Policy*, Vol. 8, No. 1 (Spring 1992), p. 131.

17. Brus, "Marketization and democratization," p. 428. See also Chen Kang cited in Jia Hao and Wang Mingxia, "Market and state: changing central–local relations in China," in Jia Hao and Lin Zhimin, *Changing Central–Local Relations in China: Reform and State Capacity* (Boulder: Westview Press, 1994), No. 14. Shirk argues that such a policy emerged out of the failure to reform the state sector. *The Political Logic of Reform*, p. 145.

18. *Socialist Entrepreneurs* (Madison: University of Wisconsin Press, 1988), pp. 16–18 and 212–18.

19. Ivan Szelenyi, "Eastern Europe in an epoch of transition: toward a socialist mixed economy?" in Victor Nee and David Stark (eds.), *Remaking the Economic Institutions of Socialism: China and East Europe* (Stanford: Stanford University Press, 1989), pp. 220 and 222 and Kornai, "The Hungarian reform process," p. 1710.

the resistance of dominant economic bureaucracies. The problem remained that of the fusion of political power and economic management.[20]

China's gradualist strategy appears to have some intellectual kinship to these earlier designs. However, the maintenance of a Leninist system should have made it vulnerable to the problems presented by the fusion of political and economic power. An exploration of the political bases of China's incremental reform becomes, therefore, a test of more general propositions about the nature of reform in socialist and post-socialist systems. Is China an exceptional case because its Leninist system has been able to sustain change along the lines of a mixed economy? Or is Chinese exceptionalism something of an illusion which obscures an underlying conformity with the fundamental logic of a Soviet-style system – the fusion of politics and economics? It is quite possible to give affirmative answers to both questions.

For some proponents of gradualism the key to resolving this apparent contradiction lies in de-emphasizing the importance of aggregated political power in favour of China's distinctive conditions. For Barry Naughton, it is "the fact that certain economic forces and institutional conditions shaped a chaotic and inconsistent set of policies into a coherent process" which makes the Chinese reform "interesting." [21] Similarly, Gary Jefferson has suggested that much of the reform initiative has come from the "bottom up" as the central party/government restricts its role to "enabling reforms" dependent on "local initiative." In this view an understanding of the course of China's economic reform requires a perspective that goes beyond a preoccupation with reform strategies to include "initial institutional conditions." As Yingyi Qian and Chenggang Xu note, China's transition is best understood as a *"path dependent evolutionary process."*[22]

20. Szelenyi, *Socialist Entrepreneurs*, p. 213 and Kornai, "The Hungarian reform process," pp. 1709–10, 1728–30. Indeed, the importance of the political system to an evolutionary alternative is apparent in Peter Murrell's recent writings on reform in post-socialist societies. He depicts the private sector playing a role vis-à-vis the planned, state sector analogous to McMillan and Naughton's "non-state" enterprises and argues this is made possible by the fact that the "old political system has vanished." The lesson is once again clear: only the elimination of the Leninist bureaucracy would make meaningful, incremental reform possible. Peter Murrell, "What is shock therapy? What did it do in Poland and Russia?" *Post-Soviet Affairs*, Vol. 9, No. 2 (1993), p. 119.

21. Barry Naughton, "What is distinctive about China's economic transition? State enterprise reform and overall system transformation," *Journal of Comparative Economics* Vol. 18, No. 3 (June 1994), pp. 472–73.

22. Gary Jefferson, "The Chinese economy: moving forward," in William Joseph (ed.), *China Briefing, 1992* (Boulder: Westview Press, 1993), pp. 48–49. See also Kang Chen, Gary H. Jefferson and Inderjit Singh, "Lessons from Chinese reform," *Journal of Comparative Economics*, Vol. 16, No. 2 (1992), pp. 214–15. Qian Yingyi and Chenggang Xu, "Why China's reforms differ: the M-form hierarchy and entry expansion on the non-state sector," (Stanford University, 1992), p. 45. This article was passed on to me after the conference paper which formed the basis for this article was completed. As will be noted, our analyses share common ground. For other analysts who have used this approach, see Dorothy J. Solinger, *China's Transition From Socialism: Statist Legacies and Market Reforms* (Armonk, NY: M. E. Sharpe, 1993), ch. 8, Victor Nee, "Organizational dynamics of market transition: hybrid forms, property rights, and mixed economy in China," *Administrative Science Quarterly*, No. 37 (1992), pp. 1–27 and Yasheng Huang "Information, bureaucracy and economic

The concept of "path dependence" is part of a broader approach known variously as "institutionalism" or "historical institutionalism" whose fundamental hypothesis is that "institutions are not just another variable ... [rather they] structure political situations and leave their own imprint on political outcomes."[23] Institutions are "sticky" and institutional inertia means that "history matters," as the "shadows of the past" embodied in institutional arrangements continue to shape present possibilities. They do so by "historical branching" or "path dependence" where "decisions at one point in time can restrict future possibilities by sending policy off onto particular tracks, along which ideas and interests develop and institutions and strategies adapt."

This approach seems particularly appropriate because it fits with the metaphor of the post-Mao reforms – "crossing the river by feeling for the stones underfoot." Most interpret this expression as stressing the importance of proceeding in an incremental manner. However, there is more to it. If you cross a river by following the stones, you are constrained by the pattern you find. You can't just cast stones where you want them, you must take them as they are and the institutions which form the political foundation of reform are, themselves, the outcome of past reforms. No reforming system starts its journey from shore, it is already somewhere in the river. This is an obvious point often missed in comparisons of China and the Soviet Union which do not note the differences in the *institutional* nature of their pre-reform political economies. Traversing the stones leading from Brezhnev's Russia takes one on a quite different route from those leading from Mao's China. The lessons of historical branching are particularly important here. The institutions of the political economy created in the past preclude certain courses even as they set the foundations for others.[24]

Franz Schurmann has distinguished between two methods of organization in Soviet-type systems: the "branch system" organized by functions and governed by specialized agencies – usually ministries – such that "command came down vertically from the centre," and the "committee system" where co-ordination was horizontal, cutting across functional

---

footnote continued

reforms in China and the Soviet Union," *World Politics*, Vol. 47, No. 1 (January 1995), pp. 102–134.

23. The following discussion draws from: Douglass C. North, *Institutions, Institutional Change and Economic Performance* (Cambridge: Cambridge University Press, 1990), John Ikenberry, "Conclusion: an institutional approach to American foreign economic policy," *International Organization*, Vol. 42, No. 1 (Winter 1988), pp. 220–243, Stephen D. Krasner, "Approaches to the state: alternative conceptions and historical dynamics," *Comparative Politics*, Vol. 16, No. 2 (January 1984), pp. 223–246 and Sven Steinmo, Kathleen Thelen and Frank Longstreth (eds.), *Structuring Politics: Historical Institutionalism in Comparative Analysis* (Cambridge: Cambridge University Press, 1992).

24. Vivienne Shue makes a similar point: "As there was no single state socialism, there will be no single 'postsocialism'," "State power and social organization in China," in Joel Migdal *et al.*, *State Power and Social Forces: Domination and Transformation in the Third World* (New York: Cambridge University Press, 1994), p. 85. Qian and Xu also make this point when they discuss the differences between China's "M-form" structure and the "U-form" structure of Eastern Europe and the Soviet Union. "Why China's economic reforms differ," pp. 16–22.

areas at a territorial level.[25] The dominance of the Soviet central organs had its roots in the 1930s. The organizational loci for the harnessing of the nation for forced draft industrialization were the central planning bodies as well as their financial and managerial arms – the ministries. Khrushchev attempted to redirect the system by empowering regional bodies (the *Sovnarhozy*) and the Kosygin reforms of 1965 sought to strengthen the enterprises. However, despite calls to strengthen the power of local soviets, the basic thrust of the last years of the Brezhnev regime was to increase centralized economic control.

On the eve of the Gorbachev reform, one commentator depicted Soviet local government as "still ... trapped by the cultural legacy of the past."[26] Localities had little experience in planning or management, few financial resources, and lacked both planning staff and instrumentalities of control. Indeed, in the judgment of one observer, they even lacked the "confidence" to use whatever attenuated powers they had. Viewing the Soviet system from the perspective of 1993, Peter Rutland has concluded that "regional coordination was clearly one of ... [its] weakest links"

From the early 1950s, the Chinese planned economy developed along a very different trajectory, culminating in the Cultural Revolution when there was a dramatic change in the nature and capacity of territorial planning at the provincial level and below that clearly set the Chinese Leninist system apart from the Soviet.[27] Some changes involved restructuring the nature of the central planning system by turning enterprises over to the localities. This transfer provided two sources of wherewithal for local development: industrial products and enterprise depreciation

25. Franz Schurmann, *Ideology and Organization in Communist China*, enlarged edition (Berkeley: University of California Press, 1968), pp. 88–90. See also Marianne Bastid, "Levels of economic decision making," in Stuart R. Schram (ed.), *Authority, Participation and Cultural Change in China* (Cambridge: Cambridge University Press, 1973), pp. 162–63. Huang presents an excellent discussion of these different approaches to planning in his "Information, bureaucracy and economic reforms in China and the Soviet Union."

26. On the weakness of local government in the former Soviet Union see Cameron Ross, *Local Government in the Soviet Union: Problems of Implementation and Control* (New York: St Martin's Press, 1987), David T. Cattell, "Local government and the provision of consumer goods and services," in Everett Jacobs (ed.), *Soviet Local Politics and Government* (London: George Allen and Unwin, 1983), Ronald Hill, "The development of Soviet local government since Stalin's death," in Jacobs, *Soviet Local Politics and Government*, Paul R. Gregory, *Restructuring the Soviet Economic Bureaucracy* (Cambridge: Cambridge University Press, 1990), ch. 7, Stephen Fortescue, "The regional party apparatus in the 'sectional society'," *Studies in Comparative Communism*, Vol. 21, No. 1 (Spring 1988), pp. 11–23 and Peter Rutland, *The Politics of Economic Stagnation in the Soviet Union* (London: Cambridge University Press, 1993).

27. Discussion of the earlier period can be found in Nicholas R. Lardy, *Economic Growth and the Distribution in China* (Cambridge: Cambridge University Press, 1978), chs. 1–4, Carl Riskin, *China's Political Economy: The Quest For Development Since 1949* (Oxford: Oxford University Press, 1987), chs. 5–7 and Schurmann, *Ideology and Organization in Communist China*, pp. 85–87 and ch. 3. The period of the Great Leap Forward is, of course, particularly important. It was during this time, as Zhao Suisheng notes, that "... local governments were empowered to approve all locally financed large- and medium-sized investment projects, to plan local production, to distribute materials, and to collect revenues," Zhao Suisheng, "China's central–local relationship: a historical perspective," in Jia Hao and Lin Zhimin, *Changing Central–Local Relations in China*, p. 26.

funds which "became the largest and most stable source of local invest-ment funds."[28]

The significance of the depreciation funds highlights the close relation-ship between enterprise supervision and income. In 1972, the county was permitted to retain 60 per cent of the profits from state industries built after that date. In addition, it would appear that considerable income from collective industries (of which more later) was retained in the county. Most of this income was included within the budget and so was techni-cally under central supervision. However, by the mid-1970s there seemed to be greater flexibility as localities were able to retain and spend any budgetary surpluses generated.[29]

The issue of budgetary management leads to the increased significance of what Thomas Lyons has called the "partitioning" of the Chinese economy.[30] The policies discussed above related to the central/local partition in what is sometimes called the state sector, the planned sector or the in-budget sector. Although not all enterprises meet all three criteria, these designations mean that they are owned by the "whole people," have their allocations within the plan and are budgeted within the plan.[31] However, there is another "partition": that between the planned sector (central or local) and the unplanned sector which was dominated by collective firms which received their allocations outside the plan and were off-budget. What the collectives had in common with the state sector was that despite their supposed origins in spontaneous worker co-operation, they were "created and managed" by governmental organi-

28. It has been estimated that between 1965 and 1970 the number of enterprises under the central ministries was reduced from 10,533 producing 46.9% of total industrial output to 500 producing only 8% of total output. Most of these enterprises were turned over to the provinces, which, in some cases, passed them on to sub-provincial jurisdictions. See Kyoichi Ishihara, *China's Conversion to a Market Economy* (Tokyo: Institute of Developing Economies, 1991), pp. 15–19 and Christine P. Wong, "The 'Maoist' model reconsidered: local self-reliance and the financing of rural industrialization," in William Joseph *et al.*, *New Perspectives on the Cultural Revolution* (Cambridge, MA: Harvard University Press, 1991), p. 188. For a discussion of depreciation funds see Barry Naughton, "Finance and planning reforms in industry, in Joint Economic Committee, *China's Economy Looks Towards the Year 2000*, Vol. 1 (Washington, D.C.: U.S. Government Printing Office, 1986), p. 607.

29. Vivienne Shue, "Beyond the budget: financial organization and reform in a Chinese county," *Modern China*, Vol. 10, No. 2 (April 1984), p. 161. On the granting of greater budgetary discretion see Michel Oksenberg and James Tong, "The evolution of central–prov-incial fiscal relations in China, 1971 to 1984: the formal system," *The China Quarterly*, No. 125 (March 1991), pp. 1–32, Akira Fujimoto, "The reform of China's financial system," *China Newsletter*, March 1980, pp. 4–5, Reeitsu Kojima, "The growing fiscal authority of provincial-level governments in China," *Journal of Developing Economies*, Vol. XXX, No. 4 (December 1992), p. 336 and Zhao Dexing, *Zhonghua renmin gongheguo jingjishi (1967–1984) (Economic History of the Chinese People's Republic, 1967–1984)* (Zhengzhou: Henan renmin chubanshe, 1989), pp. 48–49. While this was clearly at work in relations between the provinces and the Centre, it is not clear that sub-provincial bodies officially enjoyed the same privileges. David Granick, *Chinese State Enterprises* (Chicago: University of Chicago Press, 1990), pp. 40–41. Christine P. W. Wong has argued for a greater national supervision of these budgetary categories. "Fiscal reform and local industrialization," *Modern China*, Vol. 18, No. 2 (April 1992), pp. 205–207.

30. Thomas P. Lyons, "Explaining economic fragmentation in China: a systems approach," *Journal of Comparative Economics*, Vol. 10, No. 3 (September 1986), pp. 209–236.

31. Christine Wong does an excellent job of demonstrating the complexity of this classification. See "Ownership and control in Chinese industry," pp. 581–599.

zations or enterprises – rural collectives by the counties and communes, urban collectives by the cities or state factories. During the Cultural Revolution, this sector grew by between 14 and 17 per cent, almost twice that of the state sector.[32]

In the urban areas some collectives were under the supervision of, and remitted profits to, the local ministerial office with a portion of these profits staying in the locality.[33] However, there were other collectives which were managed by the locality, and which, after paying taxes, remitted all their profits to the locality for local use. Overall, from 1966 to 1977, extrabudgetary funds in the hands of the China's counties grew from 14.5 per cent of the state budget to 35.6 per cent. In one county, this type of income rose 3,000 per cent during the Cultural Revolution to become "a major factor in local planning for the county's economic development." The collective sector was thus a fast growing one which yielded considerable income outside the national budget to its governmental supervisory body. It was a central element in the robust local economies that developed in many parts of China, financed by extra-budgetary funds and producing – and allocating – a wide range of products.[34]

Equally striking, however, is the administrative expertise that developed at the local level.[35] In addition to a *managerial* function similar to that performed by ministries, localities developed techniques for performing a *co-ordinative* function more characteristic of central planning

32. Jianzhong Tang and Laurence C. Ma, "Evolution of urban collective enterprises in China," *The China Quarterly*, No. 104 (December 1985), pp. 615–640, and Wong, "Ownership and control in Chinese industry," table 5, p. 602.

33. The discussion in this paragraph draws from William A. Byrd and Qingsong Lin, *China's Rural Industry: Structure, Development and Reform* (Washington, D.C.: The World Bank, 1990), p. 343, Shue, "Beyond the budget," p. 176 and Barry Naughton, "Financial reforms in China's industrial system," in Elizabeth J. Perry and Christine Wong (eds.), *The Political Economy of Reform in Post-Mao China* (Cambridge, MA: Harvard University Press, 1985), p. 228. See also Kojima, "The growing fiscal authority of provincial-level governments in China," p. 336.

34. Barry Naughton, "The decline of central control over investment in post-Mao China," in David M. Lampton (ed.), *Policy Implementation in Post-Mao China* (Berkeley: University of California Press, 1987), pp. 51–80 and Yasheng Huang, *Inflation and Investment Controls in China: The Political Economy of Central–Local Relations during the Reform Era* (Cambridge: Cambridge University Press, forthcoming), p. 138. On the growth of extrabudgetary funds during these years see Shaoguang Wang, "The rise of the regions: fiscal reform and the decline of central state capacity in China," in Andrew Walder, *The Waning of the Communist State: Economic Origins of Political Decline in China and Hungary* (Berkeley: University of California Press, 1995), pp. 93–95. Local control over allocation of industrial output is discussed in Christine Wong, "Material allocation and decentralization: impact of the local sector on industrial reform" in Perry and Wong, *The Political Economy of Reform in Post-Mao China*, pp. 253–278.

35. The discussion in this paragraph draws from Wong, "The 'Maoist' model reconsidered," pp. 186–191, William Byrd, *The Market Mechanism and Economic Reform in China* (Armonk, NY: M. E. Sharpe, 1991), pp. 46 and 107, Audrey Donnithorne, "China's cellular economy: some economic trends since the Cultural Revolution," *The China Quarterly*, No. 52 (October–December, 1972), pp. 605–619 and Christine P. W. Wong, "Interpreting rural industrial growth in the post-Mao period," *Modern China*, Vol. 14, No. 1 (January 1988), p. 7. For a description of such overall planning in one municipality, see Marc Blecher, "Developmental state, entrepreneurial state: the political economy of socialist reform in Xinju municipality and Guanghan county," in Gordon White (ed.), *The Chinese State in the Era of Economic Reform: The Road to Crisis* (Armonk, NY: M. E. Sharpe, 1991), pp. 265–289.

bodies, bringing together different sectors of the local economy into an integrated whole. In some cases, these techniques represented adaptation to or even manipulation of the centrally planned economy such as using tax exemptions and reductions as a way of retaining funds for investment that should have been passed up to the Centre or increasing the profits of local industries by charging lower prices within the locality than without. Finally, although "going after profits" was stigmatized and the Centre's claim to agricultural raw materials made procurement difficult, local planners at the county or even commune level did develop industries to meet local needs and to generate profits for investment in other areas.

Many of the devices described above are typical of the activities that fill the interstices of any centrally planned economy (CPE). They are qualitatively different in that they were not merely coping mechanisms, but an integral part of the local economy designed to promote economic development.[36] However, local entrepreneurial behaviour went beyond these quasi-administrative actions as some administrators oversaw or facilitated market-like behaviour of economic units of quite different natures. Such behaviour included shielding private enterprise; directly marketing local output; facilitating exchanges or contracts between state and non-state economic entities; and even sponsoring market fairs or exchanges. Some authors have used terms such as "profit maximizing" or "entrepreneurial initiative" to describe these activities.[37]

Of course this was a risky business. However, local cadres took advantage of China's "sporadic totalitarian state" which was unable to maintain consistent supervision of the nation's localities.[38] As central control weakened, cadres not only promoted illicit activities, they also skirted fiscal and budgetary regulations in order to increase local development. These cadres, as well as the institutions and modes of behaviour that characterized local economic management during the Cultural Revolution, would persist into the reform period.[39]

Even given the difficulties of generalizing about *all* of China, it is apparent that the localities had resources, techniques and organization

---

36. This paragraph is based on Byrd, *The Market Mechanism and Economic Reforms in China*, pp. 5–6 and 45, Wong, "Material allocation and decentralization," p. 264, Donnithorne, "China's cellular economy," p. 616, Blecher, "Developmental state, entrepreneurial state," pp. 272–73, Yang-Ling Liu, "Reform from below: the private economy," *The China Quarterly*, No. 130 (June 1992), pp. 293–316 and Kristen Parris, "Local initiative and national reform: the Wenzhou model of development," *The China Quarterly*, No. 134 (June 1993), pp. 242–263.

37. See, respectively, Christine Pui Wah Wong, "Rural industrialization in the People's Republic of China: lessons from the Cultural Revolution decade," in United States Congress, Joint Economic Committee, *China Under the Four Modernizations*, Part 1 (Washington, D.C.: Government Printing Office, 1982), p. 407 and Donnithorne, "China's cellular economy," p. 614.

38. Liu, "Reform from below," p. 313. See also Parris, "Local initiative and national reform," p. 263. In Wuxi county local officials ignored orders to shut down local industries and concentrate on agriculture. Byrd and Lin, *China's Rural Industry*, p. 7.

39. Jean Oi notes that "Many of the local officials who are now leading rapid economic development were the same people who presided over the minimally functioning economy during the Maoist period." *Rural China Takes Off: Incentives for Industrialization* (Berkeley: University of California Press, forthcoming), p. 5.

that were lacking in the Soviet case and posed a formidable challenge to any attempt at central planning.[40] As others have noted, latent within these institutions and techniques were elements of market not found in the national, planned economy.[41] Mao's reforms thus created an institutional pattern – the "stones" – that would decisively shape the course of the reforms initiated after his death.

The Impact of China's "Non-State" Sector Industries

Strong evidence for this contention is found in the township and village industries (TVEs). These firms have been both "the main ingredient in China's transition" and the "largest and the most dynamic part" of the non-state sector which is considered to be "critical for the success" of incremental reform in China.[42] They evolved out of the economic structure discussed above, and their institutional qualities and modes of behaviour reflect that heritage.

This is apparent first in the overwhelming share of administrative ownership at *all* levels of the system. Note the use of the term "administrative." As shown earlier, the term "state" is reserved for those industries which usually fall under the national plan and budget and are controlled by the central government, provinces, cities or counties. Overall, these state industries represented 48.4 per cent of the output value of industry in 1992. Moving outside the plan, to what is called the "non-state sector," collective firms dominate with 38.2 per cent while the private sector accounts for 6.8 per cent and "others" (such as foreign investments, joint ventures) for 6.6 per cent.[43]

The distinctive heritage of China is apparent. Recall that since the 1970s collectives have not been genuine co-operatives. Although their manner of management and doing business differs somewhat from state-owned enterprises, they have remained entities owned and managed by local governments. There is nothing particularly non-state about this sector. In China's cities and counties, the two ownership types of state and collective overwhelmingly dominate, and are both managed by the state structure *at that level*.[44] At the township level or below, collective

40. This is the central argument of Huang, "Information, bureaucracy and economic reforms in China and the Soviet Union."

41. Wong, "Ownership and Control in Chinese Industry," pp. 593–96. See also, Byrd, *The Market Mechanism and Economic Reforms in China*, pp. 4–7, 44–46 and 107–109, Shue, "Beyond the budget," p. 148. On the question of dynamism in the pre-reform economy see Blecher, "Developmental state, entrepreneurial state."

42. The quotations are from McMillan and Naughton, "How to reform a planned economy," p. 138 and Qian Yingyi and Chenggang Xu, "Why China's Economic Reforms Differ," pp. 14 and 6 respectively.

43. Guojia jingji tizhi gaige weiyuanhui, *Zhongguo jingji tizhi gaige, 1993 nianjian* (*China Economic Systems Reform Yearbook, 1993*) (Beijing: Gaige chubanshe, 1994), p. 605.

44. Referring to these local collectives, one author has written, "They are essentially ministate enterprises, but the 'states' to which they belong are community governments, which supervise the enterprises through their industrial corporations." William A. Byrd (ed.), *Chinese Industrial Firms Under Reform* (New York: Oxford University Press, 1992), p. 89.

and private enterprises dominate. Although a World Bank study discovered wide variation throughout rural China, nation-wide collective industry owned and managed by the township and below represented more than 92 per cent of gross value of industrial output at this level with private industry representing 8 per cent.[45]

The shadow of the past is evident in this small private sector. The lingering suspicion of the private sector is an obvious legacy of the Cultural Revolution as is the tradition, in certain areas, of cadres sheltering private enterprise in the interest of local development and income. The growth and tolerance of the private sector thus remains directly related to its usefulness to the local state as a source of funds, employment and so on.[46] The formal legal structures needed to protect property and commercial relations in the private sector are clearly inadequate.[47] Moreover, private enterprises are constrained in their access to capital and raw materials. To avoid these problems, they frequently register as collectives or pay a "management fee" to possess some of the rights of collectives. Rather than competing with the administratively managed economy at the local level, the private sector complements it.

The ownership structure that has emerged out of China's partial reform demonstrates that the vibrant, rapidly growing "non-state" sector that has developed outside the plan can not be considered anything other than one dominated by public ownership and management.[48] Its enormous growth is neither an indication that a "capitalist revolution" has broken out from below or that the Chinese leadership has somehow renounced its Leninist

45. Byrd and Lin, *China's Rural Reforms*, p. 195.

46. These are central themes of Susan Young's writings. See her "Private entrepreneurs and evolutionary change in China," in David S. G. Goodman and Beverly Hooper (eds.), *China's Quiet Revolution: New Interactions Between State and Society* (New York: St Martin's Press, 1993), pp. 105–125 and "Policy, Practice and the Policy Sector in China," *The Australian Journal of Chinese Affairs*, No. 21, pp. 57–80. Similar points are made in David Goodman, "China: the state and capitalist revolution," *The Pacific Review*, Vol. 5, No. 4 (1992), pp. 350–59, Nee, "Organizational dynamics of market transition: hybrid forms, property rights, and mixed economy in China," Solinger, *China's Transition from Socialism*, ch. 11, Oi, *Rural China Takes Off*, pp. 131–39, and Byrd and Lin, *China's Rural Industry*, ch. 5. For a useful review by a major Chinese economic journal of the problems facing private enterprise see Joint Publications Research Service, *China Report* (hereafter JPRS-CAR), 94-001, 14 October 1994, pp. 47–51.

47. For an anecdotal discussion of this issue see Thomas P. Lyons, *Market-Oriented Reform in China: Cautionary Tales* (Ithaca, NY: Cornell University, Department of Economics, 1992).

48. This is a theme of Louis Putterman's paper in this volume. A strong statement of this case, along with a review of the relevant literature, can be found in Andrew G. Walder, "Local governments as industrial corporations: an organizational analysis of China's transitional economy," unpublished paper, pp. 10–11. See also Gordon White, *Riding the Tiger: The Politics of Economic Reform in Post-Mao China* (Stanford: Stanford University Press, 1993), pp. 76–77 and Goodman, "China: the state and capitalist revolution," p. 356 for statements of their nature along these lines. An excellent discussion of the nature of non-state enterprises can be found in Qian Yingyi and Chenggang Xu, "Why China's reforms differ." Frequent complaints in the Chinese press regarding local governmental intervention in the local economy substantiate the claims of certain Chinese economists that the collectives represent a "second state sector." Thomas G. Rawski, "Chinese industrial reform: accomplishments, prospects, and implications," *American Economic Association Papers and Proceedings*, Vol. 84, No. 2 (May 1994), p. 271. See also the remarks of the Chinese economist Wu Jinglian in JPRS-CAR 94-051, 27 October 1994, pp. 13–15.

roots and permitted capitalism to flourish.[49] The "non-state" sector is not to be confused with separateness from administrative control. It is characterized by a dependent private sector and a dominant collective sector.

The continuity with the Maoist period leads to the impact of reform policy. To stress the importance of historic institutions does not mean that policy is ignored. Institutions give shape to diverse policies. Specifically, the explosion of TVEs was the result of two reform initiatives: the decollectivization of agriculture and the fiscal reforms of the early 1980s.[50] These both provided incentives to develop the local economy and additional wherewithal with which to do so. For example, agricultural reform provided the incentive of reduced income from agricultural sales while the concurrent release of farmers supplied labour for factories. The changes in fiscal policy were more far-reaching. Although the details of the revenue sharing plan were complex, the incentives it provided to administrators at the provincial level and below were crystal clear. Governments at various levels would be able to exercise unprecedented discretion in setting their budgets, but more importantly they would have fixed obligations to pass up revenues to the next level and would have the right to retain and spend the "residual."[51]

In a Soviet-style fiscal system where industrial profits provided the bulk of governmental revenue, these fiscal reforms unleashed the potential for entrepreneurial activity inherent in the Maoist structures. Developmental goals and strategies that were earlier pursued could now be legitimately implemented and expanded. Stimulated by the incentives provided by the changed fiscal structure, unencumbered by previous restrictions and supported by the resources provided by international trade and agricultural reform, the growing collective sector has clearly expanded the scope and weight of market mechanisms in the Chinese economy during the years after 1978.[52] To this extent the localities have promoted reform in post-Mao China.

Precisely because these industries are outside the plan they, unlike state

49. The former contention is Pei Minxin in *From Reform to Revolution* and the latter is offered by Peter Murrell ("What is shock therapy? What did it do in Poland and Russia?" p. 121) as an explanation of why what appeared to be a mixed economy was developing in China despite the Leninist system.

50. On this point see also Qian Yingyi and Chenggang Xu, "Why China's reforms differ," p. 9. One could also add a third policy change – the "open door." Although Samuel Ho is probably right when he notes that this affected only the coastal provinces, it is also true that these provinces have seen some of the strongest growth in the non-state sector. Finally, of course, TVEs have been the recipients of a large amount of overseas investment and, as Lardy's paper in this volume suggests, are a major source of China's exports. Samuel Ho, *Rural China in Transition: Non-Agricultural Development in Rural Jiangsu, 1978–1990* (Oxford: Clarendon Press, 1994), pp. 69–75.

51. See Oi, *Rural China Takes Off*, ch. 2 for a discussion of the issues raised in this paragraph.

52. The discussion which follows is drawn from Byrd and Lin, *China's Rural Industry*, Ho, *Rural China in Transition*, Nee, "Organizational Dynamics of Market Transition," Anthony J. Ody, *Rural Enterprise Development in China, 1986–1990* (Washington, D.C.: The World Bank, 1992), Walder, "Local governments as industrial corporations," and Qian Yingyi and Chenggang Xu, "Why China's economic reforms differ."

industry, cannot be assured of access to means of production or sales. They must find customers as well as suppliers, and the prices at which inputs or finished goods trade are determined by negotiation. Moreover, they operate under harder budget constraints than enterprises in the planned sector. Local governments do not have the resources of a central government to support failing industries. Indeed, since industry provides a major source of budgetary income, it is logical that local authorities would have little tolerance for such enterprises.

In short, building on the techniques, infrastructure, connections and personnel of the Maoist period, local government has seized on the opportunities of the reform era to use the market to develop the local economy and enhance fiscal health. Here is the irony that Andrew Walder notes in his introduction to this collection. Those who look for the roots of the entrepreneurial and profit seeking behaviour that has been the major force for growth of the "non-state" sector must look to the legacy of the man for whom such activities were anathema. Yet, as others have argued, while emphasizing such entrepreneurial and market conforming behaviour that make China's collectives a distinctive type of public enterprise, one must not lose sight of the rest of the Maoist legacy – in particular, the dominant influence of local government in shaping the goals of these enterprises and the economic environment in which they operate.[53] China's local bureaucracies continue to intervene in ways that reflect their roots in a Soviet-style CPE. While the fiscal reforms did much to promote latent administrative entrepreneurial activity, they did not achieve the reformers' intended goal of disengaging local entities from the economy. Quite the opposite: they virtually forced localities to *intensify* their intervention in the economy.[54]

The goals of local enterprises remain those of the locality and not of the enterprise itself. This means broad development for the purposes of budgetary income and employment. As a result of the latter priority, it has not been uncommon for collectives to be overstaffed in a manner similar to state enterprises. Local governments have also pooled the income received from firms and used it to create more employment through expansion or to avoid lay-offs by supporting less successful firms. The result has been that the amount of earnings retained for expansion by the more profitable collectives has been limited.[55]

Moreover, while collective industries in China might, on average,

53. See Wong, "Interpreting rural industrial growth in post-Mao China."

54. This is the central theme of Christine P. W. Wong, "Central–local relations in an era of fiscal decline: the paradox of fiscal decentralization in post-Mao China," *The China Quarterly*, No. 128 (December 1991), pp. 691–715. Wong suggests that localities were given an additional impetus to develop economies by the fact that additional budgetary obligations were passed down to them. Victor Nee argues that "revenue-sharing arrangements forged a virtual partnership between local government and industry." "Organizational dynamics of market transition," p. 5. He also notes the more direct access to resources in the case of collective industries, p. 11. See also Walder, "Local governments as industrial corporations." For a similar point made in a Chinese economic journal see JPRS-CAR 93-077, 20 October 1993, p. 18.

55. The themes in this paragraph run through Byrd and Lin, *China's Rural Industry*.

operate under somewhat harder budget constraints than the state sector, they have still received significant market protection from their state sponsors. Local funds have been pooled to prop up less profitable enterprises. During the late 1980s when pressure from the central government to close down these industries increased, local governments were able to protect them through mergers and other forms of evasion.[56] This last strategy suggests that local governments have ways of blunting market pressures on firms in the non-state sector which derive more from bureaucratic power than financial resources.

A most important example of this has been the ability to influence the tax and banking systems.[57] The close relationship between local governments and bank branches has resulted in pressures to engage in such budget softening actions as granting preferential loans, lending beyond limits, easing loan requirements or extending loan payments. In some cases localities have established their own credit institutions. Until the tax reforms of 1994, localities down to the township acted as agents of the Centre, collecting taxes on the very enterprises that provided them with income and employment. Naturally, localities proved to be less than diligent collectors. While they could not set tax rates, they could grant exemptions or fail to report misconduct. Such manipulation of tax receipts has meant that localities were softening budget constraints at the expense of the Centre. Thus, even as they promote some types of market behaviour they frustrate others by carrying out practices rooted in their Leninist past.[58]

Chinese Reform within the Context of Soviet-style Reform

With this discussion, this article returns to its central theme: the lessons that can be gleaned from China's post-Mao experience regarding the political foundations of reform in Soviet-style systems. How is it that China can appear to be pursuing a reform path thought to be precluded by the fusion of politics and economics in Leninist systems? How can elements of a market and an aggressive, entrepreneurial sector competing with the official planned economy develop within a political system whose ethos and institutions seem inimical to their emergence? Why haven't China's attempts at incremental reform or a mixed economy

56. Oi, *Rural China Takes Off*, p. 179.

57. The very best study of how localities have manipulated the fiscal and monetary tools can be found in World Bank, *China: Macroeconomic Stability in A Decentralized Economy* Report No. 13399-CHA, 26 October 1994. See also Oi, *Rural China Takes Off*, chs. 2, 4 and 5, Yasheng Huang, *Inflation and Investment Controls in China*, ch. 4, and Singh, "Industrial policies for an economy in transition."

58. This has been noted in the Chinese press. Thus, one official in Anhui called upon localities to "change the idea of helping enterprises by relying solely on reduction of tax payment and profit delivery ... [and] help enterprises enter the market to participate in fair competition." As another article put it, the goal of local government should be to get enterprises out of the habit of "looking for the mayor rather than the market." FBIS *Daily Report: China* (hereafter FBIS-CHI), 3 May 1994, p. 48 and JPRS-CAR 93-034, 24 May 1993, p. 15.

suffered the same fate as has befallen similar attempts made in other socialist states?

The key to answering all these questions lies in a recognition of the fact that while the interdependency of economics and politics must necessarily limit the extent of incremental reform, it is also true that different varieties of Leninist systems can accommodate quite different reforms. Viewing the Chinese reform experience in a comparative Communist perspective illustrates one deceptively simple proposition: that the nature and extent of what *within* system reform can accomplish is not dependent just on reform strategy, but also on *what is within the system*.[59] It is thus not necessarily inconsistent to say both that the incremental reform of a Soviet-style economy is limited by the nature of the system, and that the very same incremental reform can bring dramatic results. Historic institutions present not only constraints but opportunities. A strategy that relies on "enabling reform" logically requires elements in the institutions of the political economy that can released.

In China's case, the basic difference from other socialist states lay in the existence of two significantly different economic systems contained within (and legitimized by) the pre-reform political economy – one managed from Beijing, the other managed at the local level. The ties of collective firms to the bureaucratic economy and their integration into locally based economies make them essentially different from the private sector in a mixed socialist economy discussed above. They are not a beleaguered enclave of private entrepreneurs in an unfriendly and (in terms of laws and institutions) inhospitable environment. They are part of a Soviet-style political economy, protected (as private enterprise is not) by their public nature and by the political tools at the disposal of their local government patrons to promote their economic success. It is this fact that has made it possible for the gradualist path of reform characterized by competition between the state and "non-state" sectors described by Naughton and others to proceed as far as it has.

The general lesson suggested in the introductory sections to this article thus seems to hold in the case of the development of the non-state sector in China: fundamental economic transformations simply do not occur in the absence of equally fundamental political changes. More specifically, it would appear that in the absence of political institutional change, this aspect of China's incremental economic reform has, in a manner predicted by the logic of Leninist systems, remained within the boundaries of that system. By seizing upon elements of market and entrepreneurialism while ignoring interventions that frustrate market development, many commentators have *overestimated* the extent of China's departure from its pre-reform Leninist roots. However, at the same time, there has been a tendency to *underestimate* the potential inherent in the particular kind

59. This argument is made by Blecher in "Developmental state, entrepreneurial state." Similar points are made in David Granick's study of the Chinese reform, *Chinese State Enterprises*, pp. 1 and 17 and Dorothy Solinger's book *China's Transition from Socialism*, parts 2 and 3.

of planned economy that developed in China during the pre-reform period. The more flexible localistic regimes that emerged during the Maoist years and which were always quick to turn to their advantage the vulnerabilities of the Centre as well as adept at using different ownership structures and managerial instruments to promote local growth, have adjusted to the opportunities of the reform period and produced startling growth.[60]

Future Developments

In much the same way as some comparisons of Sino-Soviet reforms have suffered from a slighting of the decisive impact which the distinctive Maoist heritage has had on subsequent changes, so too have many discussions of the consequences of these reforms failed to take into account the impact which their distinctive path might have on future developments. Path dependence remains a useful tool of analysis as China's leaders cross the river on the institutional stones laid down by past reforms.

In the years before the tumultuous events of 1989–91, most Western analysts saw the political constraints on economic reform described above as the Achilles' heel of a Soviet-style system capable of initiating the process of industrialization, but unable to cope with the socio-economic consequences of its own successes. As declining economic performance sapped its legitimacy, the Communist Party would find its dominance challenged by new social groups energized by economic change.[61] Post-Mao China is often seen as facing a similar crisis. However, this time it is the result not of the state-driven industrialization process but of the subsequent economic reforms which, in the words of Gordon White, brought about a "dispersion of social power" and "shift in the balance between state and society." Leninist systems were damned if they didn't reform – but also damned if they did.[62]

The events at Tiananmen in 1989 prompted assertions of a developing cleavage between state and society defined by the concept of civil society.

60. In her *Political Logic of Economic Reform* Susan Shirk deals with these issues in a somewhat different fashion. For example, although hers is an institutionalist analysis which seeks to demonstrate that some Leninist systems have a greater potential for reform than others, her emphasis seems to be on strategy. Specifically, she seeks to show how cultivating support among provincial leaders gave Deng Xiaoping the political power to affect a "market" reform in the absence of political reform. Her focus is thus more on strategy – the creation of allies for reform among the provinces – than on the impact of pre-reform structure. Moreover, it is by no means clear that the provinces are allies of reform since by her own account they sabotage the major industrial reform initiative of the 1980s (the "tax for profit" plan) and, in the end, freeze reform at a mid-point that is consistent with their bureaucratic interests. The latter point is, of course, consistent with my analysis above. However, it appears to contradict the central thesis of her book, to wit, that alliance with provinces can bring significant changes in the nature of China's Soviet style economy. For a further critique of this book see my forthcoming review in *The Journal of Interdisciplinary History*.

61. For a comprehensive review of the convergence literature of the 1960s and 1970s see William C. Taubman, "The change to change in Communist systems," in Henry W. Morton and Rudolf Tokes (eds.), *Soviet Politics and Society in the 1970s* (New York: Free Press, 1974).

62. White, *Riding the Tiger*, pp. 198–99.

For example, David Strand linked the events of that year with the historic roots of "civil society" and a "public sphere" in late imperial and republican China. In his view, and that of many others, the post-Mao economic reforms had given a new impetus to a process begun before 1949.[63] This theme stimulated a vigorous debate over whether past merchant and gentry associations could possibly be precursors of a civil society in China. For some, their close ties with the state compromised the autonomy essential in any definition of civil society. For others, the links with the state were evidence of their self-governing nature.[64]

This close relationship with the state has continued to colour – and to complicate – discussions of civil society in post-reform China. Despite evidence of social unrest, it has been difficult to find the drive for autonomy and social cohesion associated with civil society. Those studying specific societal groups ranging from the official technocratic elite to private entrepreneurs to foreign sector managers have found few impulses to seek autonomy.[65] With little pressure from below and a still dominant Leninist state – on the national and local levels – determined to contain, rather than protect, societal autonomy, commentators have been left using words like "nascent," "in the making," "sprouts" or "embryonic" to describe the signs of civil society.[66] Margaret Pearson is less circumspect, arguing that "civil society is not what is going on in China."[67] For Pearson and others, what *is* going on is the development of a form of corporatism.

The attraction of corporatism for analysts of post-Mao China is that the paradigm seems to accommodate both the changes in the nature of society brought about by economic development and the existence of the

---

63. For a useful review of the Western literature that followed Tiananmen, see Gu Xin, "A civil society and public sphere in post-Mao China? An overview of Western publications," *China Information*, Vol. VIII, No. 3 (Winter 1993–94), pp. 38–39. For a survey of Chinese views see Shu-Yun Ma, "The Chinese discourse on civil society," *The China Quarterly*, No. 137 (March 1994), pp. 180–193.

64. David Strand, "Protest in Beijing: civil society and the public sphere in China," *Problems of Communism*, Vol. XX, No. 3 (May–June 1990), pp. 1–19. Mayfair Yang also spoke of a "civil society now reemerging" as a result of the reforms. "Between state and society: the construction of corporateness in a Chinese socialist factory," *The Australian Journal of Chinese Affairs*, No. 22 (July 1989), pp. 35–38. The debate on civil society in late Qing and Republican China can be found in *Modern China*, Vol. 19, No. 2 (April 1993).

65. Li Cheng and Lynn White III, "China's technocratic movement and the *World Economic Herald*," *Modern China*, Vol. 17, No. 3 (July 1991), pp. 342–388, David L. Wank, "Private business, bureaucracy, and political alliance in a Chinese city," *The Australian Journal of International Affairs*, No. 33 (January 1995), pp. 55–71, Solinger, *China's Transition From Socialism*, ch. 11, and Pearson, *China's New Business Elites* (Berkeley: University of California Press, forthcoming).

66. Indeed, even as he made bold statements regarding the "radical social and ultimately political repercussions" of "market oriented economic reforms," Gordon White found that the organizations which have emerged (or further evolved) since the reforms have been dominated by the party/state and have shown few traces of significant autonomy. Gordon White, "Prospects for civil society in China: a case study of Xiaoshan city," *The Australian Journal of Chinese Affairs*, No. 29 (January 1993), pp. 63–87. For similar conclusions, see Shue, "State power and social organization in China," pp. 64–85.

67. Pearson, *China's New Business Elites*, p. 181.

dominant Leninist state.[68] Whereas civil society assumes limitations imposed on the state by society with the state creating the conditions for relatively unfettered development of (and participation by) autonomous associations, corporatism posits limitations imposed by the state upon society, with the state setting the ground rules for the emergence of such associations and the participation of its representatives.[69] The apparent fit with China's circumstances has made corporatism appear to be a more fruitful way to understand both the political results of partial reform and the future trajectories of the reform process. Yet, thus far, it has not realized this promise.

A major reason for this lies in the failure adequately to clarify the distinction between state corporatism and the Leninist concept of state-licensed organizations as transmission belts. Based on what Alex Pravda and Blair Ruble have called "classic dualism," Leninist organizations are expected both to mobilize societal groups for the goals of the party/state and to protect the interests of their membership.[70] Although it is recognized that during times of regime liberalization the scope for the representation of interests has expanded in China and the former Soviet Union, such expression has always been within the limits imposed from above. In order to apply corporatism successfully to China, it is necessary to distinguish it both conceptually from classic Leninism and factually from such periods of political relaxation.

Until this is done, it is not clear how much is gained by using corporatism to understand state/society relations in reform China. Attempts have been made to define the distinctive nature of "corporatism Chinese style," "Communist state corporatism" or "socialist corporatism."[71] However, like Philippe Schmitter's distinctions between state corporatism and the "Soviet monist model," these terms remain elusive and seemingly lack analytical power.[72] As with the concept of civil

---

68. See Jonathan Unger and Anita Chan, "Chinese corporatism: a developmental state in East Asian context," *The Australian Journal of Chinese Affairs*, No. 33 (January 1995), pp. 29–53. A similar process occurred more than a decade earlier in the study of the Soviet Union and Eastern Europe when dissatisfaction with the modernization/pluralism approach led some to look to corporatism. Grzegorz Ekiert, "Democratization processes in East Central Europe: a theoretical reconsideration," *British Journal of Political Science*, Vol. 21, Part 3 (July 1991), pp. 285–313.

69. The *locus classicus* for the concept of corporatism can be found in the writings of Philippe Schmitter. See his "Still a century of corporatism," *The Review of Politics*, Vol. 36, No. 1 (January 1974), pp. 93–96 and "Modes of interest intermediation and models of societal change in Western Europe," in Philippe C. Schmitter and Gerhard Lehmbruch (eds.), *Trends Towards Corporatist Intermediation* (Beverly Hill: Sage Publications, 1979).

70. This discussion is drawn from Anita Chan, "Revolution or corporatism? Workers and trade unions in post-Mao China," *The Australian Journal of Chinese Affairs*, No. 29 (January 1993), pp. 36–37. It is she who cites Alex Pravda and Blair A. Ruble, "Communist trade unions: varieties of dualism," in Alex Pravda and Blair A. Ruble (eds.), *Trade Unions in Communist States* (Boston: Allen and Unwin, 1986), pp. 1–21.

71. The first term is Unger and Chan's, the second is Chan's and the third is Margaret Pearson's. See her "The Janus face of business associations in China: socialist corporatism in foreign enterprises," *The Australian Journal of Chinese Affairs*, No. 31 (January 1994), pp. 25–46.

72. Schmitter, "Still a century of corporatism," p. 97.

society, the continuing dominance of the state makes it difficult to define significant spheres of societal autonomy.

The application of this concept is also undermined by the weak institutionalization of corporatist institutions in China. As Unger and Chan note, two significant sectors of the population – the peasants and the workers in non-state enterprises – are not included in national, state-sponsored organizations. Moreover, Pearson's claim that "foreign sector managers still choose safer, well-established, and effective clientalist strategies to maneuver their way through the bureaucracy" rather than "socialist corporatist" structures is consistent with David Wank's findings that the more influential entrepreneurs in Xiamen prefer using "personal ties" with the bureaucracy rather than the officially sanctioned, but institutionally weak, associations.[73]

Finally, the institutional weaknesses of corporatism contribute to questions regarding its utility not only for understanding the nature of post-reform China but also for conceptualizing the longer-term consequences of partial economic reform. The original paradigm of corporatism developed by Schmitter is extremely vague regarding historical change and provides little guidance. Most commentators have looked to the experiences of other East Asian countries where they have seen an evolution from earlier, authoritarian, state corporatism to later more liberal, societal corporatism.[74] Yet how this might apply to China is unclear. Pearson envisages the possibility of China remaining in a condition of "stasis" defined by socialist corporatism. Unger and Chan argue tentatively for the possibility of evolution towards more liberalized "societal corporatism" in China. However, they are vague on how this might come about and seem to fall victim to the conceptual difficulties of the paradigm when they conclude: "To the extent that China continues to loosen up politically, it is far more likely to involve such incremental shifts into societal corporatism rather than the introduction of any form of democracy." Since the line between societal corporatism and democracy is fuzzy, it is not clear how this improves on earlier paradigms assuming that economic change brings pluralism/civil society.[75]

It appears that the paradigms of corporatism and civil society are, as yet, of only limited use in conceptualizing the trajectory of China's development. This might be because they are based on the premise noted at the beginning of this section: namely, that economic change neces-

73. Unger and Chan, "Chinese corporatism," pp. 50–52, Pearson, *China's New Business Elites*, p. 187 and Wank, "Private business, bureaucracy, and political alliance."

74. Schmitter has proposed two varieties of corporatism: "societal" and "state."

75. Pearson, "The Janus face of business associations in China," p. 47 and Unger and Chan's view, "Chinese Corporatism," pp. 52–53. For the hollowness of the distinction between societal corporatism and pluralism see Youssef Cohen and Franco Pavoncello, "Corporatism and pluralism: a critique of Schmitter's typology," *British Journal of Political Science*, Vol. 17, No. 1 (January 1987), pp. 117–122 and Ross M. Martin, "Pluralism and the new corporatism," *Political Studies*, Vol. XXXI, No. 1 (1983), pp. 86–102. See also Andrew Cox, "The old and new testaments of corporatism: is it a political form or a method of policy-making," *Political Studies*, Vol. XXXVI (1988), pp. 294–308.

sarily brings a dispersal of power to society that challenges the party rule. Such an outcome is not consistent with central characteristics of the Chinese reform experience. As shown above, the principal forces for economic growth have come not from society but from jurisdictions within the state.[76] The partial reform paradigm which assumes structural change via competition between two sectors of the economy, the one (non-state) growing vigorously at the expense of the other (the state), is not only about economics. Because major components of the Chinese state – the localities and the central government, respectively – have more proximate control over (and benefit disproportionately from) each of these sectors, the course of economic reform has had real consequences for the balance of power within the Chinese state.[77] It is for this reason that some commentators consider the most important political results of economic reform are to be found not in the shifting balance between society and the state, but within the state itself.[78]

It would appear that the reforms have dispersed political and economic resources in an manner unprecedented in the history of post-1949 China. The decentralizing reforms which have caused all levels of government to have a vital stake in economic development have certainly increased the financial resources available to them, whether in the form of foreign investment, extrabudgetary funds, or taxes withheld from the Centre.[79] As Andrew Walder and others have argued, this has enhanced the administrative devolution that has accompanied economic reform as bureaucrats have developed local resources that make them less responsive to superiors. Meanwhile, because the resources available to the Centre are shrinking because of an inefficient fiscal system as well as the lower levels of profitability of state industry, Beijing's ability to act as the leading force

76. For an interesting discussion of how past state-dominated economic growth affects future trajectories see Kanishka Jayasuriya, "Political economy of democratization in East Asia," *Asian Perspective*, Vol. 18, No. 2 (Fall–Winter 1994), pp. 141–180.

77. White, *Riding the Tiger*, pp. 126–27.

78. This is a theme that has figured prominently in two recent essay collections. Goodman and Hooper, *China's Quiet Revolution* and Walder, *The Waning of the Communist State*. See, particularly, Andrew Walder, "The quiet revolution from within: economic reform as a source of political decline," in the latter for a strong argument regarding the importance of going beyond a focus on civil society to one on the state. Other useful discussions of the relationship between state and society can be found in Solinger, *China's Transition from Socialism*, ch. 11 and Elizabeth J. Perry, "Trends in the study of state–society relations," *The China Quarterly*, No. 139 (September 1994), pp. 704–713.

79. Assessing the impact of partial economic reform on China's political structure is complicated in the first instance by definitional issues; in particular, the loose manner in which the term "local government" is used to identify political jurisdictions from the township up to the province. The influence of reform policies has differed between political jurisdictions depending on the predominant type of economy ("state" at the higher levels, "non-state" below the county) and the wealth of the particular area. In addition, it is unclear how each of these political subdivisions relates to the other. Although it is likely that the views and resources of provincial authorities are influenced by the vibrant economies at the county level and below, this relationship remains opaque. See Jae Ho Chung in "Studies of central provincial relations in the People's Republic of China: a mid-term appraisal," *The China Quarterly*, No. 142 (September 1995), p. 485.

in a unitary, Leninist state has clearly declined.[80] All this has led one author to note that the crucial difference between the reform and pre-reform periods is that local governments have become an "economic interest group" rather than an "extension of the central government," while another writes of the "negotiatory relationship" that has developed between the Centre and the localities.[81]

Federalism has become a shorthand term widely used to describe these changes in the Chinese polity in much the same way as civil society and corporatism have been used to identify state/society changes. Yet like these terms it has appeared in many different guises and has often served simply to indicate the unquestioned devolution of power to lower levels. The discussion which follows will focus on one of the more ambitious and provocative uses of the term: "market preserving federalism."[82]

This paradigm explicitly shifts the debate on the implications of economic reform from the relationship between individuals and government to that among levels of government even as it seeks to explore aspects of political reform other than democratization. Specifically, the emphasis is on limiting the power of the *central* government, allowing local governments to "have authority over markets" and thereby "to foster local economic prosperity." In this view, it has been the competition among local governments, seeking to develop their own economies, that has been the major force driving robust economic growth. The "conventional wisdom" regarding the relationship between political and economic reform is therefore challenged by a perspective which sees decentralization and limits on central government intervention that might "distort markets for other purposes" as a crucial factor explaining China's economic successes.[83]

However, even advocates of this position recognize that market preservation requires more than simply unleashing the localities. It also requires a central government that can provide for "critical national public goods," most importantly, removal of internal trade barriers and monetary

---

80. For recent book-length discussions of the economic issues see Yasheng Huang, *Inflation and Investment Controls in China*, World Bank, *Macroeconomic Stability in a Decentralized Economy*, and Jia Hao and Lin Zhimin, *Changing Central–Local Relations in China*. The disparity between the central government's ambitions and the resources at its disposal is a theme of Barry Naughton's piece in this volume. It is also argued vigorously in Shaoguang Wang, "The rise of regions: fiscal reform and the decline of central state fiscal capacity in China," in Walder, *The Waning of the Communist State*. Andrew Walder's discussion can be found in his introduction to the latter, pp. 1–24 and in "The decline of communist power: elements of a theory of institutional change," *Theory and Society*, No. 23 (April 1994), pp. 297–323.

81. The quotations are from Yasheng Huang, *Inflation and Investment Controls in China*, p. 121 and Suisheng Zhao, "From coercion to negotiation: the changing central local economic relationship in Mainland China," *Issues and Studies*, Vol. 28, No. 10 (October 1992), pp. 1–22.

82. Gabriella Montinola, Yingyi Qian and Barry Weingast, "Federalism, Chinese style: the political basis for economic success in China," unpublished paper, Hoover Institution, Stanford University, 1993, revised version in *World Politics*, Vol. 48 (October 1995), pp. 50–81.

83. *Ibid.* p. 8. As Walder notes in the introduction to this volume, the authors suggest that local democratic reforms might arise out of federalism.

control.[84] China's progress towards a market system is seen at a "critical moment," as the nation's leaders face the necessity of institutionalizing a central government capable of overseeing local growth without stifling it.

Looking back over the post-Mao period, it would appear that the central government has faced the more difficult challenges in making such an adaptation to the consequences of partial economic reform. Although periods of decentralization before 1978 fostered the institutions and experience necessary to promote local development in a more market-oriented economy, there was little concomitant growth of central government instruments to manage this process. The Centre, in the pre-reform years, still relied on the economic tools of Soviet-style planning, resources furnished to it by the state industrial sector and the political prerogatives of a Leninist centre. While the localities had an adaptable institutional base from which they could exploit reform policies to enhance financial and bureaucratic resources, the central government has had to make do with more conventional instruments and declining financial resources to deal with robust local economic development.

This lag has been at the root of many of the major political/economic problems of the reform era. This is a major theme of Barry Naughton's article in this collection where he argues that the central government has not only found that its tools are no longer as powerful as before, but that it lacks the resources to develop new tools. Another example is the local "investment fever" which, in the view of most analysts, has been the principal cause of the periodic inflationary bouts that have plagued the Chinese economy and undermined the legitimacy of the central government. Beijing's continuing difficulties in regulating this investment have been attributed to a fiscal system that has allowed financial resources in the hands of the locality to grow, while those at the Centre decline; a monetary system unable to regulate the growth and allocation of money; and a central bureaucracy which cannot effectively supervise local investment.[85]

Finally, a 1994 World Bank report on the development of China's internal market concludes that progress towards greater marketization is impeded by the continuation of a "cellular" structure which has caused China to be "far from realizing the benefits of its potentially large internal market." Once again, the role of the central government is highlighted as a necessary source of tax laws, commercial regulations, redistribution of resources and so on that will allow for greater integration of what is now

84. *Ibid.* p. 26. Later (p. 30), the authors add infrastructural investment to the list of the central government's tasks.

85. Two works which explicitly address these questions are Yasheng Huang, *Inflation and Investment Controls in China* and World Bank, *Macroeconomic Stability in a Decentralized Economy*, p. 59. It should be noted that while this latter study cites the literature on "market preserving federalism," its emphasis is clearly on the need for strong central authority to complement local freedom.

a "customs union." The issue is the adaptability of economic instruments designed for other purposes: "China today is confronted by the task of transforming the economic role of its government from that required in a system of central planning, to a role more appropriate for a market economy."[86]

Indeed, some of the strongest evidence regarding the manner in which Leninist institutions have limited the capacity of the central government to function in a more decentralized and marketized economy can be found not simply in the failures of Beijing, but also in its successes. In a recent study of inflation and investment controls in reform China, Yasheng Huang argues that political control – primarily the Communist Party's power of appointment and removal – has been a "surrogate" for underdeveloped economic levers allowing Party leaders to achieve some inflation control. However, as Huang acknowledges, these political methods are blunt instruments that are less effective in regulating a national economy than specifically economic tools.[87]

The continued use of traditional centralized Party controls to deal with the growing power of the provinces is consistent with the lag that exists in the adjustment of a unitary state to the new reality of central–local relations. The central government has made only modest progress towards adapting to the new role thrust upon it by the consequences of partial reform. Indeed, the implications of the argument above are that its maintenance of Leninist institutions in the face of economic reform has done little more than provide public order amid the societal tensions caused by partial reform.[88]

This view of the challenges posed by partial economic reform to the existing structures of the central government also has implications for the provincial levels and below. Although local development has relied on some market-like mechanisms and private enterprise, the Leninist roots of the local government have been evident in their strong interventions in the economy. The result has been frequently to inhibit the operation of the market in the interests of the locality and its political authorities. Nationally, obstacles have been erected to the creation of a national fiscal and monetary system and to the achievement of market integration. At the local level, continued bureaucratic interference, the slow development of property rights, the exploitative attitude towards private enterprise and the continued prominence of clientalism (as well as corruption) suggest that, as is the case with the central government, there is a need for fundamental institutional changes in their still very Leninist

86. Kumar, *China: Internal Market Development and Regulation*, p. 167. The earlier quotation is from p. xiv.

87. Yasheng Huang, *Inflation and Investment Controls in China*, pp. 361–62.

88. For suggestions of a similar view see White, *The Road to Crisis*, introduction, and Peter Nolan, "Prospects for the Chinese economy," *Cambridge Journal of Economics*, No. 15 (1991), p. 123.

institutions if "market preservation" is to be an outcome of China's partial economic reform.[89]

In sum, as China entered the 1990s it confronted the consequences of yet another historical branch in the institutional development of its political economy. The Maoist legacy left a distinctive configuration of Leninist institutions with a potential for economic growth that could be tapped by the right set of policies. The result of the incremental economic reform has been a political economy whose principal motive force is not societal-based entrepreneurship, but entrepreneurship lodged in sub-national developmental entities. The pseudo-Marxist view that depicts economic development prompting a readjustment of state/society relations has less heuristic value than one which sees such development creating the necessity for a redefinition of the institutional structure of the Chinese state to accommodate the fundamental realignment in the balance of political institutions caused by the unprecedented economic strengthening of these administratively-rooted economic forces.

Indeed, since 1992, this issue has been at the forefront of reform discussions and policy in China. Deng Xiaoping's "southern tour" was the occasion for an entirely new stage in the reform process under the rubric of building a "socialist market economy" as well as for a new surge of local inflationary growth which highlighted the necessity for building such an economy. The tone in the relations between the central leadership and the localities became increasingly sharp as press discussions identified the intervention of local authorities in the economy as a bar to further reform and called for a strengthening of the macro-economic powers of the central government. These exhortations were backed by political action. The central Party leadership utilized their traditional Leninist political tools even as they initiated in an ambitious effort in 1994 to develop new institutions for economic management by restructuring the nation's tax and banking systems.[90]

The orientation of this "new stage" of the reform was obvious in an important article by a team of researchers from the Chinese Academy of Social Sciences. They stressed the necessity of realigning the economic

---

89. In general, while Montinola et al. recognize these kinds of problems, they appear more sanguine than I would be regarding the ability of local governments, rooted in Leninism, to support and respect markets. Jeremy Paltiel discusses the problems of political systems managing economies for which they were not "programmed" in his "China: Mexicanization or market reform," in James Caporaso (ed.), *The Elusive State* (Newbury Park: Sage Publications, 1989), p. 258. Kiren Aziz Chaudhry analyses the difficulties of a transition from planned to market economies in her "The myths of the market and the common history of late developers," *Politics and Society*, Vol. 21, No. 3 (September 1993), pp. 245–274. For a useful Chinese discussion along these lines see FBIS-CHI 94–048, 11 March 1994, pp. 50–53.

90. For a report of a confrontation between Jiang Zemin and local officials see FBIS-CHI 95–023, 3 February 1995, pp. 10–13. For other evidence of the Party Centre using its political tools see *ibid.* 94–229, 29 November 1994, p. 27, 94–238, 12 December 1994, p. 20 and 94–232, 2 December 1994, p. 10. Convenient summaries of the reform policies that emerged in 1993–94 can be found in World Bank, *Macroeconomic Stability in a Decentralized Economy*, Maurice Brosseau and Lo Chi Kin (eds.), *China Review, 1994* (Hong Kong: The Chinese University Press, 1994), chs. 9 and 10 and Toshide Mito, "1994 tax reform and the future," *China Newsletter*, No. 116 (May–June 1995), pp. 18–23.

role of government at the central and local levels and noted that in order
and noted that in order to do so it would be necessary to replace the past
"reform strategy" of "crossing the river by feeling for the stones" with a
more comprehensive one.[91] In short, the authors of this article seemed to
be concurring with Christine Wong's observation that post-Mao reforms
were approaching the "limits of gradualist reform" where further progress
required that the Chinese leadership "reinvent government."[92] This view
raises issues that provide the basis for concluding observations on the
nature of evolutionary reform in China and the relationship between
political and economic reform in Leninist systems.

As shown above, the case against gradualist or evolutionary reform is
often based on the implicit premise that the fusion of politics and
economics precludes significant movement towards a market economy
because of its incompatibility with political institutions of a Soviet-type
economy. Yet many of those who are sanguine about the course of the
post-Mao reforms question the validity of this premise, maintaining that
the key to success has been precisely the fact of economic reform in the
absence of political reform. The central argument of the earlier parts of
this article has been that, given the peculiar institutional heritage of the
Chinese economy, these two positions are not necessarily incompatible –
at least for the initial stages of reform.

What this last section suggests is that the compatibility of these two
positions is being called into question by the nature of the current stage
of the post-Mao reforms. As Thomas Rawski notes, "the future relation
between China's emerging market economy and the state is far from
settled." That the reforms in China have been able to get as far as they
have without settling this crucial question is due, in significant part, to the
Maoist legacy which facilitated an incremental approach to economic
reform in apparent defiance of the logic of Soviet-type systems. Yet, the
tasks of this stage of reform suggest that such an approach might be
reaching its limits. What remains to be seen is whether the post-Mao
reforms have created the basis for further movement towards a "socialist
market economy" or an historic branch in China's institutional development that will impede, rather than promote, such change.

Among the many issues which Deng Xiaoping has left for his successors to address is that raised by the comparative perspective taken in this
article: have China's post-Mao reforms really resolved the central question of the relationship between political and economic reform in a
Leninist system or have they simply postponed and recast it?

91. JPRS-CAR 94–035, 3 June 1994, p. 1.
92. Christine Wong, "China's economy: the limits of gradualist reform," in William Joseph
(ed.), *China Briefing, 1984* (Boulder: Westview Press, 1994), p. 52.

The Role of the Local State in China's Transitional Economy

Jean C. Oi

All states have a role in development, but this varies widely. The spectrum is defined at one end by the *laissez faire* minimalist state whose role is limited to ensuring a stable and secure environment so that contracts, property rights and other institutions of the market can be honoured. At the opposite end are the centrally planned Leninist states that directly replace the market with bureaucratic allocation and planning. Between these two extremes are the capitalist developmental states of Japan and the East Asian Newly Industrializing Countries (NICs) that are neither Communist nor *laissez faire*, but exhibit characteristics of both. The state plays an activist, rather than a minimalist, role; there is planning, but it is geared toward creating maximum competitive and comparative advantage for manufacturers within a market economy.

China's post-Mao economy suggests the emergence of yet another form of state-led development that is committed to growth and the market, but it is a developmental party-state with roots in a Leninist system and the Communist Party still at the helm. Like its once socialist counterparts in Eastern Europe and the former Soviet Union, China has increasingly abandoned central planning and moved toward market production. But unlike these states there has been little or no political reform and no headlong rush toward privatization, nor is there commitment to private property as in other developmental states.

China's is a distinctive form of state-led growth that I have termed *local state corporatism*.[1] The core of this growth is the massive upsurge in rural industry on the edges of agriculture and state industry. The state responsible for much of this growth is *local* governments that treat enterprises within their administrative purview as one component of a larger corporate whole. Local officials act as the equivalent of a board of directors and sometimes more directly as the chief executive officers. At the helm of this corporate-like organization is the Communist Party secretary.

China's reform experience is a story of path dependence altered by institutional change. The result is a hybrid strategy that utilizes capacities inherited from the Maoist state and forms found in capitalist developmental states. Whether others can replicate China's developmental experience

1. See my "Fiscal reform and the economic foundations of local state corporatism," *World Politics*, Vol. 45, No. 1 (October 1992), pp. 99–126, for further discussion of the term "corporatism." I am not concerned with the role of the central state in the vertical integration of interests within society as a whole. The corporation that I describe is constituted and co-ordinated by the *local* government, not the central authorities. For a useful discussion of this term as it specifically relates to East Asia, see Jonathan Unger and Anita Chan, "Corporatism, and the East Asian model," *The Australian Journal of Chinese Affairs*, No. 33 (January 1995), pp. 29–54.

depends less on historical legacy than on institutions. The issue is whether prospective reformers have the political capabilities that characterized the Maoist state and sufficient institutional incentives that will make it in the interests of those responsible for implementation to embrace economic development. China's reform experience is evidence for Douglass North's assertion that institutions "... are the underlying determinant of the long-run performance of economies."[2]

This article examines the constituent elements of China's local state corporatism. It shows that while the post-Mao state retains key features of the Maoist system, the decision to accommodate mandates of rapid economic development in a market context has resulted in a qualitatively new variety of developmental state and not merely a modified Leninist system. It seeks to uncover the lessons of China's recent economic development and ask whether these may be transferable to other transitional economies or developing nations.

The Maoist Legacy for Local Economic Development

The existence of problems with the pre-reform system are not necessarily good predictors of reform success. The Maoist system was plagued by economic inefficiency but this same legacy provided the foundation that allowed post-Mao China to turn in short order into an economic dynamo. Once the Maoist system was modified to allow for local initiative and the proper incentives were introduced to channel local talent toward economic development, both the central and the local state were left with an impressive array of policy instruments and political capacity similar to that found in successful developmental states of East Asia.

Unlike late industrializing countries of Africa or Latin America that are often plagued by bureaucracies lacking experience or organizational capacity,[3] the Maoist bureaucracy was an elaborate network that extended to all levels of society, down to the neighbourhood and work unit, and in international perspective it exhibited a high degree of discipline.[4] Within each level there existed an impressive organizational apparatus that could effectively transmit the state's plans to the producers by issuing quotas passed down step-by-step through several layers of government bureaucracy. Unlike the Soviet Union where the strong ministerial system by-passed local governments and transmitted plans directly to their

2. Douglass North, *Institutions, Institutional Change and Economic Performance* (Cambridge: Cambridge University Press, 1990), p. 107.

3. On the importance of what is sometimes also called the maturity of a bureaucracy, see Dietrich Rueschemeyer and Peter Evans, "The state and economic transformation: toward an analysis of the conditions underlying effective intervention," in Peter Evans, Dietrich Rueschemeyer and Theda Skocpol (eds.), *Bringing the State Back In* (Cambridge: Cambridge University Press, 1985), pp. 44–77. A useful succinct statement on effective bureaucracy as key to capacity is by Stephan Haggard and Robert Kaufman, "The state in the initiation and consolidation of market oriented reform," in Louis Putterman and Dietrich Rueschemeyer (eds.), *State and Market in Development* (Boulder: Lynne Rienner, 1992), pp. 221–242.

4. See Martin King Whyte and William Parish, *Urban Life in Contemporary China* (Chicago: University of Chicago Press, 1984); and William Parish and Martin King Whyte, *Village and Family in Contemporary China* (Chicago: University of Chicago Press, 1978).

enterprises, the Maoist system decentralized economic and administrative power to the localities.

Ideology and the goals of state intervention, not an inherent failing in the policy instruments, undermined the capacity of the Maoist state to foster economic development. Chalmers Johnson highlighted this difference when he called Communist systems "plan ideological" and capitalist developmental states such as Japan "plan rational."[5] Using similar policy instruments, the latter fosters market competition while the former, guided by a socialist ideology, replaces the market and fosters an egalitarian distribution of resources and income.[6]

China had an "industrial policy," but its all inclusive rather than selective scope caused it to hinder rather than help economic efficiency. Unlike a "plan rational" economy where state intervention is limited by a commitment to private property and the market, the Maoist state closed free markets in 1957 and created a state monopoly for the procurement and sale of almost all goods and services. Each and every factory was told which products were to be made and in what quantity, what materials should be used, where the materials should come from, how much they should cost, and where these products should be sold and for how much.

China, like East Asian NICs, had the power to "get the prices wrong," but price setting was to ensure inflation control and an equal distribution of goods and resources within a socialist ideological context, not to provide manufacturers a comparative advantage in a competitive world market.[7] Production did not hinge on costs or on sales but on the plan as determined by the planning agencies. The plan determined demand and set strict limits on consumer choice.

Maoist bureaucrats could be mobilized to action, but Maoist ideology distorted incentives when it devalued expertise not accompanied by political loyalty, or "redness." Words and actions became manifestations of political attitude – what was then termed *biaoxian*. Expression of such attitudes became intertwined with economic performance and were measured by ability to meet and exceed economic quotas.[8] Pressure to exaggerate economic performance contributed to the massive famine

5. Chalmers Johnson, *MITI and the Japanese Miracle: The Growth of Industrial Policy, 1925–1975* (Stanford: Stanford University Press, 1982); his more recent views on the Asian capitalist model and the role of the state in the economy are summarized in his "Capitalism: East Asian style" (1992 Panglaykim Memorial Lecture, Jakarta, 15 December 1992); other recent works include Robert Wade, *Governing the Economy: Economic Theory and the Role of Government in East Asian Industrialization* (Princeton: Princeton University Press, 1990).

6. Richard Applebaum and Jeffrey Henderson, "Situating the state in the East Asian development process," in Richard Applebaum and Jeffrey Henderson (eds.), *States and Development in the Asian Pacific Rim* (Newbury Park: Sage Publications), pp. 1–26, try to refine Chalmers Johnson's distinction between plan rational and plan ideological by further dividing systems into "market ideological" and "market rational." China remains in the "plan ideological" quadrant.

7. On the NICs "getting the prices wrong," see Alice Amsden, "A theory of government intervention in late industrialization," in Putterman and Rueschemeyer, *State and Market in Development*, pp. 53–84.

8. Examples of this in rural and urban areas can be found respectively in Jean Oi, *State and Peasant in Contemporary China: The Political Economy of Village Government* (Berkeley:

during the Great Leap Forward as rural cadres exaggerated production and sought to outdo each other in the sale of grain to the state, even when their own village populations had little or no grain for consumption.[9]

Changing Incentives Transform the Maoist System

Perhaps because of the dismal performance of the state in managing economic development during the Maoist period or because of the image of Communist cadres as likely opponents to reform, some have glossed over or ignored the fact that much of China's post-Mao rapid rural industrialization has been due to the work of local governments. Some observers have lumped all rural firms together as "non-state firms,"[10] portray them as "semi-private," or use them to indicate a "capitalist revolution" in China.[11] Such characterizations misrepresent the character of these enterprises and mis-identify the crucial actors in the process of China's economic reforms. Township and village enterprises, which are the most economically significant portion of rural industry, are not privately owned, nor are they forms of hybrid privatization,[12] but forms of government ownership.

Without question, a growing private sector exists; some township and village enterprises are indeed "fake collectives" – only using the collective label for protection and economic benefit.[13] But to suggest that all rural industry is partially or secretly "private" misses the essential character of the process that has spurred China's rapid rural industrialization. In the early to mid-1980s, when China's rural industry started its rapid growth, prospective private entrepreneurs, with the memory of the persecution of private enterprise during the Maoist period still fresh in their minds, were unsure of the political winds and whether policies would change. As in other countries, when the risks and costs are too great for private individuals, it was the state, in this case China's local

---

footnote continued

University of California Press, 1989) and Andrew Walder, *Communist Neo-Traditionalism: Work and Authority in Chinese Industry* (Berkeley: University of California Press, 1986).

9. Thomas Bernstein, "Stalinism, famine, and Chinese peasants: grain procurements during the Great Leap Forward," *Theory and Society*, Vol. 13, No. 3 (May 1984), pp. 339–377.

10. See, for example, John McMillan and Barry Naughton, "How to reform a planned economy: lessons from China," *Oxford Review of Economic Policy*, Vol. 8, No. 1 (1993), pp. 130–142.

11. This view is most clearly articulated in Minxin Pei, *From Reform to Revolution: The Demise of Communism in China and the Soviet Union* (Cambridge, MA: Harvard University Press, 1994), especially ch. 3.

12. The partially private nature of these firms has been suggested by Victor Nee. See, for example, his "Organizational dynamics of market transition: hybrid forms, property rights, and mixed economy in China," *Administrative Science Quarterly*, No. 37 (March 1992), pp. 1–27. This is also suggested in his earlier work, Victor Nee and Sijin Su, "Institutional change and economic growth in China: the view from the villages," *Journal of Asian Studies*, Vol. 49, No. 1 (February 1990), pp. 3–25.

13. Liu Yia-Ling, "Reform from below: the private economy and local politics in the rural industrialization of Wenzhou," *The China Quarterly*, No. 130 (June 1992), pp. 293–316.

governments, that had to step in and assume the entrepreneurial role and start rural industry.[14]

It is not surprising, however, that many would overlook the role of local government in rural industry. The institution of "the contract responsibility system" masks the heavy involvement of local officials in the crucial decision-making concerning these collectively-owned rural enterprises. Contracting suggests a degree of autonomy and allocation of property rights that simply is not present. In contrast to agriculture and land, the property rights of township and village firms remain in the hands of local governments. The contract responsibility system decentralized the day-to-day management of collective industry, but most managers are employees rather than independent entrepreneurs.[15] Those who contract enterprises are provided with lucrative incentives, bonuses, housing and other perks to be efficient and increase production, but the major decisions regarding the enterprises remain the purview of the local officials, most importantly the village Party secretary or the township economic commission and township heads. These are often the same individuals who were in office during the Maoist period. What has changed is not necessarily the personnel, but the incentives that are embedded in the institutions that shape the actions of officials.

Institutional change and the rise of rural industry. More significant than past problems is the bureaucratic capacity of the regime and whether the problems that exist on the eve of reform can be corrected with institutional adjustment. For China the issue was not whether its bureaucracy was capable of generating economic growth but whether it had the incentive to do so. At the local levels, the constraints of the state plan and Maoist fiscal system provided localities with little inducement to generate additional revenues. Localities were required to turn over all or most of the revenues generated within the locality to the upper levels, which in return provided budget allocations for expenditures. What surplus remained within the locality was subject to higher-level approval before use. Localities had incentives to try to extract as much bureaucratic slack as possible from the upper levels in the form of larger budget allocations, not to initiate growth.

Institutional changes paved the way for China's successful economic reform.[16] The post-Mao reforms marketized the economy and instituted

14. The classic statement is by Alexander Gershenkron, *Economic Backwardness in Historical Perspective* (Cambridge, MA: Harvard University Press, 1962).

15. For a description of the variations in contracting, see my "The fate of the collective after the commune," in Deborah Davis and Ezra Vogel (eds.), *Chinese Society on the Eve of Tiananmen* (Cambridge, MA: Council on East Asian Studies, Harvard University, 1990), pp. 15–36.

16. In this study I adopt North's definition of institutions as "a set of the rules, compliance procedures, and moral and ethical behavioral norms designed to constrain the behavior of individuals in the interest of maximizing the wealth or utility of principals." This definition focuses attention not only on existing structures, but also on policies, such as reform initiatives, adopted at the Centre and passed on to the local governments for implementation. Douglass North, *Structure and Change in Economic History* (New York: Norton, 1981), pp. 201–202.

changes that removed constraints on local government autonomy and injected strong economic incentives for local government to be entrepreneurial. Combined with their already extensive bureaucratic power, local governments were well situated to launch rapid economic development. Two of the most important institutional changes that prompted local governments to become entrepreneurial and develop rural industry were the decollectivization of agricultural production and fiscal reform. Both affected fiscal flows and revenue retention. The household responsibility system for agricultural production stripped village governments of the rights to income from the sale of agricultural produce. Officials in villages without a significant non-agricultural economy were left with empty coffers and little salary for themselves except for whatever fees or surcharges they could extract from their villagers. Fiscal reforms, as I have detailed elsewhere,[17] clearly defined the localities' share of the tax revenues and granted them the rights to the fiscal surplus, or residual, which the literature on agency theory posits as the most important mechanism for facilitating hierarchic control. The Chinese case illustrates the general point that "... under a range of conditions, the principal's optimal incentive structure for the agent is one in which the latter receives some share of the residual in payment for his efforts, thus giving him a direct stake in the outcome."[18]

The institutional changes made local governments in China fully fledged *economic* actors, not just administrative-service providers as they are in other countries.[19] Local governments in Maoist China also had authority to make investment decisions; the difference is that with the reforms local governments had to bear the *risks* as well as enjoy the benefits that come with entrepreneurship. The fiscal reforms hardened the budget constraint of county and township government; decollectivization of agriculture made villages heavily dependent on village industry for an independent income.

If investment decisions are made poorly, this directly affects the operating budget of the local government and the bonuses of the officials within it. The debt of a township or village factory becomes the debt of the level of government that owns the factory. Unlike the large state-

17. The essential ideas are laid out in Oi, "Fiscal reform and the economic foundations of local state corporatism." For a more detailed statement see Jean C. Oi, *Rural China Takes Off: Incentives for Rural Industrialization* (University of California Press, forthcoming). By property rights I refer to the bundle of rights over property that includes the right to sell the property, the right to the income from the property and the right to manage the property. Harold Demsetz, "The structure of ownership and the theory of the firm," *Journal of Law and Economics*, Vol. 26 (June 1983), pp. 375–390. However, in this study I focus primarily on the rights to income. For a theoretical statement on this aspect of property rights as an incentive, see Yoram Barzel, *Economic Analysis of Property Rights* (New York: Cambridge University Press, 1989).

18. For a summary of this point in the principal–agent literature see Terry Moe, "The new economics of organization," *American Journal of Political Science*, Vol. 28, No. 4 (November 1984), pp. 739–777.

19. Richard Bird makes a similar point about the difference between Communist and non-Communist local governments. See his "Intergovernmental finance and local taxation in developing countries: some basic considerations for reformers," *Public Administration and Development*, Vol. 10 (1990), pp. 277–288.

owned factories in urban areas, there is no one at the higher levels who will bail them out and subsidize their losses. If a township or village enterprise goes into the red, the money to keep it running comes directly out of local coffers; at most one might get an extension from the bank, if a loan is involved, but increasingly those at the higher levels controlling the loans also have become much more cautious in lending out limited funds and give them to those most likely to succeed (see below).

On the other hand, if investments are made wisely, local governments can meet expenses, keep a portion of the extra tax revenues (at the township and county levels) and enjoy larger amounts of extra-budgetary non-tax revenues. It is the rapid growth of the extra-budgetary revenues that has made township and village enterprises such a lucrative source of income for local governments and why they are so enthusiastically promoted.[20]

A corporate form of local economic growth. China's local development is distinguished by its reliance on existing bureaucratic networks and structure. Each level has its own goals, resources and accounting, but the levels are intimately connected. Hierarchy and obligations are explicit; those at the lower levels are subject to the directives of the higher levels; and those at the lower levels turn over to those at the higher levels a portion of their revenues. As part of a larger whole, each level has the opportunity to draw on the resources of the larger corporate body; and any one company is not dependent only on its own resources.

Village, township and county-level governments comprise the local corporate state directly responsible for the dramatic growth of rural enterprises in China.[21] These are the levels where officials have a direct role in fostering the development of rural enterprises, both collective and private. The careers and salaries of officials at these levels are directly affected by the performance and growth of their rural enterprises. The governments of these levels control the revenue flows from local economic development.

Somewhat akin to a large multi-level corporation, the county can be seen as being at the top of a corporate hierarchy as the corporate headquarters, the township as the regional headquarters, and the villages as companies within the larger corporation. Each level is an approximate equivalent to what is termed a "profit centre" in decentralized management schemes used in business firms.[22] Each successive level of government is fiscally independent and is thus expected to maximize its economic performance. In this sense, China is coming closer to the NIC

20. For details of why this is the case, see Oi, *Rural China Takes Off.*

21. This view contrasts that put forth by Qian Yingyi and Xu Chenggang who stress the independent and self-sufficient ability of townships and villages in the development of rural enterprises. Qian Yingyi and Xu Chenggang, "Why China's economic reforms differ: the M-form hierarchy and entry/expansion of the non-state sector," *Economics of Transition*, Vol. 1 (1993), pp. 135–170.

22. See Harrison C. White, "Agency as control," in John W. Pratt and Richard J. Zeckhauser (eds.), *Principals and Agents: The Structure of Business* (Boston: Harvard Business School Press, 1985), pp. 187–212.

model of development where subsidies are given to those that are judged to have the best potential or are already judged to be the best in a particular field. Like a profitable company or division within a large corporation, a highly industrialized township or village will command positive attention, be listened to at corporate headquarters and have its leaders promoted up the corporate hierarchy. It will also have more leverage to be "innovative" in its implementation of rules and regulations.

But unlike any multinational corporation or East Asian NIC, the local Communist Party secretary plays a key role in economic decision-making. But this is not Communist politics as usual. Subject to the same incentives as other local officials, Communist Party secretaries in the most industrially developed areas of the countryside are at the helm of their area's economic development. The precise role that they play varies with level of government. They are most visible at the village level where they often can be found personally intervening in the economic decision-making of the village's enterprises. They often chair the board of directors of the industrial management committee.

China's Decentralized Developmental State: Adapting Maoist Institutions for a Transitional Economy

Post-Mao institutional changes blended the entrepreneurial and governmental roles of local governments. This has had economic and political consequences. The Maoist legacy provided the political capacity for the local corporatist state, but the adaptation of this legacy to maximize local economic and political interests through rapid economic development has created a system qualitatively distinct from the original. In one sense, local officials have simply modified the Maoist system to adopt preferential allocation of resources in line with many of the successful late industrializing states. In another sense, however, the entrepreneurial interests of local governments have compromised their role as agents of the central state.

Using bureaucracy to facilitate market production. Within a local corporatist context local officials turn the administrative bureaucracy – of which they are a part – into a free channel for information and resources to facilitate market production. Rural enterprises are not entities with limited resources and avenues for information, as would be the case in a Western market system. Using information and contacts that they develop beyond the locality through their routine conduct of administrative work, local officials can provide an array of essential services to their local enterprises. This might include raw materials, but increasingly, it has become important for information about new products, technology and markets for finished goods.

The degree to which officials get involved in product development, market research and the acquisition of technology suggests that this is not the usual provision of bureaucratic service, but the activity of an entrepreneurial developmental state. The commission on science and technology or the rural enterprise management bureau, for example, spends much time and energy to represent local industries at higher-level key agencies to acquire technology, materials and funding. Officials from these county agencies may personally accompany factory managers to the higher-level bureaus to facilitate access to inputs and services. The daily routine of cadres at the county level is filled with trips to the prefecture, even to Beijing, on behalf of specific enterprises. A diary of one official from a Shandong county rural enterprise management bureau shows that during a one-month period in May 1988, he made six trips to Ji'nan, the provincial capital, one trip to Beijing, three trips to other townships and six trips to various villages.

The flow of ideas is now two-way; individual enterprises are free to do their own market research and development of product lines. But local governments remain important for facilitating the actual implementation of these ideas, regardless of the source. Local cadres use their expansive connections and bureaucratic position to secure information that will serve local economic growth, particularly as China enters the more competitive international market.[23] Here one sees how having a developed and experienced bureaucracy works to China's advantage. Embedded in the administrative hierarchy, the branches of the information network automatically multiply the higher one goes in the bureaucracy.

Using administrative power to fund corporate growth. By retaining property rights over a key portion of local industry – the township and village enterprises – local governments are able to go one step beyond what most industrial policies have the capacity to achieve: apart from directly appointing managers, they can redistribute income among different sectors and enterprises within the local corporate state. They use their power to extract profits directly from township and village-owned enterprises, and have thus developed a corporatist strategy that pools resources and debt. They can take revenue from one enterprise and use it to develop another through an informal process of "borrowing" and redistribution of debt. Local authorities may require enterprises with substantial profits to pay ad hoc surcharges, often termed "loans" or "rent paid in advance." In one township, for example, the local government took 400,000 *yuan* and 200,000 *yuan* in two separate years from its wealthier enterprises.[24] This provides local enterprises as well as local governments with an additional source of investment funds.

At one level this looks like rent-seeking: there is a flow of revenue from the enterprises to the local government, above and beyond standard tax assessments. However, and perhaps more importantly, there *also* is a substantial flow of funds and support services *from* the local government *to* the enterprises. This is a constraint or an inducement of the corporatist

23. See Jean Oi, "Cadre networks, information diffusion, and market production in coastal China," paper prepared for the World Bank Project on "Explaining Growth: Chinese Coastal Provinces and Mexican Maquiladoras," 1994, for details of these networks and how they provide information to local enterprises.

24. China interview 72388.

system, depending on whether the enterprise receives or gives. Rather than having a negative impact on China's rural enterprises, the extraction of profits from them seems to be an important mechanism that allows local governments to facilitate corporate growth. As the holders of the rights over income flows, local governments can decide, much like a corporation, how to use the profits from its various enterprises and how to redistribute income. It is more appropriate to call this profit-taking from factories to pay for expenditures and reinvestment, not rent-seeking.

Like a large corporation, villages and townships may use the profits of their richer enterprises to see poorer ones through a down-turn in the market or to start new enterprises from the profits of the more prosperous ones.[25] Profits may also be used to subsidize and bear necessary corporate overheads, including supporting industries that are not particularly profitable to provide jobs for the village's surplus labour force or because the enterprise carries prestige and thus gives "face" to the village.[26]

Theoretically, the debt is the responsibility of the guarantor of the loan, but because most loans are guaranteed by the economic commission or by the village government, the debt burden is divided among the remaining collectively-owned enterprises. Interviews reveal that in a number of localities when a collective enterprise fails and defaults on its loans, the debt is paid off by the other enterprises regardless of the specifics of the contracting system. In one Shandong township in 1987, four enterprises closed, leaving a debt of 120,000 *yuan*. The economic commission had funds to repay 60,000 *yuan* to the bank, but the remainder of the debt was divided among the other enterprises.[27]

This collective financing and debt repayment system softens the budget constraint that firms would otherwise face, but it is also a reason why township and village enterprises have been able to grow with limited funding. Each new enterprise does not have to raise all the funds it needs for its start-up operation – it can borrow funds from sister enterprises within the local corporate community. The fiscal health of an enterprise depends not only on its own internal sources of wealth and the credit that it can mobilize, but also on the financial resources of the corporate state of which it is a part. This cumulative, corporate financing offers a way to sidestep the need for outside financing. It is feasible because many of the village and township enterprises start out on a relatively small scale.

From equal treatment to preferential allocation. The local corporatist state uses Maoist policy instruments and institutions but the aims for which they are used and their application are significantly changed. A key difference between local state corporatism and its Maoist antecedent is

25. As might be expected, this direct redistribution is limited to collectively-owned township and village enterprises. The private sector might benefit from redistribution by official loans, but it is unlikely that local governments would pay the debts of the private sector.

26. See, for example, "Township enterprises should also implement reform," *Jingji cankao*, 18 November 1987, translated in Joint Publications Research Service, *China Report* (hereafter JPRS-CAR) 88–005, 18 February 1988, pp. 20–21.

27. China interview 17788.

selective targeting of enterprises for development. Subsidies are no longer given equally or to all. In this sense, China has switched to a strategy similar to targeting found in the industrial policies of the East Asian NICs. Local governments use the "carrot" characteristic of the administrative guidance found in Japan, that is, preferential allocations as an inducement for independently-owned firms to conform to state-set strategies of economic growth. However, as suggested above, local governments in China go further to maintain direct rather than indirect influence and intervene in the internal affairs of their township and village enterprises. In this sense, they may be closer to the role that government plays in the direction of the state-owned enterprises in Korea that have played such an important part in that country's economic success.

Under local state corporatism those most likely to receive this assistance are the ones deemed most capable of generating maximum benefit for the corporate good.[28] To this end, local governments have begun to rank enterprises to determine the level of services and assistance each will receive from the government and its affiliated institutions.

There are two types of selective allocation. The first grew out of the remains of national planning that still existed when rural industry began its rapid growth in the mid-1980s. Privileged access is given to favoured enterprises of items that are rationed and for which the prices are the lowest. In the past, this included anything from steel to cement to lumber. The amounts of inputs allocated to the rural areas under the plan are extremely restricted, if they exist at all. Localities make use of what remains of central allocations to further local control, but they have little discretion with regard to production materials, which are usually earmarked for specific enterprises that are producing for the national plan. By the late 1980s this was almost non-existent. The most that a locality can hope for is access to state-supplied goods that are sold at higher than rationed prices, but lower than market prices.

The second and more common type of selective allocation is privileged access to inputs that are not rationed, but simply scarce. Over time different items have fallen into this category. Fuel oil, electricity and various raw materials have topped the list. These allocations are similar to those made under administrative guidance, except that in places such as Japan the goods and resources are usually provided at below market prices. In China, this is privileged access to goods that are secured and sold at *market* prices. Like the privileged access that comes from using connections and "going through the back door," what is being given is not necessarily a cheaper price, but the chance to be first in line to buy the best available items at the posted prices. In the Chinese rural industrial context preferential access means having the chance to buy the

---

28. It should be noted, however, that the corporate good is defined more broadly than mere economic interests and profits. It may include such social interests as providing employment, but increasingly this hinges on profitability, competitiveness, and growth.

one ton of steel that the material supply bureau was able to procure at a favourable *market* price. It might also mean the opportunity to be hooked up to the special electric generator the township installed to provide its most important industries with uninterrupted power. As the market economy continues to develop, this type of selective allocation of raw materials is decreasing in importance, but it may still make a difference in an enterprise's profit margin.

What remains scarce is credit, which also falls under the second type of selective allocation. As the growing literature on the state and economic development points out, credit control is one of the most essential policy instruments that a government can possess to shape industrial growth.[29] China, like many of the East Asian NICs, is a credit-based rather than a capital-based system that allows for co-ordinated intervention necessary for an effective industrial policy. Until the reforms private loans were prohibited, as were private banks. Firms did not sell stock to raise capital; they looked to the government for their capital, as well as for all their operating budget. The state exclusively decided development through its allocation of credit and capital, as it did with other production inputs.

The emergence of private and semi-private financial institutions in the post-Mao period has weakened the hold of the central state over credit, but local authorities continue to maintain a fairly strong hold within their localities. The primary reason for this is that local governments are themselves indirectly responsible for and control a number of the sources of credit outside the official banking system that have emerged in the post-Mao period, and which are out of the reach of central regulation.[30] Local governments have continued to use their control over credit provided by the central state banking system as well as the newly emerging non-bank funds to shape local enterprise development. But they are becoming much more tight-fisted with credit, particularly those amounts that fall outside central bank control. Local bank branches and savings and loan co-operatives have incorporated a performance standard as a criterion for distribution to maximize returns on existing funds available within their locality.

From the mid-1980s, county officials began to rate enterprises annually to determine the fixed capital credit as well as the financial services available for each one at the local bank or savings co-operative. Enterprises with a credit rating (*haiding e*) are accorded the quickest approval for loans within their prescribed credit limit; automatic approval is guaranteed from the township savings and loan co-operative or the local

29. See, for example, John Zysman, *Government, Markets, and Growth: Financial Systems and the Politics of Industrial Change* (Ithaca: Cornell University Press, 1983); on the East Asian NICS see the work by Robert Wade. One of the best short statements is his "The role of government in overcoming market failure: Taiwan, Republic of Korea and Japan," in Helen Hughes (ed.), *Achieving Industrialization in East Asia* (Cambridge: Cambridge University Press, 1988), pp. 129–163.
30. See Oi, *Rural China Takes Off*, for details.

branch of the Agricultural Bank without county approval.[31] Moreover, once an enterprise is designated important, local governments try to ensure credit to it, especially during periods of centrally-mandated retrenchment when bank credit is greatly reduced and restricted. There are at least three ways this has been done.

The first is the misappropriation (*nuoyong*) of earmarked funds to those uses that will bring the highest returns – namely support for rural industry. Unfortunately for those who still farm, the funds misappropriated are often those sent by the central state through the Agricultural Bank earmarked for the procurement of agricultural products. The result has been the IOU problem, where peasants must wait for payment when they sell their grain or cotton to the state. Not all governments have engaged in this, but judging by the number of reports of IOU problems, the practice is not isolated.

A second and more legitimate way to provide increased credit for local enterprises is to license non-bank credit institutions to circumvent central regulations that restrict the lending of local banks. These institutions have only limited funds, but they too provide a crucial alternative in periods of tight credit.

A third way is to grant small loans from bureau funds. Counties, through their various bureaucratic agencies such as the tax bureau, the finance bureau and the science and technology commission, have funds they directly lend to favoured enterprises. Although banks are still the major sources of credit, local government bureaus may unilaterally provide no- or low-interest loans to help certain industries. Again, these amounts are not large, but they can be significant, particularly if a factory needs circulation funds to purchase raw materials. These sources of support and funding are critical when the upper levels of government try to rein in growth by cutting credit, as was done in the 1988–89 retrenchment. Such actions indicate an increasing divergence of interests between the Centre and the localities and the increasing ability of the local levels to circumvent central regulations.[32] Local governments, formally agents of the central state, are increasingly becoming principals in their own right.

From regulators to advocates. Granting property rights over local enterprises to local governments distorts the role of the latter as agents of the central state. On the one hand, the increased fiscal pressure to be entrepreneurial has meant that local authorities must be more vigilant to ensure that the factories make the best use of resources. But in practice this may also mean that they become more lax in their role as agents for the central state. With the transformation from administrators to en-

---

31. China interview 22688. In the rural areas, the major bank at the county level serving peasants and rural enterprises is the Agricultural Bank (*nongye yinhang*). Below the county, however, there are the branches of the Agricultural Bank, known as a business office (*yingye suo*), and the credit co-operatives (*xinyongshe*).

32. A more detailed discussion and description of other mechanisms are in Oi, *Rural China Takes Off*.

trepreneurs, local governments are shifting from regulators to advocates of their local enterprises.

The local corporate state continues the Maoist practice of planning and monitoring, but the new institutional incentives increasingly encourage local officials to carry out their regulatory functions to maximize local rather than national interests.[33] Local governments regulate the activity of contracted enterprises through plans and targets, even though China has moved away from central planning.[34] Targets for profit, output and revenue for township and village enterprises are formulated and transmitted by the bureau for the management of rural enterprises. The county finance bureau issues to its townships quotas for revenue, with built-in growth rates based largely on the number and performance of the township and village industries.

Enterprises, like bureaus and other government agencies, are required at the county and township levels to submit a large number of reports, either monthly, bimonthly, quarterly, semi-annually or annually. An extensive reporting system characteristic of the Maoist period continues to be used at these levels.[35] All township enterprises are required to send reports to the township economic commission which then submits them to the county, along with those from other parts of the township government.

But the established capacity of government to monitor its own enterprises is now used to realize *local* industrial policy. Together with maintaining ownership, local governments can more easily limit management autonomy, use enterprise profits, ration credit, and allocate investment opportunities and key inputs.[36] The owner–regulator relationship to township and village enterprises also explains why local governments are willing to invest so much time and effort in promoting these enterprises. The risks for local governments are fewer. For example when county governments invest in township or village enterprises they are in essence dealing with their subordinate levels, not with independent entrepreneurs. This differs from other developing countries, where there are two separate elites, each with its own basis of power.

Rather than the predatory role that some might assume, and unlike some political systems where local governments maintain a detached

33. For further discussion and documentation of this point see *ibid.*, especially chs. 5 and 6.

34. Local plans may or may not be mandated by upper-level quotas. Provinces send plans to the prefectures, which send them to the counties, which then send them to the townships. For example, the county still sets annual procurement quotas for agricultural goods, such as grain and cotton, and allocates the agricultural tax to the townships. Each of the specialized banks are given growth quotas for deposits by the prefectural banks. Both of these are mandated by centrally-set targets. In addition, localities, from the province on down, also set annual industrial production and fiscal targets which are not necessarily dictated by upper-level directives.

35. Only at the village level is the required preparation of reports attenuated. Townships are the administrative superiors of the villages, but townships seem only to have loose control over their villages, especially the highly industrialized, wealthy villages.

36. Christine Wong makes a similar point. See her "Interpreting rural industrial growth in the post-Mao period," *Modern China*, Vol. 14, No. 1 (January 1988), pp. 3–30.

distance from business interests, a distinctive feature of local state corporatism is that local governments and the bureaucracies that constitute them see it as part of their duty to lobby on behalf of their enterprises to maximize the interests of the local corporate state, which directly impinges on their individual well being.[37] Local officials routinely manipulate regulations to allow local enterprises to receive the maximum tax advantages and exemptions.[38] This keeps more revenue within the locality and adds to the competitive advantage of the enterprises, which also means that of the locality. Similarly, banks may exempt enterprises from penalty interest payments or extend the repayment period.

Under a local state corporatist system, the relationship between banks, finance and tax offices, and county, township and village officials is very close.[39] Local officials at the county level help secure large loans for township and village-owned enterprises. Bureaus sometimes provide services well outside their administrative domain. For example, the county tax bureau not only collects taxes and gives tax concessions, but helps enterprises train accountants and find scarce technical personnel, a pressing problem facing rural industry. It may use its connections to influence other agencies, such as banks, to bend the rules in favour of a particular enterprise. The tax bureau may allow an enterprise to repay the bank loan before taxes are assessed, in order to provide some guarantee to the bank that the enterprise can repay the loan.

Implications of the Chinese Experience: The Role of Government in a Transitional Economy

The Chinese model, while emerging from a distinctive Leninist system, holds a number of useful general lessons about reform for transitional and late industrializing economies. The first is that one cannot make broad assertions about government intervention and markets. As Wade has noted, different governments have different "capacities to guide the market."[40] In the wake of disastrous state-led development in centrally planned economies such as the former Soviet Union and Eastern Europe, there has been a rush to get government out of the economy, but a minimalist state is not necessarily the answer. The goal should be more effective government. Instead of thinking that there must be either state or market, one should instead look at the interaction of state and market

37. For a differentiated view of the rent-seeking character of different states, see Peter Evans, "Predatory, developmental, and other apparatuses: a comparative political economy perspective on the Third World state," *Sociological Forum*, Vol. 4, No. 4 (1989), pp. 561–587.

38. The reasons for this have to do with the access that local governments have to non-tax revenue. Details are laid out in Oi, "Fiscal reform and the economic foundations of local state corporatism." Further discussion is in Oi, *Rural China Takes Off*.

39. Some have criticized this relationship as too close. See, for example, "Township enterprises should also implement reform," translated in JPRS-CAR 88–005, 18 February 1988, pp. 20–21; also Xu Hao and Wang Qingshan, Research Department, Agricultural Bank of China, "China's rural financial markets: current situation and strategy," translated in JPRS-CAR 88–002, 5 February 1988, pp. 54–57.

40. Wade, "The role of government in overcoming market failure," p. 130.

and the adjustment of state actions.[41] As a number of observers have pointed out, even in the classic statements of *laissez faire* economics, there is a crucial role for states to play.[42] The recent case of China shows a regime that has evolved from bureaucratic stagnation to rapid entrepreneurial growth. The state-led growth that is occurring now in China is quantitatively and qualitatively different from that found in the Maoist period. Not all state intervention is Leninist, as the experience of the NICs has also shown.

The Chinese case points to the importance of path dependence, but it also cautions that this cannot be determined by looking a such factors as ideology or regime type. China, the former Soviet Union and East European states were all centrally planned Leninist systems, but China evolved into a distinctive decentralized form that, when coupled with the proper incentives, allowed its local officials quickly to play an entrepreneurial role. It is questionable whether local governments in the Soviet Union, even given the proper incentives, would be in as strong a position to generate economic growth quickly. When the Soviet planning system reached directly from the Centre to the enterprises, bypassing local governments, it left local officials with few resources and economic managerial skills. This plus the dissolution of the federal union and the instability of the Centre make the task of generating economic growth at the local levels distinctively different.

China's experience suggests that one should disaggregate the "state" into its component parts to distinguish between levels of government and the incentives for different levels to perform. There is a need for strong state capacity, but this capacity should exist at both the local and the central levels.

My argument lends credence to those theories that point to the importance of providing reformers with room to manoeuvre and insulation from an onslaught of political demands from society at large.[43] Unlike the USSR, which undertook political reform before beginning the task of economic restructuring, and unlike the weak authoritarian states of Africa and Latin America, China maintained its ability to rein in economic activity after reforms began. Not only is the political strength of a regime on the eve of reform crucial to determining its capacity to structure economic change, but a regime must also ensure that it retains sufficient capacity to control the course of reform. Unlike the former Soviet Union, China has tenaciously held on to its political power to decide the *content* and *speed* of reform.

41. A useful discussion of this general point is in Dietrich Rueschemeyer and Louis Putterman, "Synergy or rivalry?" in Putterman and Rueschemeyer, *State and Market in Development*, pp. 243–262.

42. See, for example, Paul Streeten, "Markets and states: against minimalism," *World Development*, Vol. 21, No. 8 (August 1993), pp. 1281–98; and Kiren Aziz Chaudhry, "The myth of the market and the common history of late developers," *Politics and Society*, Vol. 21, No. 3 (September 1993), pp. 245–274.

43. See, for example, Rueschemeyer and Evans, "The state and economic transformation," pp. 44–77; also Haggard and Kaufman, "The state in the initiation and consolidation of market oriented reform."

A practical lesson to be learned from the Chinese experience may be that reforming regimes should not be too quick to judge incumbent bureaucrats when trying to reform, merely because they have been associated with poor economic performance. In China it is the Communist Party first secretaries who are leading much of the rural industrialization. Institutional context and incentives matter. The Chinese case suggests that reformers need to craft incentives that will make it in the interests of those in bureaucracy and those involved in production to see reforms succeed. In China, altering fiscal flows and property rights overcame the inertia that many associate with Communist officialdom.

This also suggests that more is needed than just incentives for successful economic growth. Producers are not left to fend for themselves in the market context. The growth that is occurring in China is based on a corporatist strategy that spreads risks and resources to maximize local community interests. This gives competitive advantage to local enterprises. In today's modern economic environment infrastructural support needs to be defined more broadly than roads and the provision of electricity to include the provision of market information and technology.[44]

The success of local governments as entrepreneurs suggests that privatization is not the only way to stimulate economic growth. However, this is not to say that government ownership is the best or should be the only form of enterprise. China's continuing success may also be due to the fact that as development has progressed, local officials have provided increasing support to private enterprise. As has been shown elsewhere, by the late 1980s a strong public–private co-operation was developing, resulting in what some have called a symbiotic relationship between the private enterprises and local officials.[45] This growing public–private co-operation brings China closer to the successful developmental state model of the East Asian NICs.

A decentralized strategy does not come without costs. As is common in late industrializing countries, there is a tension between the need to decentralize and the deteriorating effect this has on the need for a strong central state. But apart from the usual problems, there is an additional twist to the Chinese case. The policy instruments that have effectively allowed local governments to pursue preferential allocation and targeting are linked to a strong central state. The question is whether the localities can continue to grow in power without fatally damaging the strength of the Centre. Perhaps one of the best outcomes would be a

44. North, *Institutions, Institutional Change and Economic Performance*, especially pp. 76–77.
45. See Dorothy Solinger, "Urban entrepreneurs and the state: the merger of state and society," in Arthur L. Rosenbaum (ed.), *State and Society in China: The Consequences of Reform* (Boulder: Westview Press, 1992), pp. 121–142; David Wank, "From state socialism to community capitalism: state power, social structure, and private enterprise in a Chinese city," Ph.D. dissertation, Harvard University, 1993; and his "Private business, bureaucracy, and political alliance in a Chinese city," *The Australian Journal of Chinese Affairs*, No. 33 (January 1995), pp. 55–74. Liu Yia-Ling, "Reform from below," also points toward such an alliance.

formalized and institutionalized division of power along the lines of a federal system.[46]

There is also a lack of economic co-ordination that comes with decentralized economic development.[47] While it has been shown that China continues to exhibit a lack of regional specialization,[48] this problem may be mediated by the information that flows through the vast government bureaucracy to the local enterprises. The government-owned foreign trade corporations are probable sources that will help interpret the export market. Neither the enterprises nor their local governments operate blindly in a vacuum. One also would expect that competition will shake out the market.

Finally, a number of questions leave open the sustainability of Chinese economic growth. One has to ask whether the reason why China's reforms have succeeded to the extent that they have and why the local decentralized developmental state has been able to lead this success is the type of production undertaken by rural industry. Much of the production, particularly at the early stages, required relatively little expertise and start-up cost; entrance barriers were low. This allowed individuals who only a few years earlier were in the fields to adapt fairly easily to industrialization. This may also explain why China has been able to pursue a developmental state strategy without an elite central bureaucracy of the type that exists in Japan and Singapore. For other countries with less room for growth on the fringe of the economy or for other countries trying to generate growth through the development of more sophisticated products, China's decentralized strategy may be less suitable. For China itself, the question is how long local elites can spearhead rapid economic growth. Part of the problem may be alleviated by the provision of technology through joint ventures and the information diffusion through the bureaucratic network, but a major challenge for China's reformers is to ensure that those who now have the incentive will continue to have the institutional and technical support necessary to continue their entrepreneurial efforts. Institutional change created the necessary environment for successful reform to begin and growth to occur, but continued institutional change is necessary to ensure that growth continues down the right path.

46 See Gabriella Montinola, Yingyi Qian and Barry R. Weingast, "Federalism, Chinese style: the political basis for economic success in China," *World Politics*, Vol. 48 (October 1995), pp. 50–81.

47. See, for example, Christine Wong, "Central–local relations in an era of fiscal decline: the paradox of fiscal decentralization in post-Mao China," *The China Quarterly*, No. 128, (December 1991), pp. 691–715; and Christine Wong, "Fiscal reform and local industrialization: the problematic sequencing of reform in post-Mao China," *Modern China*, Vol. 18, No. 2 (April 1992), pp. 197–227.

48. Anjali Kumar, "Economic reform and the internal division of labor in China: production, trade, and marketing" (Washington, D.C.: The World Bank, March 1994).

Implications of China's Reform Experience*

Thomas G. Rawski

As reform approaches the end of its second decade, the prospect of an interpretive summary of China's recent economic experience becomes irresistible. The analyst may plausibly hope to separate trend from cycle and pick out key elements in the kaleidoscopic jumble of events. China's unique combination of enormous size, large and unexpected economic gains, unorthodox policies, hybrid institutional structures and formidable challenges to future economic advance adds to the promise of such a review. This article begins with a summary of reform outcomes, followed by discussions of the reform process, the implications of recent reform experience and China's economic prospects. It concludes with a hesitant excursion into the realm of "lessons" from China's reform experience.

Reform Outcomes

There is no need to rehearse the quantitative details of China's economic gains. Reform has propelled China to the top of the world growth league.[1] Beginning with the onset of reform in the late 1970s, China has experienced rapid and virtually uninterrupted growth of every plausible measure of economic growth or material welfare. Macroeconomic fluctuations, often described as cycles of boom and bust, remain mild by international standards. Reform has produced no readily identifiable groups of losers whose income and material welfare have declined.

This growth spurt coincides with striking qualitative change. The profit motive appears everywhere. Even large state industrial firms show clear signs of adapting to the culture of the market. Despite the continuation of various forms of subsidy, agents throughout China's economy are increasingly forced to live with market-generated financial outcomes. Domestic industries, formerly insulated from international market trends by a wall of state protection, find themselves buffeted by international market forces.[2] Domestic institutional arrangements bend in the face of external pressures. These developments continue to reshape individual attitudes, expectations and behaviour at every level of Chinese society.

* The ideas developed in this article reflect the influence of ongoing collaboration with Gary H. Jefferson and Yuxin Zheng. I have also benefited from conversations with Edward Green, Nicholas Lardy, Cyril Lin, Alvin Roth, Julius Rubin and Jan Svejnar, as well as detailed comments from Michael W. Michalak and several conference participants. None of these colleagues necessarily agrees with what follows.

1. Official Chinese statistics undoubtedly overstate the pace of recent growth. Plausible downward adjustments would not alter this or other statements advanced here.
2. In textiles, for example, "fluctuations in international market prices directly affect domestic price movements." See Dong Yunliang, "This year's changes in domestic prices of textile products and their consequences," *Jiage lilun yu shijian* (*Price Theory and Practice*), No. 10 (1994), p. 24.

Yet China's transition to a market system remains far from complete. Three outstanding issues, to be treated below, illustrate this point. State enterprises, most in the industrial sector, shelter an army of redundant but tenured workers. The banking system remains suspect. With estimates of non-performing loans running as high as 40 per cent of total borrowing[3] and new "policy" (that is, non-commercial) loans adding to the stock of dubious assets, even Chinese sources now suggest the possibility that the main banks have negative net worth.[4] A flurry of problems involving foreign firms has drawn attention to limited enforcement of property rights and commercial agreements. Similar difficulties affect purely domestic transactions.

The Process of Chinese Economic Reform[5]

Conventional policy advice pictures economic reform as a series of changes imposed by decree, much in the style of central planning. Many economists counsel governments to implement rapid and simultaneous change across a broad range of economic and social arenas.[6] They recommend "early and comprehensive price decontrol," "rapid privatization of small enterprises" and "full commercialization and privatization" of finance.[7] Divergence between this advice and the recent history of dynamic economies in Japan, Taiwan, Korea and Singapore is rarely considered.

Reform in China did not follow conventional lines. Orthodox recommendations take the creation of United States-style market arrangements as the objective of reform. But in China, the objective of creating a "socialist market economy" emerged only in the 1990s. The idea of a market outcome received little consideration during the first decade of reform. The initial reform goal was to improve performance by tinkering with the socialist system. Even the slogan *mo shitou guohe* (crossing the river by stepping from stone to stone) exaggerates the systematic component of China's early reforms by suggesting a firm objective – the far

3. One report mentions "bad debts" of "nearly 1 trillion *yuan* in 1994, 40% of the country's total bank loan" (Wang Xiaozhong, "Bold, new moves needed to make headway," *China Daily*, 9 January 1995, p. 4). Another notices: "Statistics indicate that defaulted loans account for 11 to 15% of total bank loans" ("This year's reforms to focus on state enterprises," *China Daily*, 30 January 1995, p. 4). A third states that "16.7% or 400 billion … in loans have been defaulted (Sun Shangwu, "Workers' interest is priority," *China Daily*, 17 January 1995, p. 4). Any of these figures is high by international standards.

4. "The ratio of liabilities to assets of China's State-owned enterprises is nearly 70:30 … banks have to bear nearly all the operation risks of State enterprises, which would probably lead banks to bankruptcy" (Tong Ting, "Overseas funds aid state firms," *China Daily*, 30 December 1994, p. 7).

5. This section summarizes ideas developed in Gary H. Jefferson and Thomas G. Rawski, "How industrial reform worked in China: the role of innovation, competition and property rights," *Proceedings of the World Bank Annual Conference on Development Economics 1994* (Washington, D.C.: The World Bank, 1995), pp. 129–156.

6. Farid Dhanji, "Transformation programs: content and sequencing," *American Economic Review*, Vol. 81, No. 2 (1991), pp. 323–28, offers a particularly clear statement of this view.

7. International Monetary Fund *et al.*, *The Economy of the USSR: Summary and Recommendations* (Washington, D.C., 1990), pp. 24–26, 32.

bank of the river – where none existed. In the absence of clear goals, policy announcements from the Centre remained partial and tentative. The Centre ratified but did not direct the momentous shift from collective to household farming. Central initiatives in the reform of industry focused on incremental relaxation of controls over state-owned enterprises. Even the revolutionary "open door" strategy, which shattered long-standing barriers to China's participation in the world economy, concentrated on expanding trade and investment activity in a few provinces and special zones along China's south-east coast.

China's reforms typically involve what might be termed "enabling measures" rather than compulsory changes. Instead of eliminating price controls, reform gradually raised the share of sales transacted at market prices. Instead of privatization, there was a growing range of firms issuing shares. Production planning does not vanish, but its span of control gradually shrinks. This open-ended approach invites decentralized reactions that the Centre can neither anticipate nor control. Governments at all levels become participants, sometimes even followers, as well as leaders of reform. Reform unfolds as a process replete with interactions among governments, enterprises, workers and consumers rather than a sequence of events in which the state makes decisions to which businesses and individuals react. The steep decline in the ratio of government revenue, especially central revenue, to national product illustrates the importance of unforeseen outcomes.

The nature of the reform process is perhaps best seen by looking at a schematic representation for industry, which is both the largest sector of China's economy and the source of the most intractable policy dilemmas. What emerges is a picture of economic momentum arising from a virtuous circle of reform, a cumulative and mutually reinforcing process of interaction among market-leaning institutional change, technical innovation and economizing behaviour. The dynamics of partial reform in China's industry unfold as a succession of responses to imbalance and disequilibrium on the part of both enterprises and governments, much in the spirit of Albert Hirschman's analysis of unbalanced growth.[8] The sequence of responses that transforms partial reform into improved performance is simple and direct.

Government initiates partial reform measures. Chinese industry includes several types of firms – joint ventures, state firms, urban collectives, township–village enterprises and private producers – each with its own technical capabilities and institutional constraints. There is a distinct hierarchy of capabilities, product quality and labour costs, all of which are highest in joint ventures and state-owned firms. Competition occurs within a framework of "product cycles" in which low-wage firms increase sales and profits by imitating goods introduced at higher levels of the hierarchy; advanced firms strive to maintain their advantage by upgrading the quality and variety of their products. Reform begins when the government implements partial reform measures that reduce entry bar-

---

8. *The Strategy of Economic Development* (New Haven: Yale University Press, 1958).

riers and lower the cost of many types of transactions. These initiatives have a differential impact on the opportunity sets available to various groups of firms. Partial reform accelerates the domestic product cycle by facilitating the transmission of cost pressures and technologies up and down the hierarchy of industrial enterprises.

Partial reform destabilizes outcomes and intensifies competition. The unequal impact of reform efforts destabilizes the existing division of industrial resources and product markets among different types of firms. Competition in industrial product markets intensifies. China's early re-forms allowed rural industry, formerly confined to fabricating local materials and serving local buyers,[9] to burst into markets that they had coveted for years. China's southern provinces, excluded from large-scale investment during three decades of central planning, used the new "open door" policy to promote industrial growth with the aid of capital, skill and commercial contacts from overseas Chinese. Defence conversion brought strong new entrants into a number of civilian sectors. Finally, China's long-standing policy of building "complete sets" of state-owned indus-tries in most provinces provided a ready-made source of competition.

Competition reduces profitability. Stronger competition diminishes flows of profits created by entry barriers and market segmentation. At the micro-level, reduced profitability limits the growth of wages and bonuses for some firms; others are thrown into a position of financial loss. At the macro-level, erosion of profits limits the growth of revenues accruing to local and provincial authorities and to the central government. Reform brought dramatic reductions in industrial profits. The dominance of the public sector made governments the chief victim.

Tax and profit deliveries from industry, which provided 83 per cent of fiscal revenue in 1980, lagged far behind the growth of output. The ratio of industrial tax revenues to total industrial output tumbled from 20 per cent to 4 per cent between 1978 and 1993.[10] Widespread tax evasion exacerbated the fiscal consequences of falling profits. This decline in earnings affected all segments of domestic industry. Profit rates for township–village enterprises fell even faster than for state industry.[11] The decline in earnings increased the number of unprofitable firms, with losses concentrated primarily, but by no means exclusively, in the state sector.

Enterprises respond to financial pressures. Firms react to financial stress by choosing one or more of the following strategies: restructuring operations; lobbying for further deregulation to facilitate profit-seeking; lobbying for subsidies or official intervention to restore the initial

9. Dwight H. Perkins *et al.*, *Rural Small-Scale Industry in the People's Republic of China* (Berkeley: University of California Press, 1977).

10. *Zhongguo tongji nianjian 1994* (*China Statistical Yearbook*, hereafter *Yearbook*) (Beijing: Zhongguo tongji chubanshe, 1994), pp. 215, 375.

11. The data for the township–village sector include all enterprises, not just industry. See Thomas G. Rawski, "An overview of Chinese industry in the 1980s," in Gary H. Jefferson and Inderjit Singh (eds.), *Reform, Ownership, and Performance in Chinese Industry* (forthcoming), Table 12.

financial position. The dimension of market opportunities and the scale and accessibility of official subsidies influence micro-level decisions to emphasize one or another response to financial pressures.

Governments react to financial pressures and enterprise lobbying. Governments also face financial pressures that reduce their share of total output and destabilize the distribution of fiscal revenue across regions, missions and administrative levels. Officials face conflicting enterprise lobbying efforts, some demanding further autonomy and deregulation, others seeking protection from the effects of earlier reforms.

Governments' declining share of economic output is a key link in Chinese reform dynamics. As they lack funds to provide all firms with "soft budget constraints," central officials repeatedly faced an unwelcome choice between escalation of fiscal deficits and forcing state enterprises to seek sustenance from market activities rather than from the state. Central officials frequently, although not always, selected the latter option. Provincial and local governments, whose share of revenues rose at the expense of the Centre, also restricted subsidies. Again, competition provides an explanation. Provincial and local governments compete for foreign and domestic investment. With little access to credit markets, local governments fear that large subsidy payments will cripple local competitive strength by delaying vital infrastructure projects.

Feedback effects accelerate the impact of reform. The induced responses of firms and governments further erode entry barriers and reduce transaction costs. Beneficial feedback effects accelerate every dimension of the reform process by intensifying competition, further diminishing profits and motivating additional reform efforts on the part of enterprises and governments. These changes initiate more rounds of technical development, economizing efforts and reform increments.

Experience reforms attitudes and expectations as well as behaviour. This entire process affects the attitudes of enterprise personnel and government officials toward the direction and outcome of reform. Changing attitudes affect the objectives and strategies of all participants. The experience of partial reform created pro-market sentiment among former advocates of central planning. Susan Shirk finds that managers of large-scale industry "changed from lazy conservatives coddled by the state to active reformers challenging the state."[12] The thinking of government officials and political leaders experienced similar gradual changes.

The rise of pro-market sentiments among the political and administrative elite represents the biggest feedback of all. In the early 1990s, these reactions coalesced into a stunning reversal of deep-seated attitudes. Ideas that only ten years earlier stood outside the limits of permissible discussion now took centre stage. Ambitious bureaucrats began to resign

12. *The Political Logic of Economic Reform in China* (Berkeley: University of California Press, 1993), p. 288. See also Thomas G. Rawski, "Progress without privatization: the reform of China's state industries," in Vedat Milor (ed.), *The Political Economy of Privatization and Public Enterprise in Post-Communist and Reforming Communist States* (Boulder: Lynne Rienner, 1994), pp. 27–52.

their official posts to pursue private business careers.[13] China's Communist Party formally announced a national goal of creating a decentralized market economy.[14]

This remarkable change in outlook, combined with intense fiscal pressures, has sparked a series of policy innovations aimed at relieving governments of the burden of supporting loss-making enterprises. Although official documents avoid terms like "ownership reform" or "privatization" to describe these changes, recent initiatives amount to a policy of gradual and induced privatization. Ministries, provinces and localities have begun to lease state-owned industrial firms to private agents (including foreign companies). Some loss-making firms are forced to merge with stronger enterprises, with substantial loss of jobs[15]; others are auctioned off to the highest bidder. The government has also begun to support the reorganization of state enterprises into limited-liability entities owned by government, corporate and private share-holders.

Although this analysis focuses attention on endogenous or bottom-up aspects of the reform process, it does not imply that China's recent industrial experience consists only of induced responses to the initial tranche of partial reforms. The mix of top-down initiative and bottom-up reaction is itself a variable element within the reform mechanism. In the 1980s, when the Centre lacked clear objectives, initiative gravitated to lower levels. In the 1990s, a new elite consensus favouring market outcomes stimulated a volley of centrally-directed reforms affecting taxation, banking and corporate governance. China offers a shifting array of forces in which many policy changes, such as the partial commercialization of bank lending and the reduction of budgetary appropriations for industrial research, probably represent a combination of bottom-up response and independent central initiative.

This capsule account summarizes developments more fully described by Naughton and others.[16] In essence, institutional changes arising from partial reform created a virtuous circle in which the growing intensity of competition not only rewarded winners and punished losers but, by slowing the growth of tax revenues, diminished the state's ability to protect losers from the consequences of high cost, poor quality, neglect

13. Kathy Chen, "Chinese bureaucrats take hopes private," *Wall Street Journal*, 26 January 1994, p. A10.

14. "China's central government decision on resolving several problems concerning the establishment of a socialist market economic system," *Renmin ribao (People's Daily)*, 17 November 1993, p. 1.

15. One report notes that "the biggest problem with mergers are the job losses." Many of the enterprises acquiring loss-making firms "are only interested in obtaining the equipment and extra space," which creates a "problem of redundancies." See Huang Zhiling, "Mergers revive loss-making firms," *China Daily*, 16 April 1994, p. 4.

16. Barry Naughton, *Growing Out of the Plan: Chinese Economic Reform, 1978–1993* (New York: Cambridge University Press, 1995); Kang Chen, Gary H. Jefferson and Inderjit Singh, "Lessons from China's economic reform," *Journal of Comparative Economics*, Vol. 16, No. 2 (1992), pp. 201–225; John McMillan and Barry Naughton, "How to reform a planned economy: lessons from China," *Oxford Review of Economic Policy*, Vol. 8, No. 1 (1993), pp. 130–143; and Alan Gelb, Gary H. Jefferson and Inderjit Singh, "Can Communist economies transform incrementally?" *NBER Macroeconomics Annual 1993* (Cambridge, MA: MIT Press, 1993), pp. 87–132.

of customers and other legacies of planning. State firms, stung by competition and only partially compensated for lost earnings, pressed for further deregulation and sought relief from costly social obligations from which their collective rivals largely escaped. These pleas brought fresh increments of deregulation, stronger competition, additional erosion of profits, slower growth of government revenue, and so on.

Implications

History matters. The foregoing sketch highlights the importance of specific initial conditions – the decentralized nature of Chinese economic planning, the pre-reform growth of rural industry, the dispersion of large-scale manufacturing facilities, and the availability of commercial information, technical knowledge and funds from overseas Chinese communities – in propelling a virtuous circle of institutional change, market competition, financial pressure, innovation and further incremental reform. More distant historical patterns also influenced the outcome of reform. Consider the unexpected rural economic boom that followed decisions by China's leaders to allow the restoration of household farming and rural market activity. This growth spurt is widely attributed to the flowering of pent-up entrepreneurial energies. But where did these energies come from? Important elements of the rural market economy persisted throughout the collective era. The revival of market dynamism in rural China was an extension of ongoing activities. It did not crucially depend on individual or collective memory of economic patterns prior to 1949.

Rural industry entered the reform era with a substantial base of 1.5 million commune and brigade enterprises employing 28.3 million workers.[17] Village studies show continuous household participation during the collective era in markets for building materials, sideline products and brides. From the perspective of household finances the scale of transactions was large. In Guangdong, the sale of one litter of piglets "provided a family with almost as much income as the husband could earn in half a year's work in the collective fields," while the cost of materials for building a house "could easily amount to 1,000–2,000 *yuan*" – equivalent to several years' collective wages for a strong man. Furthermore, these markets were volatile: growing prevalence of marriages within single villages caused bride prices to plunge from "a thousand *yuan* and up...to a modest 100–300 *yuan*" within "a couple of years."[18]

Market skills did not disappear under the collective system. The communes themselves nurtured a class of official entrepreneurs who commanded public respect because of their ability to "work the system" to the advantage of their constituents. These talents fuelled the post-reform growth of rural industry, where over 70 per cent of persons responsible for creating and managing industrial enterprises "formerly

17. Data for 1978 are from *Yearbook 1994*, pp. 361–62.
18. Anita Chan, Richard Madsen and Jonathan Unger, *Chen Village Under Mao and Deng* (Berkeley: University of California Press, 1992), pp. 173, 191, 194.

served as cadres for townships or villages or in different sectors at the basic levels."[19] The survival of business skills in rural communities enabled reform to draw on China's "abundance of small-time entrepreneurs."[20]

Martin King Whyte's contribution to this volume shows how scholars of China once viewed Chinese social structures as inimical to economic growth. Mounting evidence from the work of Gary Hamilton, Whyte and others supports the opposite view that Chinese society contains elements that facilitate successful adaptation to the modern market economy.[21] China's reform experience, especially in its rural dimension, offers fertile ground for pursuing this elusive but significant line of inquiry.

Marshallian economics is not enough. Economic theory offers valuable perspectives for evaluating any economy. Claims that the Tiananmen massacre of June 1989 heralded the failure of China's reforms illustrate the danger of proceeding with no coherent economic perspective. But discussions of socialist reform often overstep the limits of economic theory. Problems cluster in two areas: substitution of ideal types for practical objectives and excessive reliance on what might be termed Marshallian economics.

Reform aspires to improve economic performance, leading to higher material welfare and better life chances. Reform aims to *alleviate* problems and to *relax* constraints. Replicating the economic achievements of Japan, Taiwan or Korea would represent a huge success. Each of these economies prospered despite the cost of protection, corruption, waste, distortion and monopoly. Dynamic economies can overcome the burdens of mismanagement and policy errors. The task of reform is to encourage dynamism and to limit the drag imposed by foolish policies and defective institutional structures. Nothing remotely approaching perfection is required.

Discussions of socialist transition easily slip into a rhetoric of policy extremism. Reformers are advised to replicate the institutional framework of the United States economy or, more precisely, a highly idealized version of this system. Even though no major market in the American economy escapes the heavy hand of government intervention, veteran policy analysts advise Russia to pursue "immediate and comprehensive price deregulation," so that sellers can "set whatever prices they choose" as a "necessary condition for all the other reforms that we advocate."[22]

19. Jiao Ran, "Facing the challenge," *Zhongguo xiangzhen qiye* (*China Township Enterprise*), No. 11 (1994), p. 27.
20. Tim Wright, "Growth of the modern Chinese coal industry: an analysis of supply and demand," *Modern China*, Vol. 7, No. 3 (1981), p. 325.
21. Gary Hamilton (ed.), *Business Networks and Economic Development in East and Southeast Asia* (Hong Kong: University of Hong Kong Centre of Asian Studies, 1991); Martin King Whyte, "The Chinese family and economic development: obstacle or engine?" unpublished paper, 1995; Thomas G. Rawski, "Social foundations of East Asian economic Dynamism," unpublished paper, 1994.
22. Alfred E. Kahn and Merton J. Peck, "Price deregulation, corporatization, and competition," in Merton J. Peck and Thomas J. Richardson (eds.), *What is To Be Done:*

The idea of necessary conditions or prerequisites, thoroughly discredited by scholars of economic history[23] and development,[24] recurs again and again. Equally common is what Harold Demsetz terms "the *nirvana* approach," in which the imperfectness of arrangements observed in actual economies is taken as sufficient reason to invoke the superiority of an unexamined alternative.[25] Since "partial reform is fraught with pitfalls," some writers leap to embrace the mythic goals of "true markets" or a "true market mechanism," as if this could banish all difficulty.[26]

Economic reform, even the tentative and partial reforms initiated by China's central government, massively restructures the organization of economic life and the conduct of everyday business. The consequences of these shifts are often obscured from view, and sometimes take years to play out, but they gradually pervade society from top to bottom, and eventually produce fundamental and dramatic change. Relations between buyers and sellers, producers and consumers, or workers and managers; attitudes towards work, education and personal responsibility; links between elites and masses or between citizens and the state – all these and more are deeply influenced as the consequences of reform unfold.

To deal with this shifting landscape, economists often deploy a theoretical vision based on what might be termed a Marshallian approach. Alfred Marshall is revered for his systematic exploration of "marginal analysis," which focuses on the consequences of particular changes in price, cost or tastes by assuming that other relevant factors remain fixed (*ceteris paribus*) while the consequences of the specified disturbance unfold. Marshallian analysis of reform issues poses a sharp conflict between rigour and relevance. Marginal analysis is a powerful tool for investigating the consequences of incremental change against a stable institutional backdrop, but it is not intended for studying systems in the midst of massive socio-economic change.

Application of marginal analysis reveals that China's economy is riddled with distortions that undoubtedly limit the growth of productivity and output. It is tempting to conclude that "partial reforms will not suffice."[27] But this makes sense only if progress requires the eradication

footnote continued

Proposals for the Soviet Transition to the Market (New Haven: Yale University Press, 1991), pp. 21, 40.

23. Alexander Gerschenkron, *Economic Backwardness in Historical Perspective* (New York: Praeger, 1965), chs. 1–2.

24. Albert O. Hirschman, "Reflections on economic development policy," observes that "the search for components that have to be in place" continues even though "we should have noticed that whenever development occurs, it does so in the absence of one or several of these 'required' components or preconditions" (in Robert E. Asher *et al.* (eds.), *Development of the Emerging Countries* (Washington, D.C.: Brookings, 1962), p. 41).

25. "Information and efficiency: another viewpoint," in D.M. Lamberton (ed.), *Economics of Information and Knowledge* (Harmondsworth: Penguin, 1971), p. 160. Peter Nolan advises me that this concept originated with Karl Popper.

26. Kevin Murphey, Andrei Schleifer and Robert Vishny, "The transition to a market economy: pitfalls of partial reform," *Quarterly Journal of Economics*, Vol. 107, No. 3 (1992), pp. 905–906; János Kornai, *The Socialist System: The Political Economy of Communism* (Princeton: Princeton University Press, 1992), p. 496.

27. Richard E. Ericson, "The classical Soviet-type economy: nature of the system and implications for reform," *Journal of Economics Perspectives*, Vol. 5, No. 4 (1991), p. 25.

of all distortions, a view that conflicts with experience as well as theory. It overlooks Dudley Seers' warning that "weaknesses in administration" make it impossible to deploy top-quality policy staff "on all fronts at the same time."[28] Governments may be well advised to concentrate on measures that promise to maintain the momentum of growth and ignore many harmful distortions, simply because the cost of identifying and remedying distortions often exceeds the benefit.[29]

Reform amid confusion. Chinese reform is often criticized for its unsystematic, even chaotic, approach. There is no "coherent or predetermined blueprint."[30] The rules are not clear. This ambiguity increases uncertainty, encourages corruption and raises costs. In addition to technical and market risks, would-be investors must shoulder extra burdens arising from the fluid policy environment. This reduces the incentive to invest.

Consistent evidence of excessive rather than inadequate demand for investment suggests that regulatory uncertainty may contribute more than a simple drag on investment. The standard argument about "investment hunger" emanating from state firms operating under "soft budget constraints" rings increasingly hollow as more and more state enterprises feel the grip of market discipline. Furthermore, the share of fixed investment financed through official grants and domestic loans to state-owned entities, which fell to 19.3 per cent in 1993, is no longer large enough to determine aggregate investment trends.[31]

Focus on the absence of clearly defined rules arises from thinking about reform as an *event* that government imposes on society in the mode of central planning. This perspective may be appropriate in the resolution of massive macroeconomic instability of the sort visible in Russia during the early 1990s.[32] But stabilization is only one aspect of economic reform, which also includes liberalization of prices and markets as well as "deep institutional change."[33] Recent experience of deregulation, privatization and deficit reduction in the main market economies confirms that institutional change requires a lengthy reform *process* involving the passage of time as well as extensive interaction among governments, enterprises and

28. Dudley Seers, "Why visiting economists fail," *Journal of Political Economy*, Vol. 70, No. 4 (1962), p. 331.

29. Perfection is prohibitively expensive in industry as well. U.S. firms often neglect to cost out alternative manpower arrangements because the cost of doing so exceeds probable benefits (Michael J. Piore, "The impact of the labor market upon the design and selection of productive techniques within the manufacturing plant," *Quarterly Journal of Economics*, Vol. 82, No. 4 (1968), p. 611).

30. Qimao Fan and Mark E. Schaffer, "Enterprise reforms in Chinese and Polish state-owned industries," London School of Economics, Development Economics Research Programme, STICERD, CP No. 13, April 1991, p. 21.

31. *Yearbook 1994*, pp. 139, 145.

32. Jeffrey Sachs, "Russia's struggle with stabilization: conceptual issues and evidence," in *Proceedings of the World Bank Annual Conference on Development Economics 1994* (Washington, D.C., 1995), pp. 57–80.

33. Leszek Balcerowicz and Alan Gelb, "Macropolicies in transition to a market economy: a three-year perspective," in *ibid.* pp. 21–44.

citizens. This outcome bears no resemblance to the notion of shock therapy in which centrally determined reform policies drive unwilling agents toward market outcomes.

An entirely different perspective arises from Douglass North's study of early market systems in Western Europe.[34] North traces the origins of commercial property rights to the efforts by ambitious rulers to expand their domains. Expansion required large revenues that could come only from large-scale commerce. Merchants, unable to match the military strength of the rulers, relied on mobility and diversification to limit their exposure to arbitrary exactions. The law of contract and the protection of private property arose from a gradual and incremental process of accommodation between rulers and merchants.

North's perspective offers a fresh vision of China's reform experience. China, like Europe, has many governments. Reform has brought the ratio of government revenue to national output crashing down from 33 per cent in 1978 to 15 per cent in 1993.[35] Governments at all levels find it difficult to fulfil their traditional obligations while dealing with environmental clean-up, telecommunications infrastructure and other new requirements. As a result, government bodies negotiate informal local agreements about commercial property rights and official prerogatives with foreign and domestic companies; these pacts often differ widely from conventional procedures and official regulations.

Statistical analyses show that loss-making firms are most likely to obtain greater managerial autonomy.[36] They also link enterprise autonomy with higher productivity growth and greater reliance on contract workers and performance wages.[37] These associations provide a quantitative reflection of an environment of ad hoc, decentralized reform in which governments seek to shed the burden of subsidizing weak enterprises by offering partial grants of property rights. They show how loosely co-ordinated local decision-making, conducted in the absence of clear central policy direction, has pushed enterprises, managers and workers from extreme dependence upon state largess toward increasing financial self-reliance and responsiveness to market forces.

Simultaneous unco-ordinated negotiation in many jurisdictions has produced the current wide variety of commercial regulation that businesses find both tempting and frustrating. This seeming confusion can be viewed as the sort of market for institutions proposed by James Buchanan, who insists that commerce "is not competitive by assumption

34. Douglass C. North, "Institutions," *Journal of Economic Perspectives*, Vol. 5, No. 1 (1991), pp. 97–112.

35. Christine P. W. Wong, Christopher Heady and Wing Thye Woo, "Economic reform and fiscal management in China," draft paper, May 1993; Wanda Tseng *et al.*, *Economic Reform in China: A New Phase* (Washington, D.C.: International Monetary Fund, Occasional Paper No. 114, 1994), p. 23. Revenue data are adjusted to standard international definitions. Borrowing is excluded from revenue.

36. Jefferson and Rawski, "How industrial reform worked in China."

37. Theodore Groves, Yongmiao Hong, John McMillan and Barry Naughton, "Autonomy and incentives in Chinese state enterprises," *Quarterly Journal of Economics*, Vol. 109, No. 1 (1994), pp. 183–209.

or by construction," but "*becomes* competitive, and competitive rules *come to be* established as institutions emerge" to shape behaviour.[38]

China exemplifies this "process of becoming." Institutional arrangements are worked out through bargaining and experimentation. Reform is driven by fierce regional rivalries and by the culture of envy that permeates China's economy. There is a cacophony of complaints about unfairness. A 1993 survey found that "72.4 per cent of enterprise managers feel they are treated unfairly in competition ... most enterprises reported that their counterparts get preferential policies."[39]

Two decades of reform experience have taught firms and managers to evaluate alternative institutional arrangements in the same way that they analyse the profit consequences of different product designs, machines or compensation arrangements. The "market for institutions" resembles commodity and asset markets in that chaotic appearances conceal important regularities. There is a predictable sequence of events. Reform begins with conventional standard arrangements (or a limited range of permissible variation). An experimental phase creates new alternatives. The range of observed outcomes expands rapidly. Eventually, the experimental success of specific new arrangements leads to institutional closure. The range of outcomes shrinks as competing jurisdictions scramble to implement successful policies and institutions.

This perspective makes sense of many reform phenomena. The dismantling of communes and the spread of special export zones are typical examples. In 1991, nobody knew what to do about redundant workers in state factories. By 1993, it was widely understood that state factories could transfer large numbers of workers onto the payrolls of newly created service establishments without risking major disruption or political censure. The delay in winding down the current round of inflationary pressures reflects another aspect of institutional closure, as thousands of jurisdictions race to replicate the infrastructure investments that have brought foreign capital and buoyant growth to China's south-east coast.

At any moment, the customs and regulations that govern business life seem both heterogeneous and unpredictable. Chinese commerce, with its legions of grafters and "fast-buck artists," displays a streak of wildness. This "cowboy capitalism" limits China's ability to draw on the world's deepest pools of funds to satisfy its immense capital requirements. Any province that can create a system of business legislation, regulatory practice, courts and financial institutions that appeals to overseas equity investors will attract capital inflows on a far larger scale than the foreign investments of the recent past. If one jurisdiction succeeds in this venture – Shanghai and Guangdong seem the most likely candidates – the ensuing institutional closure could sweep the vestiges of socialism from China's polity with astonishing speed.

38. James M. Buchanan, *What Should Economists Do?* (Indianapolis: Liberty Press, 1979), p. 29.
39. Liu Weiling, "Enterprise managers upset by 'unfair' regulations," *China Daily*, 18 September 1993, p. 2.

China's market for institutions, like markets everywhere, appears wasteful. If some central authority could determine the best price for steel sheets or the best arrangement for organizing the manufacture of steel, vast savings in time and effort would accrue. Ironically, economists who never question the benefit of decentralized price determination now advocate the central planning of institutions. China's approach to institutional change, which represents a historical outcome that was neither anticipated nor welcomed by China's central leaders, has surely expanded the achievements of reform far beyond what could have been accomplished by top-down initiatives dependent on political consensus among national leaders.

The Centre cannot hold. The reform literature exaggerates the role of central governments, often assuming that central officials are uniquely committed to the social good. China's size and heterogeneity, coupled with the superior accessibility of publications and informants sympathetic to the interests of the Centre, can tilt discussions towards an excessively centralized view of the reform process.

Fiscal weakness is both an unintended consequence and a powerful engine of China's reform. The most difficult reform task is to force state enterprises and their employees, the principal clients of China's central government and Communist Party, from comfortably protected niches into the hurly-burly of market competition. The declining revenue share of the state, especially the Centre, was essential in motivating a serious push towards this difficult and unpalatable objective.

The interests of reform seem best served when the economy stands at the brink of dangerous levels of excess demand. It is when deficits and price pressures seem to threaten frightening instability that the Centre mounts a concerted effort to transfer enterprises from the rolls of official clients into the marketplace. In 1989–90, when a political crisis intensified economic alarm bells, there was for the first time a willingness to allow anonymous market forces to undermine the position of state-sector units and workers within the inner ring of government clients. In 1993–94, an upsurge of inflation elicited a barrage of tough measures that shattered long-standing barriers to market pricing of energy products and, again breaking new ground, aimed the big capitalist guns of credit restriction, bankruptcy and layoffs directly at money-losing state enterprises.

From this perspective, another consequence of fiscal austerity, its contribution to the unexpected flight of elite Chinese from the civil service, may substantially influence the long-term prognosis for reform. The declining prestige attached to official employment certainly increases the prospect for a market-leaning outcome to the still-unresolved issue of government's role in designing China's economic future.

The erosion of insuperable obstacles. The nature of China's reform dynamics must influence the perception of threats to the continued buoyancy of China's economy. As noted above, it is not necessary to eradicate obstacles, only to reduce the resulting costs and distortions to tolerable levels. Furthermore, the uneven pace of reform, with long periods of seeming inaction followed by quick changes in outlook or behaviour, makes it difficult to determine whether amelioration of real or potential obstacles is under way.

One standard argument against gradualism is that slow change gives conservatives an opportunity to organize blocking coalitions. This is surely relevant for China, where enterprise leaders have gained only a portion of the autonomy promised in the July 1992 regulations for state industrial firms.[40] Nevertheless, warnings that reform would perish because of bureaucratic resistance have all but ceased. This is because prolonged exposure to the reform process has convinced growing numbers of officials that the opportunities created by market expansion far outweigh its costs. As new perceptions permeate China's administrative establishment, the bureaucracy, like some giant ocean vessel, swings gradually from opposition toward manipulative participation. Most recently, with large numbers of officials departing to "test the waters" (*xiahai*) of business, announcements of large reductions in the civil service – unthinkable only a few years ago – have become routine.[41]

A larger example concerns the complex and intertwined issues surrounding the reform of state-owned industrial enterprises and the reorganization of China's banking system. The task of reform is daunting. Many state enterprises are hopelessly uneconomic. The number of redundant employees is crudely but plausibly estimated at 10–40 million.[42] Bank assets include large stocks and, worse yet, continuing flows of unrepayable loans. Producers often continue to supply non-paying customers in the expectation that the banks will eventually extend loans to unwind the resulting chains of inter-enterprise claims.

The difficulties, although formidable, can be exaggerated. Reports of big losses in state industry come from fiscal data that understate profits. With taxes and fees absorbing an estimated 86 per cent of declared profits in state industry,[43] tax fraud is endemic. Concealed profits may exceed

40. "Text of regulations on transforming state enterprises," U.S. Department of Commerce, Foreign Broadcast Information Service, *Daily Report: China*, 28 July 1992, pp. 27–36. On the limited impact of these reforms, see "Executives of major firms meet in Beijing to discuss the program of enterprise reform," *Zhongguo gongye jingji yanjiu* (*Research in China's Industrial Economics*), No. 2 (1993), pp. 4–10.

41. Cao Min, "State to cut 2m jobs in year-long slim plan," *China Daily*, 17 December 1994, p. 1; Wang Rong, "Guangdong to cut government staff by 40,000," *China Daily*, 21 January 1995, p. 3.

42. Gu Shutang and Cao Xuelin, "Create the circumstances to overcome difficulties: on enlivening state enterprises to escape contradictions," *Jiage lilun yu shijian* (*Price Theory and Practice*), No. 2 (1993), pp. 13–14. Huang Xiaohui, Yan Changle and Lou Xuesong, "Thoughts on the reform and development of large and medium-sized state enterprises," *Zhongguo gongye jingji* (*China Industrial Economics*), No. 2 (1995), p. 50. These figures refer to redundant workers in all state enterprises, not industry alone.

43. "Statistics from 1980 to 1993 show that the profits tax, energy transportation funds and budgetary adjustment funds collected from State industrial enterprises averaged 86% of their total profits" ("State firm is base of economy," *China Daily*, 21 January 1995, p. 4).

reported earnings.[44] Genuine losses arise from price controls, defence conversion and the burden of officially-mandated social expenditures as well as business failure. Claims that "China's banks do what central and local governments tell them" seem considerably inflated.[45] They conflict sharply with interview materials and published reports indicating the banks' increasingly commercial orientation. Press reports routinely describe the quandary faced by enterprises whose credit lines have been severed.[46] Enterprise managers offer a worm's-eye view of bank behaviour that emphasizes credit ratings and ability to repay.

Despite the exaggeration of difficulties and the very real accomplishments of state industry in raising output, productivity, exports and technological capabilities, persistent weaknesses may yet stall the entire reform process (see below). But the limited progress of reform may conceal underlying movement toward institutional closure that could reduce the prospects for "stagflation" or macroeconomic instability arising from weaknesses in state industry and banking. Ingredients in this emerging cluster of reform initiatives include the following:

(i)   Dispose of hopelessly uneconomic enterprises via auction, merger or closure. Workers whose jobs disappear will receive compensation, retraining, and/or offers of alternate employment.

(ii) Relax controls over the dismissal of redundant workers as unemployment insurance and other social support programmes expand.

(iii) Concentrate non-commercial bank lending in new "policy banks," allowing the ordinary banks (zhuanye yinhang) to expand the application of commercial criteria to industrial lending.

(iv) Strengthen the capital position and balance sheets of the commercial banks by assigning them shares in state enterprise assets during the reorganization of bankrupt firms and the restructuring of viable units.[47]

Even though implementation of these reforms could take years, the existence of feasible and promising policy responses can serve to focus central policy deliberations, guide regional and local experimentation,

44. Wang Haibo, "Now is the time to strengthen the unity between high speed growth and raising efficiency," Zhongguo gongye jingji yanjiu (Research on China's Industrial Economics), No. 10 (1992), p. 26.

45. Robert Cottrell, "A vacancy awaits: a survey of China," Economist, 18 March 1995, p. S–10.

46. Fu Jian, "Stockpiles hurt healthy development," China Daily, 5 January 1995, p. 4, reports banks "decreasing or stopping credits to certain enterprises" with excessive stockpiles. According to Su Ning and Lu Zhongyuan, "Because the specialized banks day-by-day increase their attention to the safety, liquidity and profitability of their funds, some old enterprises seek for loans but find no suppliers, and face bankruptcy and closure" ("Fiscal difficulties of state industries and the way out," Caimao jingji (Finance and Economics), No. 8 (1994), pp. 17–20.

47. "China's largest bankrupt enterprise, a freight container producer" in Wuhan, was sold for 42 million yuan to the International Business Section of the Hubei Branch of the Agricultural Bank of China, its main creditor. "Bankrupt enterprise sold to bank," China Daily, 23 January 1995, p. 7.

and introduce an element of stability into expectations about future arrangements.

The emergence of schematic solutions also clarifies the relative magnitude of specific obstacles to continued growth. From this perspective, the presence of perhaps 30 million redundant tenured workers becomes a costly nuisance rather than a threat to China's economic viability.[48] The unchecked spread of the debt-chains (*sanjiaozhai*), which now extend beyond the state sector[49] and threaten to undercut the credibility and control capabilities of China's central bank, seems much more dangerous to growth and stability.

Can Gradual Reform Continue?

The discovery of plausible approaches to resolving difficulties does not ensure that China's economy can maintain its forward momentum. Making predictions about China's medium- and long-term economic prospects is difficult, partly because there is little debate among proponents of opposing views. One group of writers (including this author) focuses on reform achievements. Despite scepticism about the potential of China's approach to reform, these researchers produce detailed evidence to show how gradual reform has worked for China. The unspoken implication is that gradual reform can continue to produce impressive results.

Pessimists attempt, with limited success, to pick holes in the optimists' empirical evidence. They recite the problems (including those mentioned in this article) confronting China's economy – a weak tactic because there are no problem-free economies. The most convincing aspect of this approach is the authors' instinctive sense that China's economic mechanism cannot sustain continued growth.

The instincts of the pessimists need to be confronted with the empirical knowledge of the optimists. Might current trends unfold in directions that drain the economy's powerful momentum? This article is no place for an extended discussion of China's economic prospects, but it can include a brief examination of the plausibility of significant erosion in the pace of growth and identify areas that might contribute to a slowdown.

To see why a dramatic reduction in growth might occur, it is only necessary to consider the position of state-owned industry, a sector whose contributions are widely misunderstood both within and outside China. The financial surplus of state industry is China's largest source of tax

---

48. In percentage terms, this backlog of on-the-job unemployed is no larger than Japan's cadre of three million corporate window-sitters (*madogiwazoku*). See Christopher Wood, *The End of Japan Inc.* (New York: Simon & Shuster, 1994), p. 19.

49. Figures presented in Wu Yunhe, "Economic setting advances," *China Daily*, 28 January 1995 p. 4, imply that state enterprises account for two-thirds of outstanding debts at year-end 1994, but contributed only 43% of the 1993–94 increase. Debts of state firms rose by 38% during 1994, while debts of enterprises outside the state sector jumped by 263%.

revenues.[50] This surplus is also expected to support a large work force (including millions of redundant employees), satisfy the housing, educational, health and pension costs of tens of millions of dependents and retirees, and contribute to the financing and development of the joint venture and collective sectors, all in addition to supplying capital for its own restructuring and technical development.

With the after-tax profit rate for state firms stuck in the vicinity of 3 per cent,[51] the ability of state industry to fulfil multiple obligations *and* accelerate the pace of technological change is open to question. Nicholas Lardy's discovery that China has received no significant net capital inflow and Barry Naughton's description of inefficiencies in China's banking system underscore the importance of ascertaining the capacity of domestic industry to finance its own restructuring and technical development.

In addition to the hierarchies of technology and cost mentioned earlier, Chinese industry can be visualized in terms of a ladder of financial capability, with firms and industrial branches ranging from robust strength to permanent insolvency. If large numbers of firms slip down this financial ladder, not just individual firms but localities, industrial sectors or the whole industrial system can experience a declining capacity to generate self-sustaining growth. Pressure on profitability is unlikely to slacken. The expansion of joint ventures, the maturation of collective industry, the gradual emergence of Chinese private industry and continued steps in the direction of import liberalization all point to further intensification of competition in the markets for Chinese industrial output. Efforts to focus corporate resources on purely industrial tasks will meet stiff resistance, as when the State Education Commission urges state firms "to continue running their primary and high schools" – at enterprise expense.[52]

Enterprise reforms do not occur in isolation. Transferring state firms to private owners may be difficult without agreement on the financing of social burdens traditionally entrusted to state industry. Since state firms are China's main taxpayers, it is difficult for the state to assume these burdens without fuelling inflation. But inflation threatens to undermine China's banks, which could then endanger the supply of credit to finance industrial expansion and reform. Now that China's regions and localities have developed a considerable appetite for autonomy, even well-crafted central reform initiatives may be difficult to implement.

Research based on current data from large numbers of enterprises offers the most promising opportunity to penetrate this thicket of issues.

---

50. Tseng *et al.*, *Economic Reform in China*, note (p. 29) that 80% of China's direct tax payments in 1991 came from state enterprises. In 1993, the state sector contributed 308 billion *yuan* to government revenues; revenue from collectives, private firms and "other" entities (including foreign-linked enterprises) was only half as large (*Yearbook 1994*, p. 215).

51. Profit rate is the ratio of after tax profits to the sum of net value of fixed assets and average value of quota circulating funds. Data come from *Yearbook 1994*, p. 399 and *Zhongguo gongye jingji tongji nianjian 1993* (*Statistical Yearbook of China's Industrial Economy 1993*) (Beijing: Zhongguo tongji chubanshe, 1994), p. 66.

52. He Jun, "State firms urged to finance education," *China Daily*, 4 April 1995, p. 1.

It is necessary to move beyond debates about industry-wide *averages* (such as for productivity growth) to look for patterns of organization and behaviour that have pushed enterprises on to trajectories of self-sustaining development. The search for patterns of success should begin with an open mind; for China, as for Japan and Korea, there is no reason to expect winning resource combinations to replicate successful arrangements observed in other economies.

What Are the Lessons of China's Reform Experience?

To anyone familiar with the cant and fraud associated with previous rounds of "learning from China," an invitation to expatiate on the lessons of China's reform experience mixes opportunity with danger. Yet China's reform experience can enlarge perceptions of the possibilities and pitfalls of socialist reform, as well as the scope and content of economic theory. This article therefore concludes with a summary of what might be learned from the brief history of China's economic reforms.

Reform means improvement, not perfection. Successful reform moves economic institutions in directions that facilitate improved economic outcomes. Some aspects of economic performance, such as output, incomes, employment, exports and productivity, are readily quantified. Others, such as innovative effort, links between contribution and reward, and the balance between market-directed profit-seeking and bureaucratically-oriented "rent-seeking," are more difficult to measure. The recent development of China's economy provides an array of evidence pointing to performance gains in many dimensions of economic life. The magnitude of beneficial change swamps any doubts about data quality.

Successful reform does not require the removal of all obstacles. Any effort to abolish all policy and institutional blockages is doomed by the same information gaps that limit the transformative capacity of central planning. Wise reform strategy identifies the most pressing shortcomings and concentrates resources on the relaxation of binding constraints. Limited administrative capacity ensures the presence of diminishing returns in institutional change. Attempting more may accomplish less. The survival of enterprise subsidies, redundant workers, soft credits and other leftovers from the plan era only confirms the obvious: reform is not complete. To judge the robustness of the reform process requires a move beyond mere enumeration of difficulties to evaluate the chances that current shortcomings can seriously undercut future economic performance or fritter away the momentum of reform. Such judgments necessitate a quantitative frame of mind (to gauge the scale of negative forces) even when measurement is impossible.

Appraising the durability of reform is a practical matter of comparative economics. It is comparative because the best available yardsticks come from existing human economic experience. Is "full commercialization and privatization" of banking essential to the reform enterprise?[53] Perhaps not, since government-controlled banks account for more than 80 per cent of bank loans and deposits in Taiwan, while Korean banks "remain subservient" to the Ministry of Finance and the central bank.[54] And it is practical because comparing real economies with the vacuous perfection of textbook abstractions leads to an "economics of nirvana" that is devoid of useful policy consequences.

Gradual reform initiated but not directed or controlled from above, is feasible and may be highly effective. Early in the recent spate of reforms, a survey of Russia's prospects led representatives of international organizations to the following viewpoint: "Ideally, a path of gradual reform could be laid out which would minimize economic disturbance and lead to an early harvesting of the fruits of increased economic efficiency. But we know of no such path...."[55] China's recent experience shows that gradual reform that leads to "early harvesting of the fruits of increased economic efficiency" can happen. Even if published statistics exaggerate China's economic gains as well as the losses suffered in Eastern Europe and the former Soviet Union, the contrasts in performance are unmistakable.

Initial conditions count. This review of China's reforms emphasizes the importance of economic, institutional and social inheritance in shaping the potential of alternative policy strategies and the outcome of actual reform initiatives. It rejects the idea that "one size fits all." In China's case, the implications of what Ohkawa and Rosovsky[56] term "social capability" extend far beyond the widely remarked availability of capital and business expertise from Hong Kong and Taiwan.

The importance of initial conditions should not divert attention from commonalities among the ex-socialist nations. In their haste to find Chinese experience irrelevant to problems of reform in Eastern Europe and the former Soviet Union, for instance, Sachs and Woo exaggerate the consequences of China's relatively large farm sector by emphasizing that "China began reform as a peasant agricultural society ... fac[ing] the classic problem of normal economic development, the transfer of workers from low-productivity agriculture to higher-productivity industry."[57] For them, the chief characteristic of pre-reform China is backwardness, not socialism. A perceptive essay by Dwight Perkins shows the limited

53. International Monetary Fund *et al.*, *The Economy of the USSR*, p. 32.

54. Ya-hwei Yang, "Taiwan: development and structural change of the banking system," pp. 302–303 and Yung Chul Park and Dong Won Kim, "Korea: development and structural change of the banking system," p. 195, both in Hugh T. Patrick and Yung Chul Park (eds.), *The Financial Development of Japan, Korea, and Taiwan* (New York: Oxford University Press, 1994).

55. International Monetary Fund *et al.*, *The Economy of the USSR*, p. 2.

56. Kazushi Ohkawa and Henry Rosovsky, *Japanese Economic Growth: Trend Acceleration in the Twentieth Century* (Stanford: Stanford University Press, 1973), ch. 8.

57. Jeffrey Sachs and Wing Thye Woo, "Structural reforms in the economic reforms of China, Eastern Europe, and the former Soviet Union," *Economic Policy*, April 1994, pp. 102–103.

validity of this distinction,[58] which in any case brushes aside China's whole apparatus of state control: 83,700 state-run industrial enterprises, 74 million subsidized and tenured workers in the state sector,[59] the automatic priority claim of state entities on funds for investment or research, college graduates, foreign exchange and scarce materials.

Chinese initial conditions *are* different. They may be so different that Chinese-style reform cannot generate favourable outcomes elsewhere. But any such conclusion must rest on sustained comparison between Chinese reform mechanisms and corresponding possibilities elsewhere.

Official policy is only part of the reform story. Research and policy advice typically overstate the significance of official actions, especially policies of the central government, in determining reform outcomes. Preoccupation with the concerns of the Centre inclines the analyst towards the central planning approach to reform, which portrays bureaucrats as operating on society in the fashion of surgeons reshaping the organs or limbs of a comatose patient.[60] The resulting preoccupation with "optimal" programme design injects an element of fantasy into many discussions of socialist transition.

This is not to deny the essential function of public policy. But if reform is a *process* rather than an event, policy decisions represent only one aspect of a complex dynamic that revolves around *interactions* among reform initiatives, decentralized responses to specific policies, economic trends associated with underlying socioeconomic forces, and changes in perceptions and attitudes within and outside the policy elite. Initial conditions influence both the range of feasible reform measures and the impact of policies actually implemented. The same policy will yield different results if implemented under different circumstances.

Recognition of the common sense inherent in these assertions is essential to any effort to interpret the past two decades of Chinese reform experience. The image of central policy as the hammer of reform that reshapes the economy cannot explain the profound consequences of partial reform, nor can it illuminate the sequence of events that led China's Communist Party to embrace market economy ideas that languished far beyond the limits of permissible discussion only a few years earlier.

Disciplinary tools are inadequate. Marshallian analysis is best suited to the analysis of incremental or marginal changes in market systems operating under stable institutions. Recent studies focused on the impact of strategic behaviour, organizational issues and information problems

---

58. Dwight H. Perkins, "Economic systems reform in developing countries," in Dwight H. Perkins and Michael Roemer (eds.), *Reforming Economic Systems in Developing Countries* (Cambridge, MA: Harvard University Press, 1991), pp. 11–54.

59. Data for 1978 from *Yearbook 1985*, pp. 216, 305.

60. See, for example, János Kornai, *The Road to a Free Economy* (New York: W. W. Norton, 1990), pp. 176–78.

challenge the applicability of standard analysis even to modern market economies.[61] The relevance of standard analytic results to China, where the institutional structure is neither uniform nor stable, is open to question.

This difficulty is nowhere more evident than in issues of state enterprise reform. Stiglitz finds "no scientific basis" for identifying full and early privatization as a cornerstone of effective reform.[62] The presence of government regulation eliminates the presumption that private firms are more efficient than public entities.[63] Desirable enterprise behaviour is most likely when competition creates pressures to economize and innovate and when governments allow unsuccessful firms and their workers to suffer the consequences of failure. If government is unwilling or unable to succour the victims of competition, enterprises must learn to compete regardless of ownership. This explains the success of America's public universities. If government offers subsidies, protection or employment guarantees to failed firms and their workers, the distinction between public and private ownership is again blurred. Performance is likely to depend more on market conditions than on ownership.[64]

But the market conditions must be real, not imaginary. It does no good to insist that, for reform to succeed, "the enterprise needs clear objectives, it should face the correct prices for its inputs and outputs, the managers should have the correct incentives, which in turn requires that their performance can be monitored."[65] If success means improvement rather than perfection, this is nonsense. Without precise numerical relations for evaluating trade-offs among current and future profit, risk levels, environmental outcomes, executive pay and a host of other priorities, there can be no clear objectives for multinational corporations. The notion that actual market economies manufacture "correct" prices is simply wrong. Should we travel to Paris, Chicago, Tokyo or Hong Kong to locate the "correct" price of petrol, wheat, steel or a visit to the doctor? If sustained and beneficial development required "correct" managerial incentives, individual proprietorships would have driven corporations into extinction before the Second World War.

Economic theory itself has entered a period of reform and transition. New theories incorporating strategic behaviour, organizational concerns and information problems upset traditional verities, including Adam Smith's "invisible hand" results – the bedrock of economics for more

61. For a summary, see Joseph Stiglitz, *Whither Socialism* (Cambridge, MA: MIT Press, 1994).

62. *Ibid.* p. 261.

63. Jean-Jacques Laffont and Jean Tirole, "Privatization and incentives," *Journal of Law, Economics, & Organization*, Vol. 7 (1991), special issue, pp. 84–105.

64. Summarizing empirical comparisons of public and private firms producing similar products, John Vickers and George Yarrow observe that "the most important point to emerge is the importance of competitive conditions and regulatory policies, as well as ownership, for incentives and efficiency" ("Economic perspectives on privatization," *Journal of Economic Perspectives*, Vol. 5, No. 2 (1991), p. 118.)

65. David M. Newbery, "Transformation in mature versus emerging economies: why has Hungary been less successful than China?" *China Economic Review*, Vol. 4, No. 2 (1993), p. 110.

than two centuries. Even under standard assumptions, they "*remove* the widespread belief that markets are necessarily the most efficient way of allocating resources."[66] Like engineers who find that weeks of observation and testing on the factory floor are not enough "to separate the essentials for the process from the witchcraft,"[67] economists cannot fully specify the central determinants of market performance. There is no agreed answer to the question "what is a market system"? Efforts to transform former socialist nations into high performance economies create unparalleled opportunities to study this and other fundamental issues.

Research on Chinese experience can strengthen the foundations of economic analysis. In economics, the Chinese surely qualify as the world's leading experimentalists. The 20th-century economic history of China, Taiwan, Hong Kong, Singapore and the overseas Chinese diaspora spans the entire gamut of economic regimes from virtually unrestricted competition (nominal tariff protection, tiny government and free banking in China during the early pre-war decades) to rigid state micromanagement (in 1982, restive researchers in Canton insisted that "even toilets require approval from Beijing").

The Chinese view of themselves as exceptional ensures the continued accumulation of valuable evidence. Unlike the Poles, whose reform seeks to adopt the basic institutions of European capitalism,[68] the Chinese are not content with aspiring to match foreign achievements. They trumpet their intention to surpass the West by developing a "socialist market economy with Chinese characteristics," and initiate bold experiments that involve genuine institutional innovation. Such experiments often fail. The Great Leap Forward of 1958–60, which caused a great famine, is the most obvious example. Others succeed, like the "barefoot doctors" of the 1960s and 1970s, whose ministrations contributed to large improvements in mass welfare (life expectancy rose dramatically between the censuses of 1953 and 1982) long before the World Bank urged low-income nations to focus on the "basic needs" of their citizens.

The consequences of more recent experimentation speak directly to the central concerns of microeconomic theory. China's dual price structure flourished during the decade beginning in 1984. Commodity flows were partitioned into plan and market components, with the latter transacted at more-or-less uncontrolled prices. Once the share of output exchanged becomes substantial (say one-third), so that anyone can easily learn the market price of coal, wheat, yarn or any other commodity, how closely does the resulting semi-market system approach the information requirements of a full market system? Is it possible that most of the efficiency gains from allowing prices to signal scarcity and glut accrue before the

66. Stiglitz, *Whither Socialism*, p. 32.
67. Piore, "Impact of the labor market," p. 605.
68. Jeffrey Sachs, *Poland's Jump to the Market Economy* (Cambridge, MA: MIT Press, 1993).

share of marketed output reaches 50 or 60 per cent, and that the benefit of raising the market share to 80 or 90 per cent may not offset the social dangers of rapid price liberalization?

The explosive growth of China's township and village enterprises, which now employ roughly 100 million workers and contribute 40–50 per cent of China's production and export of manufactures, challenges widely-held conceptions about ownership and property rights. An elaborate vocabulary of denial obscures the uncomfortable reality that these firms, widely described as collectives, TVEs, non-state, quasi-private or even private enterprises, are typically owned and controlled by local governments. Indeed Chinese journals are filled with complaints about the lack of clearly-defined property rights in rural industry.[69] As Stiglitz notes, "traditional economic theory ... would suggest that this system is a recipe for economic failure. Yet the success is palpable," suggesting that property rights, a staple building block of standard economic theory, may "play a far less important role than is conventionally ascribed to them."[70]

The reform of state-owned industry provides a final intersection between economic theory and research on China's economy. Aghion, Blanchard and Burgess conclude that it may be impossible for the state to impose privatization on unwilling enterprise communities. They propose to set aside hard budget constraints so that "selective debt write-downs can be used to buy off coalitions adverse to restructuring or unbundling" of state enterprises that combine production with social responsibilities, because "giving managers a share in the privatized firm leads them to act closer to value maximization."[71] Stiglitz finds "little reason for the government not to retain a large minority interest" in enterprises undergoing privatization.[72] Although these authors are perhaps unfamiliar with efforts to "corporatize" China's state enterprises, the resonance between their theory-based inferences and recent Chinese reform initiatives is unmistakable.

China's reforms have unleashed a process of growth and institutional change that has moved its vast economy to the brink of a market system in less than two decades. The extent of these economic achievements, although exaggerated by official measures, is immense. Flagrant imbalance between Peking's partial and tentative policy initiatives and the magnitude of subsequent change directs attention to the mechanism of domestic economic change. It also challenges popular views about appropriate strategies for socialist transition and contributes to growing scepti-

69. "Property rights of township and village collective enterprises are vague, everybody has some part, nobody asks questions, the responsibility for property rights is not clear" ("Ministry of Agriculture offers opinions on reforming the property rights system of township and village enterprises," *Zhongguo xiangzhen qiye* (*China Township and Village Enterprise*), No. 5 (1994), p. 4.

70. Stiglitz, *Whither Socialism*, p. 176.

71. Philippe Aghion, Olivier Blanchard and Robin Burgess, "The behaviour of state firms in Eastern Europe, pre-privatization," *European Economic Review*, Vol. 38, No. 3–4 (1994), pp. 1327–49.

72. Stiglitz, *Whither Socialism*, p. 186.

cism concerning fundamental tenets of economic theory. Recent economic gains are intimately linked with China's unusual socio-economic inheritance. It is possible, but by no means necessary, that other ex-socialist nations could benefit by incorporating specific aspects of Chinese transition patterns into their own reform strategies.

China's political leaders and business managers know that, despite many achievements, vast potential remains untapped, especially in the financial sector and its chief clients in state-owned industry. Their efforts to realize these latent opportunities will maintain, and perhaps increase, China's rapid pace of institutional change, with results that promise to contain as many surprises as have emerged during the past two decades. As the world's second- or third-largest economy, China deserves careful investigation. Its unique combination of blazing growth and unorthodox policy demands close attention. And its penchant for creating new combinations of material resources and institutional arrangements ensures that research on China's economy will continue to produce abundant intellectual rewards.

Index